Tools, Techniques and Strategies for Reflective Second & Foreign Language Teacher Education

Paul Voerkel • Mergenfel A. Vaz Ferreira
Nancy Drescher
Editors

Tools, Techniques and Strategies for Reflective Second & Foreign Language Teacher Education

Insights from Contexts Around the World

J.B. METZLER

Editors
Paul Voerkel
Schmalkalden University of Applied
Sciences
Schmalkalden, Germany

Mergenfel A. Vaz Ferreira
Faculdade de Letras, Setor de Alemão
Federal University of Rio de Janeiro
Rio de Janeiro, Brazil

Nancy Drescher
Department of English
Minnesota State University
Mankato, MN, USA

ISBN 978-3-662-68740-6   ISBN 978-3-662-68741-3 (eBook)
https://doi.org/10.1007/978-3-662-68741-3

© The Editor(s) (if applicable) and The Author(s), under exclusive license to Springer-Verlag GmbH, DE, part of Springer Nature 2024

This work is subject to copyright. All rights are solely and exclusively licensed by the Publisher, whether the whole or part of the material is concerned, specifically the rights of translation, reprinting, reuse of illustrations, recitation, broadcasting, reproduction on microfilms or in any other physical way, and transmission or information storage and retrieval, electronic adaptation, computer software, or by similar or dissimilar methodology now known or hereafter developed.

The use of general descriptive names, registered names, trademarks, service marks, etc. in this publication does not imply, even in the absence of a specific statement, that such names are exempt from the relevant protective laws and regulations and therefore free for general use.

The publisher, the authors, and the editors are safe to assume that the advice and information in this book are believed to be true and accurate at the date of publication. Neither the publisher nor the authors or the editors give a warranty, expressed or implied, with respect to the material contained herein or for any errors or omissions that may have been made. The publisher remains neutral with regard to jurisdictional claims in published maps and institutional affiliations.

This J.B. Metzler imprint is published by the registered company Springer-Verlag GmbH, DE, part of Springer Nature.
The registered company address is: Heidelberger Platz 3, 14197 Berlin, Germany

If disposing of this product, please recycle the paper.

Foreword

I was supposed to attend the AILA congress in the Netherlands and was really looking forward to presenting my paper, but then the COVID-19 pandemic arrived in 2020 and the conference was canceled and rescheduled to 2021 and in an online format. Thus, I had no choice but to cancel, and so I missed the pleasure of hearing my colleagues present on this interesting theme. Then, I was pleasantly surprised and honored to be asked to write this foreword for a collection titled, *Tools, Techniques, and Strategies for Reflective Second & Foreign Language Teacher Education*, yes, the same title of the thematic section for which I was supposed to present at AILA. I was presented with the chance to read what I missed, and I must say, it was my loss to have missed these wonderful papers that you now will have the pleasure of reading.

The collection, or anthology as the editors call it, includes nine presentations from the AILA 2021 conference under the theme that is now the title of the book. The title of the collection indicates that the focus of the papers will be broadly on embracing the concept of reflective practice in second and foreign language teacher education and suggests various tools, techniques, and strategies that can be implemented for the development of pre-service (as well as in-service teachers) to help them in their teaching careers. This is a very important focus because pre-service language teachers will need to be able to adapt to a variety of different challenges throughout their teaching careers, and I believe that empowering them with the tools of reflective practice will help them become successful throughout their careers.

At present, many current TESOL teacher education programs provide theories in general and some methods courses that TESOL teacher educators presume will be useful when they go teach. However, often when they are plunged physically into the real world of classrooms, the contents of their education program are of no help, and they are forced into developing quick fixes through a process of blind experimentation rather than any deep reflection. On the contrary, teacher education should prepare learner teachers to become reflective practitioners so that they can become adaptive professionals throughout their careers. Thus, a key element of second language teacher education is engaging learner teachers in reflective practice, especially as it can act as a bridge between theory and practice for learner teachers as adaptive professionals where they can reflect on, evaluate, and adapt their own practice (Farrell, 2021). Such a reflective approach to second language teacher education will help learner teachers move more smoothly through the phases of adaptation they will experience during their early career years and into their in-service years.

Reflection can be operationalized by encouraging developing second language teachers to reflect on their *philosophy, principles, theory, practice,* and *beyond practice* (Farrell, 2022), because such structured reflective opportunities can enable these learner second language teachers to grow professionally throughout their careers. This holistic framework encompasses much of Dewey and Schon's work but adds the element of the teacher who is doing the reflecting in stage 1, philosophy which enables teachers to examine the teacher-as-person. Stage 2 entails reflecting on principles or a teacher's deeply held assumptions, beliefs, and conceptions of language teaching and learning. Stage 3 explores a teacher's planning and the activities and methods they want to use in their lessons as they reflect-*for*-action. Stage 4 is where teachers look at what they actually do in their practice as they reflect-*in*-action and *on*-action. The final stage is often neglected in second language teacher education and entails teachers' critically reflecting on the moral, political, emotional, ethical, and social issues that impact practice both inside and outside the classroom. For me, reflective practice is the epicenter or heart of teaching.

Tools, Techniques, and Strategies for Reflective Second & Foreign Language Teacher Education exhibits many examples of the above framework in different ways. This collection expertly put together by knowledgeable editors Nancy Drescher, Paul Voerkel, and Meg Ferreira from three different continents who show their passion for encouraging reflective practice among learner language teachers. The collection of nine chapters fills gaps in the literature on implementing reflective practice in language education by providing valuable practical insights and theoretical developments concerning this importance yet complex concept of reflective practice.

For example, many of the authors in this collection make the case for incorporating writing of some form (e.g., writing responses, portfolios, and rubrics) into teacher education courses as a way of encouraging learner teachers to engage in reflective practice. I am a big fan of writing as reflection because the act of writing has a built-in reflective mechanism; teachers must stop to think and organize their thoughts before writing and then decide on what to write. After this they can "see" their thoughts and reflect on these for self-understanding and development (Farrell, 2013). Action research has a reflexive relationship with reflection and is included in this collection where the tools of action research were encouraged to help learner teachers engage in their own research. Reflective practice is also presented in more broader definitions where learner teachers are encouraged to reflect on their professional development such as the European Portfolio EPOSTL tool, as well as the development of learner teachers' overt ELF awareness. Affectivity as a key element in the professionalization of reflective teachers is also covered, as is perceptions of experts in the field of teacher education about their daily practices as well as their ideas about the education of reflective primary pre-service teachers in the subject of English in the German university context. The anthology ends with a broad exploration of the linguistic and pedagogical beliefs that are embedded in second language teacher education (SLTE) in Chile to unmask their hidden ideologies with the overall idea of improving reflection within instructional practices.

This somewhat eclectic collection of very interesting papers all have a common core: to educate and encourage learner language teachers to engage in reflective practice in their teacher education programs and throughout their teaching careers. There is growing research evidence within SLTE that encouraging learner language teachers to engage in reflection is making a positive impact on their careers because teachers recognize the developmental value and transformative potential in reflective activities (Farrell, 2021). Thus, the goal of SLTE is to produce reflective practitioners who are educated in the habits of reflection and provided the necessary tools to be able to accomplish this. Many of these tools are exhibited in this important anthology that teacher educators in a wider context will find very useful for their own practices. Reflective practice is more than a method, it is a way of life—we evolve as language teachers throughout our careers as we construct and reconstruct our practice.

Brock Univerity, St. Catharines, Canada   Thomas S. C. Farrell
July 2023

References

Farrell, T. S. C. (2013). *Reflective writing for language teachers*. Equinox Publishing Ltd.

Farrell, T. S. C. (2021). *TESOL teacher education: A reflective approach*. Edinburgh University Press.

Farrell, T. S. C. (2022). *Reflective language teaching*. Cambridge University Press.

Contents

1 **Introduction: Tools, Techniques, and Strategies for Reflective Second & Foreign Language Teacher Education** 1
Paul Voerkel, Mergenfel A. Vaz Ferreira, and Nancy Drescher

2 **Reflective Writing and Self-assessment of Language Teaching Performance** 7
Alfredo Urzúa and Nancy Drescher

3 **Applying Peer Rubric Feedback in Foreign Language Teacher Education: Fostering Pre-service Teachers' Oral Feedback Skills Through Facilitating Reflective Moments** 31
Olivia Rütti-Joy

4 **Developing J-POSTL Elementary for English Language Teacher Education in Japan: Challenges and Opportunities** 53
Fumiko Kurihara, Takane Yamaguchi, Sakiko Yoneda, Eri Osada, and Rie Adachi

5 **Tools of Action Research in Undergraduate Teacher Education: Experiences from Brazil**................................... 73
Paul Voerkel

6 **Developing a Critical Reflection Stance Towards Language Teaching Practice: European Portfolio for Student Teachers of Languages and Reflective Tasks in Language Education**........ 95
Larisa Kasumagić-Kafedžić and Selma Đuliman

7	**ELF-Aware Teacher Development: The Case of the ENRICH Continuous Professional Development Course**...........	117
	Yasemin Bayyurt, Lucilla Lopriore, and Stefania Kordia	
8	**Affection as a Professional Knowledge in German as a Foreign Language Teachers' Initial Education in Rio de Janeiro**...........	145
	Mergenfel A. Vaz Ferreira and Anelise F. P. Gondar	
9	**Teachers as Researchers: Voices from Experts**..................	161
	Sonja Brunsmeier	
10	**A Corpus-Based Analysis of Ideologies in Chilean SLTE Policies**...	177
	Rodrigo Arellano	
11	**Epilogue: Tools, Techniques, and Strategies for Reflective Second & Foreign Language Teacher Education**................	199
	Paul Voerkel, Nancy Drescher, and Mergenfel A. Vaz Ferreira	

Abbreviations[1]

AILA	Association Internationale de Linguistique Appliquée/International Association of Applied Linguistics
AR	Action Research
CEFR	Common European Framework of Reference for Languages
CPD	Continuous Professional Development
DLL	Deutsch Lehren Lernen (Program "Learn to teach German," developed and run by Goethe-Institut)
EAL	English as an Additional Language
EAP	English for Academic Purposes
edTPA	Educative Teacher Performance Assessment
EFL	English as a Foreign Language
ELE	English Language Education
ELF	English as Lingua Franca
ELP	European Language Portfolio
ELT	English Language Teaching
EMF	English as a Multilingua Franca
EPOSTL	European Portfolio for Student Teachers of Languages
ES	Elementary School
FL	Foreign Language
GFL	German as a Foreign Language

---

[1] The contributions in the anthology come from different regions and contexts and therefore take up reflection from quite diverse perspectives. One of the consequences of this is that heterogeneous settings, theories and concepts are used and described, often with different names and technical terms. For a better overview, the following are terms used more than once in the papers and can be found there as abbreviations.

J-POSTL	Japanese Portfolio for Student Teachers of Languages
NA	Needs Analysis
PCM	Partial Credit Model
PEP	Practice Exploration Project
PIBIC	Programa Institucional de Bolsas de Iniciação Científica (Public scholarship for undergraduate students for doing research work)
PIBID	Programa Institucional de Bolsa de Iniciação à Docência (Public scholarship for undergraduate students for Teaching)
PRLCP	Profession-Related Language Competence Profiles
PRLC-R	Profession-Related Language Competence Assessment Rubric
RBL	Research-Based Learning
SAD	Self-Assessment Descriptors
SLTE	Second Language Teacher Education
TESOL	Teachers of English to Speakers of Other Languages
TFL	Teacher Feedback Literacy
TLC	Teacher Language Competence
WL	World Languages

Introduction: Tools, Techniques, and Strategies for Reflective Second & Foreign Language Teacher Education

Paul Voerkel, Mergenfel A. Vaz Ferreira, and Nancy Drescher

1 First Considerations

This anthology attempts to link the theoretical discussion about reflection in academic teacher training to the practical developing competence (underlying ability) and competencies (actionable skills) needed for classroom success with concrete examples as well as studies that help us understand some of the underlying and sometimes unnamed assumptions and beliefs that guide our teaching of teachers. It offers a collection of insights and tools that aim to guide teacher educators in the teaching of reflective practice and help them to integrate reflection into their students' everyday actions in order to ensure the quality and further development of

---

P. Voerkel (✉)
Schmalkalden University of Applied Sciences, Schmalkalden, Germany

M. A. Vaz Ferreira
Department of Anglo-Germanic Languages, Federal University of Rio de Janeiro, Rio de Janeiro, Brazil

N. Drescher
Department of English, Minnesota State University, Mankato, MN, USA
e-mail: nancy.drescher@mnsu.edu

© The Author(s), under exclusive license to Springer-Verlag GmbH, DE, part of Springer Nature 2024
P. Voerkel et al. (eds.), *Tools, Techniques and Strategies for Reflective Second & Foreign Language Teacher Education*,
https://doi.org/10.1007/978-3-662-68741-3_1

their work. The anthology itself is organized around specific tools, broader applications in specific contexts, perceptions, and policies.

Within the framework of applied linguistics, teacher training has become increasingly important during the last decades and, thus, forms an intersection with foreign language didactics. Within this connection, reflection has been increasingly considered a fundamental aspect for teacher education.

More than 40 years ago, Donald Schön postulated, in his book on the "Reflective Practitioner" (1983), that it was necessary to consciously add reflectivity to accompany teacher action in teacher development and professionalization, and especially as attention has been focused on teacher research (cf. Legutke & Schart, 2016), the importance of reflection in teacher action research has become even clearer. This need is all the more important as studies on concrete measures and procedures of reflection, e.g., on micro-teaching and the associated negotiation and communication processes, clearly show the effectiveness of reflection for the improvement of teaching (cf. Hattie, 2013: 134–136).

In addition to applied linguistics, foreign language didactics has also increasingly discovered the topic of reflection. Particularly in Europe, the discipline is thus making significant inroads into the field of teacher education and is having a major impact on it. Concepts and examples of reflection are increasingly being discussed from the perspective of foreign language didactics, both for the training of teachers in the school sector and for adult education (cf. Bechtel & Rudolph, 2022).

2 The AILA Congress Section: From Papers Submissions to Pandemic Turnaround

This background framed the proposal for a thematic section at the AILA congress planned in the Netherlands with the title "Tools, Techniques, and Strategies for Reflective Second & Foreign Language Teacher Education," which was adopted in the summer of 2019.

The AILA organizers could not have chosen better when they published the main title of the conference: "The dynamics of language, communication, and culture in a changing world." Indeed, the world was changing fast during the first months of 2020. With the beginning of the Covid Pandemic that struck humanity worldwide, many things became uncertain, and planning across all areas of life was affected drastically. Included in the many changes across the globe was the abrupt shift in both the date and mode of the AILA Congress. The entire congress was postponed for one year, to August 2021, and switched from face-to-face presentations to mainly online contributions.

Because of the new date and conditions, some participants had to cancel their participation in the conference. Nevertheless, there were nine presentations from different countries and backgrounds held in the section. There were participants from Latin America (Brazil, Chile, and Mexico), from Europe (two speakers from Germany, an international trio from Greece, Turkey, and Italy, and a project from Southeastern Europe, from Bosnia-Herzegovina), from Asia (namely a collaborative project from Iran and another from Japan) and even from the United States and Australia. While we regret that there were no contributions from Africa and that participants from Eastern Europe had to withdraw, it was still visible that teacher education and the process of reflection are important issues all over the world.

We are now happy to join a mosaic of pieces and experiences from around the world and to introduce the book.

3 About the Chapters in This Anthology

This anthology attempts to link the theoretical discussion about reflection in academic teacher training to the practical developing competence (underlying ability) and competencies (actionable skills) needed for classroom success with concrete examples as well as studies that help us understand some of the underlying and sometimes unnamed assumptions and beliefs that guide our teaching of teachers. Thus, the book brings together both theoretical studies and practical experiences of foreign and second language teacher education and professional development that focus on the issues pointed to above. It offers a collection of insights and tools that aim to guide teacher educators in the teaching of reflective practice and help them to integrate reflection into their students' everyday actions in order to ensure the quality and further development of their work. The anthology itself is organized around specific tools, broader applications in specific contexts, perceptions, and policies.

The first section contains three contributions and opens with the chapter *Reflective writing and self-assessment of language teaching performance* by Urzúa and Drescher, who used teachers' performance-based assessment data to explore how language teacher candidates write reflective responses and to identify ways to support this type of writing. The authors described an investigation of reflective writing that aims to determine levels and dimensions of reflection as well as common discourse moves and steps in teacher candidates' reflective writing through the development and use of a specially tailored, user-friendly rubric. It is followed by a chapter by Rütti-Joy, *Applying peer rubric feedback in foreign language teacher education: Fostering pre-service teachers' oral feedback skills through fa-*

cilitating reflective moments. In this chapter, the author discussed the practice of effective feedback as one of the most influential factors impacting student achievement. She highlighted the importance of language teachers acquiring linguistic and practical skills, such as teacher feedback literacy, that are considered highly specific to the development of reflective teachers. The paper in this sense presents an intervention study that investigated the development of pre-service language teachers' oral feedback skills in the target language, English, while focusing on the language and content-related aspects of their feedback performances. The next chapter, entitled *Developing Portfolios for English Language Teachers in Japan: Challenges and Opportunities*, by Kurihara, Yamaguchi, Yoneda, Osada, and Adachi, began by presenting a brief overview of English language education in Japan and the implementation of English as a compulsory subject in Japanese elementary schools. From the focus on English teacher education for elementary school, the paper highlighted the development of the Japanese Portfolio for Student Teachers of Languages: Elementary (J-POSTL Elementary). It also presented examples of the implementation of J-POSTL Elementary and examines the opportunities and challenges this tool provides in the growth of teachers' competencies in the area of reflection.

The anthology moves to broader contexts of application within teacher development courses with the chapter *Tools of Action Research in Undergraduate Teacher Education: Experiences from Brazil* by Voerkel, who presents a study that examined the extent to which the tools in Action Research can be a useful instrument in the development of reflective teachers in teacher education programs even at undergraduate level. To this end, he presented a course offered to German teacher education students in Brazil and investigated, through a retrospective survey, the impact of the course on further activity as a German teacher. In the next chapter entitled *Developing a Critical Reflection Stance towards Language Teaching Practice: European Portfolio for Student Teachers of Languages and Reflective Tasks in Language Education*, Kasumagić-Kafedžić and Đuliman focused on a Bosnian context and examined the use of the EPOSTL tool in language teaching pedagogy courses and how students used this document to reflect on their own linguistic and didactic competencies as well as in planning and assessing their own professional development by keeping a record of their teaching experiences provided for them as in-class simulations, in-class observations, or in-class and school practice teaching. Bayyurt, Lopriore, and Kordia then presented, in the chapter *Developing the ELF-aware teacher: The case of the ENRICH Continuous Professional Development Course,* an original Continuous Professional Development (CPD) Course for EFL teachers with an overt ELF-aware orientation. The establishment of mentoring partnerships and transnational teacher communities was highlighted in both phases, aiming at promoting critical reflection on one's views, attitudes, and practices, encouraging constructive dialogue, and providing, when appropriate, intellectual challenge and emotional support. In this chapter, they emphasized the challenges and opportunities encountered throughout the course development and implementation, as well as on the implications for teacher development.

The focus of the anthology then turns to the perspectives of teachers and experts in the field with the chapter *Affection as a Professional Knowledge in German as a Foreign Language Teachers' Initial Education in Rio de Janeiro* by Ferreira and Gondar, who highlighted the results of a previous study on teacher professionalization in Rio de Janeiro that pointed to affectivity as a key element in the professionalization of reflective teachers. This chapter aimed to discuss the relevance of affectivity in the initial education of teachers of German as FL by revisiting a survey conducted with future GLF teachers and drawing on a theoretical framework of teachers' knowledge, reflection, and affectivity in teacher's practices. Also focusing on the perspective of pre-service teachers and experts, Brunsmeier in her chapter *Teachers as Researchers: Voices from Experts* attempted to show how universities actually "translate" contemporary demands into their everyday pre-service teacher instruction and why they opt for one or another seminar concept. Brunsmeier presented, by means of problem-centered interviews, the perceptions of experts in the field of teacher education. She provided insights into their daily practices as well as their ideas about the education of reflective primary pre-service teachers in the subject of English in the German university context. Finally, the chapter *A Corpus-Based Analysis of Ideologies in Chilean SLTE Policies*, by Arellano, explored the linguistic and pedagogical beliefs that are embedded in second language teacher education (SLTE) based on a mixed study that aimed at reviewing a multi-layered set of SLTE policies in Chile to unmask their hidden ideologies. To do so, the research employed corpus-based techniques using keywords in context to determine the most frequent words and their placements in official documents such as the national SLTE standards, SLTE curricula, and their program descriptions. This policy analysis revealed the potential for improving reflexivity and reflection within instructional practices.

We hope that by examining reflection for second and foreign language teacher education and exploring the theoretical studies and practical insights we—and those interested in reading the texts included here—will be able to rethink our practices and ensure the quality of our everyday work. We would like to thank all the contributors for their terrific collaboration! A special thanks as well goes to the publishers who supported the initiation of this anthology in a very positive way. Have a nice reading!

References

Bechtel, M., & Rudolph, T. (Eds.). (2022). *Reflexionskompetenz in der Fremdsprachenlehre r*innenbildung. Theorien – Konzepte – Empirie*. Peter Lang.

Hattie, J. (2013). *Lernen sichtbar machen. Überarbeitete deutschsprachige Ausgabe von "Visible Learning"*, besorgt von Wolfgang Beywl und Klaus Zierer. Baltmannsweiler: Schneider Verlag Hohengehren.

Legutke, M., & Schart, M. (Eds.). (2016). *Fremdsprachendidaktische Professionsforschung: Brennpunkt Lehrerbildung*. Narr.

Schön, D. (1983). *The reflective Practitioner. How Professionals Think in Action*. Temple Smith.

Paul Voerkel is a passionate language teacher. He studied German as a Foreign Language, History, Hispanic Studies and Educational Sciences at the University of Leipzig (Germany) and received his PhD on teacher education in Brazil at Jena University (Germany). Since 2007, he has been active at various universities in Germany, Ecuador and Brazil, among others as an invited DAAD lecturer. At present, he works as a the Head of the Department of Studies and International Relations at Schmalkalden University of Applied Sciences. His research interests include teacher education, methodology-didactics, cultural studies, and language policy. Contact: paul.voerkel@gmail.com.

Mergenfel A. Vaz Ferreira has been an Associate Professor of German Language at the Federal University of Rio de Janeiro since 2011. Between September 2022 and July 2023, she was a Visiting Professor at the Friedrich Schiller Universität Jena with a grant of the German Academic Exchange Service (DAAD). She holds a master's and PhD in Language Studies from the Pontifical Catholic University of Rio de Janeiro and her main areas of interest are the processes of teaching and learning additional languages/cultures, focusing mainly on the education of teacher's additional languages and didactic approaches for additional languages from a critical and decolonial perspective. Contact: megvazferreira@letras.ufrj.br.

Nancy Drescher is a full Professor in the Teaching English to Speakers of Other Languages at Minnesota State University, Mankato. She has a Ph.D. in Applied Linguistics from Northern Arizona University. Her teaching focuses on English language teaching, teacher education, sociolinguistics, and literacy. Her main research interests include teacher development, educational policies, and reflection. She has taught English at the K-12 level in the United States and overseas and currently works primarily at the university level. Contact: nancy.drescher@mnsu.edu.

Reflective Writing and Self-assessment of Language Teaching Performance

Alfredo Urzúa and Nancy Drescher

1 Introduction

Teacher reflection is considered one of the dominant paradigms in language teacher education programs, which increasingly aim to incorporate ways of promoting more reflective dispositions among teachers-in-training (Farrell, 2016; Gun, 2011; Zeichner & Liu, 2010). The ability to reflect is also a major component in evaluative processes in language teacher education (e.g., National Board for Professional Teaching Standards, 2010), including high-stakes assessments, such as those used for teacher licensure. In order to respond effectively to reflective assignments and assessments based on reflective writing, it is essential for teachers to understand what reflection entails and how to compose reflective texts. In addition, assessing teachers' reflective writing presents many challenges, not only due to the difficulties in arriving at a consensus in defining reflection, but also because multiple models of reflection exist (Korthagen, 2010). Many reflection-focused studies rely on models that characterize reflection according to types or levels. In the study reported here, we adopted a similar approach in that we used models based on levels and dimensions previously identified by Ward and McCotter (2004) and Jay and

---

A. Urzúa (✉)
Department of Spanish and Portuguese Languages and Literatures, San Diego State University, San Diego, CA, USA
e-mail: aurzua@sdsu.edu

N. Drescher
Department of English, Minnesota State University, Mankato, MN, USA
e-mail: nancy.drescher@mnsu.edu

© The Author(s), under exclusive license to Springer-Verlag GmbH, DE, part of Springer Nature 2024
P. Voerkel et al. (eds.), *Tools, Techniques and Strategies for Reflective Second & Foreign Language Teacher Education*,
https://doi.org/10.1007/978-3-662-68741-3_2

Johnson (2002). However, our goal is not only to examine the various ways in which teacher candidates compose their reflections, but also to develop a user-friendly rubric to appraise these texts and identify discourse moves and steps (Swales, 1990) that might support their understanding of reflection and reflective writing so future teacher candidates are better equipped to generate this type of discourse in academic and professional contexts.

2   Reflection and Teachers

As is well known, two traditions underlie most work on reflective teaching to date: the work of John Dewey (1933) and that of Donald Schön (1983, 1987). Despite key differences between the Deweyan and Schönian traditions (Fendler, 2003) and criticisms of how the concept of reflection has been applied to teaching, Anderson (2020) highlights the notion that reflection constitutes an important part of teacher thinking and that there is a "generally positive impact of reflection on language teacher cognition and practice" (p. 481). For novice and experienced teachers alike, this impact includes a greater understanding of self and an increased awareness of their beliefs (Farrell, 2016). However, despite the central role assigned to reflection in teacher education and professional development, there is still much debate about how to operationalize reflective thinking and what constitutes reflective discourse (Anderson, 2020; Korthagen, 2010). Fendler (2003) has also highlighted the "many historical and discursive complexities of the concept," as well as "tensions in the discourse of reflection" (p. 17). Nevertheless, this has not deterred teacher educators and researchers from trying to better understand, define, model, and operationalize reflection and reflective thinking, as the vast literature in this area clearly shows.

Despite the aforementioned challenges, various definitions of reflection have been proposed. Richards (1990), for instance, refers to reflection as "the conscious recall and examination of experience as a basis for evaluation and decision-making as a source for planning and action" (p. 5), while Hatton and Smith (1995) define it as "deliberate thinking about action with a view to its improvement" (p. 40). Larrivee (2008) describes it as a process that leads to "an examination of both personal and professional belief systems" (p. 90) that guides decision-making and problem solving, and Collier (2010) defined it as "a process of inquiry that encourages an understanding of the interactive nature of theory and practice" (p. 48). In attempting to capture recurrent elements in various definitions, Quinn et al. (2010) defined teacher reflectivity as "a purposeful activity fostered over time that requires awareness of self and self-perception, is developmental and occurs in stages, and is based in experience that connects to other meaningful experiences" (p. 28). More recently, Farrell (2020) defined language teacher reflection as the systematic examination of principles and practices about teaching and learning, as well as related assumptions, beliefs, and values. This kind of reflection involves analysis and evaluation of practice in order to make evidence-based decisions regarding changes and improvements in teaching. It is this last view of reflection that we adopted in our study.

Models of reflection typically involve distinct aspects, levels, or dimensions. Reflection, thus, can be conceptualized in relation to a temporal frame as retrospective or prospective (Schön, 1983, 1987; Killion & Todnem, 1991). It can also include various types of levels, such as technical, interpretative, and critical (Van Manen, 1977) or factual, prudential (evaluative), justificatory, and critical (Zeichner & Liston, 1987). Other models distinguish between descriptive, dialogic, comparative, and critical reflection (Hatton & Smith, 1995; Jay & Johnson, 2002) or between routine, technical, dialogic, and transformative reflection (Ward & McCotter, 2004). To the latter, the authors also included dimensions of reflection, which refer to the focus or content of reflection, related processes of inquiry or problem solving, and actual or planned changes occurring as a result of engaging in reflection. In general, many models depict reflection as consisting of levels that range between descriptive and factual, on one end, and critical and transformative, on the other. These reflections can occur, using Schön's framework, while teaching (reflection in action), after teaching (reflection on action), or in relation to future actions (reflecting for action). Farrell (2020) also considers another level, that of reflecting beyond practice, which links practice to broader sociopolitical issues, such as educational policies.

2.1 Reflection in Teacher Education

Zeichner and Liu (2010) consider that an important shift occurred when, instead of focusing on training teachers to enact certain teaching methods or techniques, efforts started to center on the need to educate teachers to "understand the reasons and rationales associated with different practices" (p. 67). This shift constituted a catalyst for research on teacher thinking to emerge and for the notion of reflective practice to start permeating teacher education programs. How to prepare reflective teachers became the key question, and the main goal was to move away from a view of teachers as technicians to a recognition that to grow as competent and effective teachers, it was necessary to adopt and develop dispositions and skills that help examine one's own teaching practice and learn from it (Farrell, 2016). At present, it can be said that reflection is considered *essential* for teachers to be able to organize and examine their experiences, knowledge, beliefs, and plans in order to evaluate themselves, their teaching and their students' learning, and to make changes and improvements (Farrell, 2006, 2011, 2020; Leung, 2009). It is through reflection that teachers can analyze their teaching context, their own actions and those of colleagues and students to guide their professional development.

Reflection also serves a mediating function between theory and practice for teachers-in-training. Akbari (2007) considers that reflective teaching has the potential to create a balance between theory and practice and emphasizes that the purpose of reflection "is not rejection of theory, but promotion of practical knowledge to the level of theory" (p. 202). For this connection between theory and practice to occur, teachers need opportunities to reflect systematically on their classroom practices to "promote understanding and self-awareness and to make changes when necessary" (McDonough, 2006, p. 33). Given the key role that reflection plays in teacher training and development, it is not surprising that the National Board for Professional Teaching Standards (2010) has included it as one of nine World Language Standards, stating that "effective reflection stimulates a teacher's creativity, guides personal growth, contributes to content knowledge and classroom skills, and enhances students learning" (p. 43).

On the other hand, even within a context in which researchers and practitioners agree upon the importance of teacher reflection, it is still the case that most teachers are generally not trained to be reflective (Tsui, 2007). As Freese (2006) shows in her longitudinal case study analysis of Ryan, a novice teacher, reflection is not necessarily something done willingly and easily; it may not occur spontaneously and it involves challenges, self or externally imposed, whether because of preconceived notions, lack of readiness, resistance to requests for change, unrealistic expectations, or fear of failure, among many other possible factors. Rodgers (2002) has also pointed out that, without specific training, teachers, especially novice teachers, might find it difficult to differentiate between description and interpretation. Similarly, Gun (2011), highlighting the importance of 'reflection training' in teacher education programs, states that "although teachers are constantly encouraged to 'reflect' on their teaching, they are unable to do so effectively unless they are specifically trained in how to reflect" (p. 126).

Studies on teacher reflection often focus on a core set of activities or techniques that seem to foster a reflective stance or disposition. Typically, these involve activities such as focused conversations or interviews (e.g., Urzúa & Vásquez, 2008), group discussions (e.g., Farrell, 2011), dialogue journals and other forms of written or oral narratives (e.g., Reiman, 1999), as well as prompted reactions (orally or in writing) to audio- or video-recorded classroom teaching (e.g., Gun, 2011). What all these activities have in common is that they offer the possibility of articulating teachers' thoughts and opinions about their plans and expectations, including the identification of problems and evaluation of possible solutions. In this study, we focus on language teachers' written reflections of their own teaching. We analyze their reflections in terms of levels and dimensions and offer a quantitative overview of findings. We also explore their reflections in a more qualitative manner, adopting a genre perspective that allows the identification of common discourse patterns related to such levels and dimensions.

2.2 Reflective Texts from a Genre Perspective

The notion of genre has proven useful to understand the characteristics of texts in context and how they are generated and processed in specific communicative situations (Hyland, 2002). Genres are comprised by texts with shared features such as purpose, content, linguistic patterns, meta-linguistic choices, text structure, and organization. Of course, variation across texts within a genre can be expected as well. One way in which texts within a specific genre can be explored is by determining the typical 'moves' and 'steps' used during the composing process to express a particular communicative function. For example, Swales (1990) identified typical moves and steps commonly occurring in introductions to research articles. These patterns are not fixed as some moves and steps are optional, resulting in the type of variability that is inherent to any groups of texts comprising a genre, from more to less prototypical. This variation, Devitt (2015) states, "necessarily occurs every time someone performs a genre in a particular text" (p. 45). In our case, the genre in question is teacher candidate written reflections on their own classroom practice. These reflections have common aspects, which we will describe in terms of "moves and steps" (Swales, 2004), while each text can also be considered a 'unique performance' in response to the prompts found in the assessment.

A move, according to Swales (2004), is a "discoursal or rhetorical unit that performs a coherent communicative function in a written or spoken discourse" (p. 228). These moves can occur in a single clause or in several sentences, as the concept refers to a functional unit and not to a formal one. However, some grammatical features (e.g., specific verbal forms; use of first-person pronouns) may be associated with certain moves. In addition, some lexical items can 'signal' moves, such as the phrase 'in conclusion.' Finally, Swales shows that move identification "tends to be a bottom-up process [...] influenced by intuitions derived from our schemata about the structuring of text-types and genres" (p. 229). He further explains that steps help to construct moves. In other words, a move is realized via various steps, which have particular communicative purposes, such as description, justification, gap identification, purpose, summarization, etc.

Devitt (2015) proposes that in order to support the development of the skills needed to compose texts within a particular genre, instruction can "lead students to examine not just similarity within genre but also differences" (p. 44). Therefore, in this study, we include a qualitative analysis of the data in which we identify typical ways in which the text authors, i.e., teacher candidates, compose their reflective texts, and highlight some of the moves (i.e., action, problem/solution, and change) and steps (description, explanation, evaluation, and analysis) that characterize their reflections from a genre perspective. Our main goal is to illustrate the shared features found in the sample of texts analyzed by examining teachers' reflective writing about their own teaching practice within the context of a performance assessment.

3   Methodology

Teacher reflection is expected across a range of contexts and for a variety of purposes. However, it is in the context of formative and summative assessment that teacher educators often encounter this type of writing. For teachers-in-training, it becomes important to demonstrate their ability to reflect, especially as part of high-stakes testing situations. In this study, we analyzed reflective texts composed for the edTPA (Educative Teacher Performance Assessment), which is a national performance assessment used in the US for initial teacher licensure, concentrating on a sample of texts generated by language teacher candidates in response to Task 2 in the edTPA, which focuses specifically on instruction. These are the guiding questions formulated for the study:

1. Are there distinct levels and dimensions of reflection found in language teacher candidates' writing about their teaching and their students learning (edTPA-Task2)?
2. What percentage of discourse accounts for different levels and dimensions of reflection in the data analyzed?
3. What common discourse patterns (moves/steps) can be identified through the lens of levels and dimensions of reflection?

3.1 The Data

As mentioned, the data used for the study comes from the edTPA, a well-known performance assessment. At present, more than 900 educational institutions use the edTPA as a significant part of their initial teacher preparation programs, which makes it "the most frequently used instrument in the United States for assessing teacher candidates' teaching effectiveness" (Davis & Armstrong, 2018; p. 18). During the student teaching process, teacher candidates are asked to complete a portfolio as part of their graduation requirements in preparation for licensure. This portfolio includes three to five lesson plans, instructional materials, video recordings of the teachers' classroom instruction, and reflections or commentaries. There are three main parts or tasks: (1) planning, (2) instruction, and (3) assessment. In each task, teacher candidates are asked to reflect, in writing, using prompts included in each section to guide their reflections. The instructions they receive direct them to focus on their thinking, based on their knowledge of pedagogy and their students' needs (SCALE, 2019a).

We chose to use the edTPA as a source of data for our study because this assessment is a widely used measure of pre-service teachers' knowledge, pedagogy, and ability to reflect on their teaching. We assume this assessment inspires candidates to engage in teaching and reflection to the best of their ability, while acknowledging that their reflections may be affected by the fact that these are generated as part of a standardized assessment. Nonetheless, given that this assessment constitutes an integral part of the licensure process for many teachers in the US, including language teachers, we believe the data can be both informative and helpful to better understand how teacher candidates reflect in writing and to explore the characteristics of their reflective texts. For this study, we specifically focused on the edTPA task 2 (Instruction), which allowed us to examine candidates' reflections on their instructional practice. There are four different sections that teachers are asked to reflect on in task 2: (2) promoting a positive learning environment, (3) engaging students in communication in the target language, (4) deepening students' language proficiency, and (5) analyzing their teaching (including changes needed).

3.2 The edTPA and Reflection

The literature on the edTPA indicates that reflection is an integral part of this assessment. According to the Stanford Center for Assessment, Learning, and Equity (SCALE, 2019b), the edTPA aims to provide candidates with opportunities to demonstrate a reflective disposition or stance, and it is expected to constitute a reflective experience for preservice teachers where they can demonstrate their knowledge, skills, and abilities embedded in real teaching with real students in real classrooms. More specifically, in relation to language teachers, the SCALE (2019c) instructs candidates that the commentaries they write as part of their portfolio should both explain and reflect on each component, i.e., planning, instruction, and assessment (p. 2) as well as reflect upon the relationship among them (p. 3). Moreover, teacher educators also see the edTPA as inherently involving reflection. Davis and Armstrong (2018), for instance, report that their survey participants, 17 teacher educators in 11 content areas, were "particularly vocal" about reflection being one of the strengths of the edTPA.

It has been noted, however, that most teacher candidates find the kind of reflection elicited by the edTPA difficult to articulate (Micek, 2017) and that strong reflective writing skills are necessary to complete such assessment successfully. Conversely, if these skills are lacking, candidates will struggle to develop the edTPA reflective commentaries (Denton, 2013; Troyan & Kaplan, 2015). Thus, it has been recommended that teacher preparation programs provide support for the edTPA with particular focus on reflective writing, including working with rubrics (Okraski & Kissau, 2018). We agree with this recommendation and with Troyan and Kaplan's (2015) position that more research is needed "to understand the complexities and the variations in teacher candidates' reflective writing trajectories as programs and states increasingly move toward the edTPA" (p. 387).

3.3 Data Files

The data used for analysis in this study consisted of 12 edTPA task 2 reflective responses or commentaries (henceforth referred to as 'files') from teacher candidates in the fields of English as an Additional Language (EAL) and Word Languages (WL). Six files in each area, previously cleaned of all identifying information, were chosen randomly from an available pool of texts at one of the researcher's institutions. In task 2, teacher candidates are limited to writing no more than six single-spaced pages. However, the number of words in each of the four sections comprising task 2 can vary considerably, as shown in Table 2.1. As can be observed, most files ranged between 2000 and 3500 words, with only two files below 2000 (files EAL-4 and WL-11) and one file (WL-12) with more than 3500 words. The average number of words per file was 2704.

As shown in Table 2.1, section 4 elicited more writing (10,220 words) in comparison to the other sections, followed by sections 5, 3, and 2, in descending order. As a reminder, section 4 deals with extending and deepening language proficiency in the

Table 2.1 Number of words per file (Task-2 sections)

File	Section 2	Section 3	Section 4	Section 5	Totals
EAL-1	676	461	965	1136	3238
EAL-2	574	511	826	1102	3013
EAL-3	503	584	843	1293	3223
EAL-4	259	521	666	304	1750
EAL-5	408	572	908	622	2510
EAL-6	384	377	697	561	2019
WL-7	522	1029	792	588	2931
WL-8	381	668	687	357	2093
WL-9	472	499	754	1029	2753
WL-10	416	500	1323	1201	3440
WL-11	188	493	586	470	1737
WL-12	610	1305	1174	655	3744
Totals	5393	7520	10,220	9318	32,451

target language, while section 5 calls for an analysis of the teacher's instruction as shown in the lessons observed. Sections 2 and 3 refer to promoting a positive learning environment and communicating in the target language, respectively.

4 Analysis

4.1 Rubric Used in the Study

The rubric for our study was based on Jay and Johnson (2002) and Ward and McCotter (2004). Drawing on Schön's views of reflective practice, Jay and Johnson (2002) proposed a typology of reflection that could be used to link theory and practice by connecting teachers' actions and experiences to their evolving knowledge. Their typology includes three dimensions. The first is called *descriptive reflection*, which focuses on identifying and defining a 'problem' (i.e., anything puzzling, troubling, or interesting) and making sense of it. The second dimension is termed *comparative reflection* and it calls for understanding others' point of view, which often requires questioning one's own values and beliefs. The third dimension, *critical reflection*, refers to the integration of the information gathered in the other two dimensions to make decisions or take actions, taking into consideration not only the situation at hand but, ideally, the broader context of schooling.

In a more detailed manner, Ward and McCotter (2004) designed a rubric to evaluate teacher reflection and determine levels and dimensions of reflection. Using a grounded theory approach to develop the rubric, they proposed four levels of reflection. *Routine reflections* tend to be concerned with the self rather than students' learning. Similarly, *technical reflections* do not focus on students' learning nor consider multiple perspectives, although the focus shifts from the self to teaching tasks and there is more discussion of problems. These lower levels of reflection are unlikely to generate change or new insights. A deeper level of reflection involves consideration of the views of others, a focus on the process of learning, careful consideration of alternatives, and the emergence of new insights, which are all part of the level termed *dialogic reflection*. Lastly, at the deeper level of *transformative reflection*, teachers question established practices, conventional beliefs, and their own personal assumptions about teaching and learning. These levels can be found across three dimensions: *focus* (e.g., focus on self, on students, on the impact of broader concerns), *inquiry* (e.g., considering multiple perspectives), and *change* (e.g., new insights arriving from situated experiences).

Our rubric was modified from the one originally proposed by Ward and McCotter (2004) in connection with the dimensions proposed by Jay and Johnson (2002). The modifications resulted from an iterative process of using the rubric and making decisions regarding the suitability of the original descriptors to code the type of data included in the files. After a process of coding, recoding, and discussions to refine its descriptors, the final rubric (shown in Table 2.2) was generated. The goal here was to create a rubric with clear, user-friendly descriptors that future teachers and teacher educators could use to better understand, create, and assess reflective writing.

Another important corollary of the rubric generated for the analysis was that it allowed us to examine the discourse generated by the teacher candidates in terms of moves and steps, as described by Swales (2004). Given that the rubric consists of specific communicative functions (i.e., describing, explaining, evaluating, analyzing) and that these help to construct broader concerns on the part of authors (i.e., actions taken, issues noticed, problems solved, improvements made), this provided us with a helpful heuristic to explore and understand the data from a qualitative perspective. In our rubric, the moves correspond to the dimensions of action, problem solving, and change, while the steps correspond to the descriptors within each level of reflection (e.g., behavior, reasons, problems, responses, strengths, connections, etc.).

4.2 Data Coding

The rubric described above (Table 2.2) was used to manually code the data. Responses to the edTPA task 2 prompts were coded by identifying text segments,

Table 2.2 Coding rubric (based on Jay & Johnson, 2002; Ward & McCotter, 2004)

	Describing	Explaining	Evaluating	Analyzing
Actions What happened? How did it happen?	*Behavior:* Describing teacher and student actions in lessons observed	*Reasons:* Explaining purpose or reasons behind actions	*Observations:* Evaluating teacher and student actions	*Realizations:* Analyzing actions and formulating insights or new understandings that go beyond current classroom and students
Problem – Solution What issues are noticed? How are they noticed and/or dealt with?	*Routines:* Describing routine-like actions and expressing generalizations	*Problems:* Explaining issues as puzzling, troubling, problematic, worth noting	*Responses:* Evaluating issues and ways to respond and/or consider alternatives	*Connections:* Analyzing actions in relation to theories, research, and/or expert knowledge
Change Why did it happen in a certain way? What improvements can be made?	*Circumstances:* Describing actions as resulting from circumstantial (other) factors	*Causes:* Explaining why something worked or did not work	*Changes:* Evaluating ways to improve outcomes and/or strengths and weaknesses	*Beliefs:* Analyzing one's own assumptions and belief system regarding teaching and learning within a societal context

or 'chunks,' that expressed any of the functions included in the rubric. Segments or chunks could range in length from a few words to several sentences, with the end of a chunk signaled by a change in the function being expressed, so that a sentence could include more than one code, e.g., description of a behavior followed by an evaluation. First, each data file was coded independently by the researchers, with a percent agreement ranging between 64% and 94%, with ten out of the twelve files above 70% percent. Differences in coding were then discussed and agreed upon so that a final coding for each file could be generated for both levels and dimensions of reflection. After this, the number of words coded similarly, per levels and dimensions, was counted, and the corresponding percentage of the total number of words calculated. These percentages provided an overview, in summarized form (see below), of the amount of description, explanation, evaluation and analysis in each file, as well as the amount of discourse focused on actions, problem/solution, or change.

5 Results

5.1 Quantitative Results

Table 2.3 shows the amount of discourse in each file devoted to each level of reflection, as a percentage of the total. Because some of the responses included language that simply reproduced the prompt, there was a need to take these phrases out of the total count and represent that use separately. This language is shown in the column labeled *prompt language*. We decided to give these chunks a separate code and include the corresponding percentages as they represent, in a way, a specific discourse move within a response (see example 1 in the qualitative results section below). As can be observed in Table 2.3, in seven out of the 12 files, a higher percentage of the text was coded as descriptive, and in two files (EAL-6 and WL-8), description accounts for almost half of the writing.

Another noticeable pattern is that, in all cases, the level of 'analysis' accounts for the least amount of discourse in the files, ranging from less than 1% to a maximum of 13.16%. It is, therefore, clear that this is the level of reflection most neglected and where more attention is needed. There was also variation in the way the discourse was distributed across levels of reflection in each file. We can see, for instance, that there were files that did not include as much descriptive reflection and, instead, more emphasis was put on explanatory (EAL-2) or evaluative (EAL-1 and 3, WL-9) reflection. In addition, in two files (WL-9 and EAL-3), the discourse includes as much evaluation and analysis as description and explanation, resulting in more balanced responses in terms of including different types of reflective writ-

Table 2.3 Percentage of discourse per levels of reflection

File	Description	Explanation	Evaluation	Analysis	Prompt lang.
EAL-1	25.69%	23.78%	35.21%	10.56%	4.76%
EAL-2	19.18%	35.75%	29.61%	8.16%	7.30%
EAL-3	19.11%	22.34%	38.91%	13.16%	6.48%
EAL-4	33.20%	31.31%	24.80%	0.69%	10.00%
EAL-5	24.66%	28.17%	32.87%	3.98%	10.32%
EAL-6	43.98%	24.67%	17.43%	1.78%	12.13%
WL-7	35.69%	25.90%	25.45%	12.45%	6.69%
WL-8	47.15%	25.75%	16.28%	6.13%	4.69%
WL-9	28.91%	17.25%	36.51%	12.35%	4.98%
WL-10	33.82%	32.13%	27.96%	6.09%	0.00%
WL-11	41.65%	23.13%	21.02%	5.68%	8.52%
WL-12	37.19%	22.73%	25.37%	8.82%	5.88%

ing in them. Finally, if we consider the files with more description as being less reflective than those where more discourse was distributed among the other three levels, then files EAL-2 and EAL-3 would be good exemplars, both with less than 20% of the text coded as descriptive.

Before moving on to the results regarding dimensions of reflection, it is worth pointing out that even when teacher candidates were responding to the same prompts, their responses could be quite different, as shown in excerpts 1 and 2. These reflections were both elicited by a prompt asking teachers to "describe how your instruction linked students' prior learning with new learning" (task 2, section 3b). As excerpts 1 and 2 illustrate, in some cases the response incorporates mostly descriptions, while in others it builds on the description with other levels such as explanation and evaluation.

Excerpt 1—Descriptive

> Lesson two was designed to allow the students to incorporate their own cultural and personal assets into the lesson. The students are able to talk about any subject they want and use any fruit they want. One student who is very interested in all things military, talked about a tank that ate many other 'fruit tanks' and became a more advanced tank. Student 3 talked about a Pacman that was eating its way through fruit to become bigger and stronger because of his interest in that videogame. A third student decided to go the humorous route and talked about a little man who ate a bunch of fruit and became a sumo wrestler. By encouraging my students to inject their own assets and personality into the lesson, I created an effective exercise that the students enjoyed. (sample 11).

Excerpt 2—Descriptive, explanatory, evaluative

> By following the reading curriculum in Lessons 1 and 2, I built upon students' familiarity with the leveled readers and use of weekly vocabulary words. I incorporated a new routine into this familiar context by adding the numerous pre-written comprehension questions, but students caught on quickly to the change and seemed eager each time they got to look through their question slips to see if it was their turn (e.g., clip 2 2:17–2:25, 2:54–2:57). The learning segment was structured to allow for connections between prior learning and new learning, such as reviewing the week's vocabulary words with an interactive Smart Board game in Lesson 1 before encountering them in the text, or orally recounting the story so far before resuming the leveled reader in Lesson 2 (clip 2 0:00–0:59).
>
> In order to support students' learning of new words, I provided some realia (a yeast packet, a sponge) to give them a more tangible idea of these words' meanings. Later, when those words came up again either in further vocabulary discussion or in the read-

ing, I could refer back to those objects to remind the students of that experience and the meaning they had learned (e.g. clip 1 0:41–0:46, 4:13–4:21). (sample 3).

In excerpt 1, even though there is an initial statement indicating the overall objective of the activity, the response consists mostly of descriptions of what students did, ending with a brief and unsupported evaluation of the activity (i.e., it was effective and students enjoyed it). In contrast, in excerpt 2, the response explains not only how and why actions were taken (e.g., students are eased into new routines within previously established activities by means of pre-written comprehension questions in order to connect prior and new learning), but also linked to future actions, in the last sentences, adding an element of prospective reflection to the response.

Similar percentages to those calculated for levels of reflection were also calculated for dimensions, i.e., actions, problem/solution, and change. The results are shown in Table 2.4. The use of prompt language in responses is also indicated.

As can be observed in Table 2.4, most of the discourse in the responses focused on actions, that is, what teachers and students did, what the purpose behind those actions were, and how instructors assessed those actions. Percentages in this dimension range between 39%, in EAL-2, to a high 67%, in WL-8. The latter was also the file with the most descriptive language, while the former was one in two files with little description. Table 2.4 also shows that in 8 out of 12, there was a considerable amount of discourse, between 23% and 44%, dealing with problem identification and solving or referring to situations that, if not problematic, they were at least worth noting; for instance, file EAL-2, which can be contrasted with

Table 2.4 Percentage of discourse per dimensions of reflection

File	Actions	Problem/Solution	Change	Prompt language
EAL-1	50.80%	28.44%	16.03%	4.76%
EAL-2	39.63%	44.41%	8.66%	7.30%
EAL-3	43.44%	32.61%	17.47%	6.48%
EAL-4	52.23%	11.20%	26.57%	10.0%
EAL-5	43.47%	25.98%	20.24%	10.32%
EAL-6	49.53%	15.11%	23.18%	12.13%
WL-7	59.91%	24.19%	9.21%	6.69%
WL-8	67.11%	23.03%	5.17%	4.69%
WL-9	56.41%	13.40%	25.21%	4.98%
WL-10	56.57%	30.50%	12.93%	0.00%
WL-11	60.28%	18.35%	12.84%	8.52%
WL-12	60.75%	25.67%	7.70%	5.88%

file EAL-4, where only about 11% of the discourse deals with problems and possible solutions. In relation to the 'change' dimension, i.e., chunks discussing why actions happened in certain ways and what improvements can be made in one's instruction, teaching skills, or belief system, the percentages tend to be relatively low, ranging between 5% and 26%. Overall, in most files, more than half of the discourse was focused on teachers' and students' actions, with lower percentages devoted to problem-solving and change.

5.2 Qualitative Results

As mentioned earlier, the dimensions in the rubric, i.e., actions, problem/solution, and change, represent discourse moves and within each of these moves we have different steps related to each level of reflection: describing, explaining, evaluating, and analyzing (see Table 2.2). In this section, we present examples of reflective responses in task 2 of the edTPA to illustrate how teacher candidates structured and organized their responses and how moves can comprise different sets of steps. The examples presented in this section are divided by moves and the steps are indicated to the right of each discourse segment or chunk.

Actions: As the quantitative results indicated, one of the frequent discourse moves found in the files was 'action,' used to comment on what happened and how it happened. Four steps are associated with this move: describing behavior, explaining reasons, evaluating observations, and analyzing realizations (see Table 2.2). Some teacher candidates did not go beyond the step of 'describing behavior,' which denotes a lower level of reflection, as they simply describe their own actions or that of their students, at times connecting these to language used in the prompt, as in (1), but without further elaboration.

(1)	*I demonstrated mutual respect for and rapport with students*	prompt
	by calling them each by name and giving them ample time to think rather than demanding responses (sample 3, 2a)	describing behavior

In other instances, the step of 'describing behavior' was built upon by adding steps such as 'explaining reasons' (2) or 'evaluating observations' (3), thus presenting their actions in a slightly more elaborated -and thus more reflective- manner.

(2)	*I also encouraged the students to write down the words that were not already in their packet,*	describing behavior
	to use as a future resource (sample 9, 3a)	explaining reasons

(3)	*One student brings in one of the ELL vocabulary words from Lesson 1, ingredients, when I am explaining the new word fermentation in relation to yeast. He says, "Or like ingredients or something"*	describing behavior
	showing that he understands the concept of fermentation changing things and knows that ingredients change in the process of cooking, as well as demonstrating the ability to effectively use this vocabulary word (sample 3, 4c)	evaluating observation

In reading the teacher candidates' responses, we noticed that, through a process of elaboration, i.e., by adding steps, a particular behavior being described could be complemented with an explanation (reason), an evaluation of the behavior (observation), and/or with an analysis of the situation (realization), and in this way reach deeper levels of reflection, as illustrated by example (4).

(4)	*When student 3 asks me how I am doing and I respond that I am well and I correct him on his pronoun use,*	describing behavior
	I am providing him with a brief reminder of the differences between American and German culture: the difference between formal and informal use of 'you.'	explaining reasons
	This is an intentional correction and I always correct this mistake.	describing routines
	This is an important cultural difference and discussing it in a meaningful way is an effective way to reinforce acquisition of this German cultural practice. By relating American and German culture to each other, the students are able to make connections between their own cultural practices and German cultural practices.	evaluating observations
	This also reinforces an important perspective of respect in German. If one uses the wrong 'you' form with a stranger, it can be seen as disrespectful and insulting to both the native speaker and the person communicating with them. This is a communicative skill that is transferable to language use within the target culture on a regular basis and being able to recognize the distinction between formal and informal enables these students to develop their communicative proficiency while making distinctions between their own culture and the target culture. (sample 11, 4c)	analyzing realizations

Furthermore, actions can also be accompanied by other moves, such as 'problem/solution,' where teacher candidates refer to issues or situations that they deemed peculiar, unexpected, problematic, or simply worth mentioning, as well as references to 'change,' the other major move, which includes possible causes, evaluations of changes and/or one's strengths or weaknesses, improvements, or reconsideration of perspectives and beliefs. As can be seen in (5), adding steps as-

2 Reflective Writing and Self-assessment of Language Teaching Performance

sociated to these moves offers much insight into a teachers' thinking and reflecting disposition. Actions are not only described but explained and discussed in light of related issues or problems, possible responses, and evaluations.

(5)	*I begin the class by asking "What do you remember about the Flint news article?" and I receive responses from two students with higher speaking proficiencies in the class. The girl says, "I remember the Great Lakes."*	describing behavior
	At this point I should have stopped and asked, "Tell me more," but instead I rushed ahead	evaluating changes
	and fill in how the Great Lakes connects to Flint. The boy responds with "polluted" and I ask him, "What is polluted?"	describing behavior
	I again could have asked, "Tell me more." This simple question could have elicited a way both students could have demonstrated their understanding of the news article.	evaluating changes
	I rushed through that formative assessment	analyzing realization
	I can see that a third student, sitting in the second row	describing behavior
	had more to share, but I didn't hear him	explaining problem
	I also could have had students "turn and talk" to their partner about what they remembered about the news article before opening it back up to the whole class. By first practicing their response in a smaller setting like with a partner and hearing what their partner remembered	evaluating changes
	students who are not as confident to speak up in front of the whole class (like some of my students in the front row who are at different language proficiencies and some of whom struggle to read in their first language and are considered SLIFE)	explaining problems
	may have volunteered more readily or I could have called on each table to share something. (sample 1, 5a)	evaluating changes

While we found that moves and steps did not necessarily occur in a particular order, depending on the candidate's writing style, it was often the case that the reflections were built from lower to higher levels, i.e., from mere description to explanation and evaluation, and from including just one dimension, i.e., action, to including multiple dimensions of reflection, i.e., starting with activity and purpose, followed by the problem/response, and leading to evaluation and ideas for change, but this was by no means uniformly found, as the quantitative results show.

Problem/Solution: The second move found throughout the files is 'problem/solution.' Four steps were identified in connection with this move: describing routines, explaining problems, evaluating responses, and analyzing connections. The following examples provide some insight into these steps. The first, describing routines, refers to describing issues in a detached manner. As shown in (6), this occurs when the description seems uncomplicated, routine-like, or expected, often expressed with definitive statements and generalizations.

(6)	*In lesson plan one, I challenge the student to roll their "R's" I try to do this whenever I am teaching a lesson.* (sample 4, 2a)	describing routines

Another step in the 'problem/solution' move was 'explaining problems.' These are instances in which teacher candidates noticed something that needed attention, often explaining how/why issues may be context-specific, interesting, relevant, unexpected, or worth-exploring. As illustrated in (7), this step often, but not always, occurred with a 'solving' step, evaluating responses, where teachers address the problem or try to understand it by considering possible solutions and alternative ways to improve learning or teaching outcomes. This step could also include making a concrete plan for future teaching in response to a situated problem or for a specific type of student.

(7)	*When this student still seems to be uncertain of how to respond,*	explaining problem
	I elicit a response in the target language by giving him an example. I say "Por ejemplo, yo soy una persona cómica. Jajaja. ¿Cómo eres tú? The student then responds correctly with "Oh. Yo soy una persona interesante." (sample 7, 4a)	evaluating response

Yet another step within the 'problem/solution' move is 'analyzing connections,' depicting a deeper level of reflection. It involves inquiry and engagement with critical texts, research findings, or experts to (re)interpret issues and situations (8). In this step, the aim is to consider information from other sources as a way to shed light onto -and thus more fully understand- a particular issue or problem.

(8)	*According to Krashen's theories about Comprehensible Input from 1981, Second Language Acquisition and Second Language Learning. University of Southern California: Pergamon Press Inc., if the input that the students are receiving is not comprehensible, it is not helping them learn. In order for the students to acquire the language, they must be able to understand what is being said to them,*	analyzing connections
	and judging by my student's reactions in my lessons,	evaluating responses
	they did not understand everything. (sample 11, 5b)	explaining problems

2 Reflective Writing and Self-assessment of Language Teaching Performance

In addition to occurring with multiple steps, the 'problem/solution' move can also occur with other moves. Because reflective papers can be expected to have a very loose structure, moves may appear and re-appear at different times, given the nature of a lesson where actions, problems, evaluations, or analysis may be realized at any point in the lesson, and thus in the reflection. Example (9) shows a candidate going back and forth between 'action' and 'problem/solution' moves with multiple steps in each move.

(9)	*After some initial resistance,*	explaining problem
	the girl and boy in the middle in the front row can be seen working together to find matching cause and effect relationships in the Learning Center.	evaluating observation
	In the front row, but closer to the wall this girl and boy who also share differences across linguistic, cultural, and gender lines	explaining problem
	are seen working patiently through the task.	evaluating observation
	Noticeable due to her quickness in oral responses and higher volume is a female student (Student H) in the second row and closer to the camera,	explaining problem
	who can be seen working well with a quieter male student closest to the camera in the second row from a diverse linguistic and cultural background.	evaluating observation
	The partner work seen both in Clip 1 with rereading and in Clip 2 with the Learning Center	describing behavior
	demonstrates general rapport among students and adds a challenge and support to engage in the learning tasks.	prompt language
	Clip 2 also shows the easy rapport I have with students	evaluating observation
	through positive and appropriate physical contact, smiles, and easy use of first names. When reading with a student in the front row (4:18–7:47)	describing behavior
	I demonstrate strong rapport and responsiveness to her needs.	prompt lang.
	by getting on her level, giving a lot of positive feedback, actively listening and responding to her questions and pronunciation and reading challenges.	describing behavior
	I know she has a great desire to learn, but has some challenges orally expressing what she knows and lacks confidence.	explaining problem
	I believe this extra one-on-one attention helped strengthen our relationship and her ability to feel safe and heard in our classroom	evaluating response
	where she is not as likely to speak up in front of the whole class. (sample 1, 2a)	explaining problem

Change: In the move labeled 'change,' teacher candidates analyzed their teaching, suggested possible changes, or proposed new ways to think about their instruction. This move also had four distinct steps that occurred with various frequencies: describing circumstances, explaining causes, evaluating changes, and analyzing beliefs. The step labeled 'describing circumstances' was one of the least frequently found. It refers to instances in which candidates blamed problems or failure on other factors or people, thus outside their control, as shown in (10).

| (10) | *Another missed opportunity came in lesson 3 where many of my students were absent for various excused reasons. Students 1 and 2 were among them. I would have liked to have had them in class to encourage the development of their communicative proficiency, especially because I found many aspects of that lesson to be very helpful for the other students in the class. Although there is nothing I could have done to make the students be in the class that day, I feel like it was a missed opportunity because I was not able to help them learn that day.* (sample 11, 5a) | describing circumstances |

The two steps more commonly found in the texts were 'explaining causes,' in which teacher candidates offered possible reasons why something worked or did not work, and 'evaluating changes,' in which they assessed their own contributions to the success or failure of lessons and ways to improve future outcomes accordingly. When explaining causes, teacher candidates commented on factors affecting relative success or failure of their teaching actions and its outcomes. This was generally explained in terms of previous knowledge rather than revelations and explicitly mentioned success or failure, as shown in (11).

| (11) | *I knew this would resonate with students because dealing with conversationally dominant people is a very common occurrence in life. Especially when a person is young. This example allows students to interpret the terminology easier, because they are able to see how this information applied to real-life, and not just the classroom or a business setting.* (sample 2, 3a) | explaining causes |

In 'evaluating changes' candidates also had an opportunity to examine their own personal teaching effectiveness in terms of learning from current classroom experiences, as shown in (12).

| (12) | *I would like to be sure to give students more time to be able to have the same attention that the rest of the class is being given.* (sample 8, 5b) | evaluating changes |

Finally, the step called 'analyzing beliefs' was not found in the texts but would have involved candidates analyzing their own assumptions and belief systems regarding teaching and learning. We looked for instances where candidates challenged their own personal assumptions and reframed their personal belief system regarding teaching and learning. A possible reason this step was not found could be that candidates, in addition to reflecting on their teaching and the students' learning, were attempting to express their established teaching philosophy in this formal assessment, rather than questioning existing beliefs and practices in order to further develop these.

6 Conclusions and Implications

Based on the findings presented above, it can be said that the teacher candidates' responses, for the most part, included elements of reflection at various levels, ranging from descriptive to analytical, as well as reflective commentaries that point to the three dimensions examined: actions, problem/solution, and change, as conceptualized in previous models of reflection (e.g., Ward & McCotter, 2004; Jay & Johnson, 2002). On the other hand, the examination of the data, both quantitatively and qualitatively, also shows that there is considerable variation in the way teacher candidates composed their reflective responses. It was clear that most samples show a preponderance of descriptive and explanatory reflection, with fewer instances of deeper levels and dimensions of reflection, that is, evaluation and analysis. Our findings, thus, align with arguments that teacher candidates need more support on how to reflect in a deeper, more sophisticated manner, so that they can improve their ability to respond to self-assessments of their teaching practice, especially if this is an integral part of their teacher education, licensure procedure, or teacher development program.

In a profession such as teaching, in which new members are asked to demonstrate their preparation and readiness, in part, by demonstrating their ability to reflect, in writing, about their practice, it is imperative that the construct of reflection be presented in a clear and easy-to-understand manner. In other words, teachers need to know what it means to reflect, and what are ways in which reflective texts can be composed. To support teacher candidates, as well as teachers in training, we believe that a rubric such as the one designed and used in this study can serve as a tool to make reflection more transparent. First, by showing that reflection on teaching involves specific moves and steps, and secondly, by illustrating what these moves and steps look like in discourse. Teachers need to know, and possibly be explicitly taught, that describing what happens in the classroom is usually not enough to demonstrate deep reflective thinking, as this also requires offering reasons or explanations for teaching and learning actions, evaluating such actions, and analyzing them. In addition, it would be helpful to show that analyzing one's practice must also establish connections between practice and theory, classroom decisions and pedagogical research, and between problems and solutions. Finally, it is also necessary to tie these elements to potential areas for change (based on strengths and weaknesses).

In addition to using a teacher-friendly rubric, we believe that teacher educators can use the discourse patterns (moves and steps) we identified in this study to illustrate how reflections of teaching performance can be composed, as well as how descriptive reflections can move towards deeper levels of reflection by integrating description, explanation, and evaluation with some of the more complex reflecting elements, such as analysis, change, connection to theory and research, and examination of beliefs and assumptions. We surmise that showing how moves and steps are variously deployed by teachers when attempting to compose a reflective text can demystify a process that is often vague and confusing, especially when this occurs in high-stakes situations such as the edTPA and other forms of teacher assessment, formal and informal.

References

Akbari, R. (2007). Reflections on reflection: A critical appraisal of reflective practices in L2 teacher education. *System, 35*, 192–207.

Anderson, J. (2020). Key concepts in ELT. *ELT Journal, 74*(4), 480–483.

Collier, S. T. (2010). Reflection as a social problem-solving process. In E. G. Pultorak (Ed.), *The purposes, practices, and professionalism of teacher reflectivity* (pp. 45–71). Rowman & Littlefield Education.

Davis, K., & Armstrong, A. (2018). Teacher educators' initial impressions of the edTPA: A "love-hate" relationship. *SRATE Journal, 27*(2), 18–25.

Denton, D. W. (2013). Responding to edTPA: Transforming practice or applying shortcuts? *AILACTE Journal, 10*, 19–36.

Devitt, A. J. (2015). Genre performances: John Swales' 'Genre Analysis' and rhetorical-linguistic genre studies. *Journal of English for Academic Purposes, 19*, 44–51.

Dewey, J. (1933). *How we think*. D.C. Heath and Co.

Farrell, T. (2006). Reflective practice in action: A case study of a writing teacher's reflection on practice. *TESL Canada Journal, 23*(2), 77–90.

Farrell, T. (2011). Exploring the professional role identities of experience ESL teachers through reflective practice. *System, 39*(1), 54–62.

Farrell, T. (2016). The practices of encouraging TESOL teachers to engage in reflective practice: An appraisal of recent research contributions. *Language Teaching Research, 20*(2), 223–247.

Farrell, T. (2020). *Reflective teaching*. TESOL Press.

Fendler, L. (2003). Teacher reflection in a hall of mirrors: Historical influences and political reverberations. *Educational Researcher, 32*(3), 16–25.

Freese, A. R. (2006). Reframing one's teaching: Discovering of teacher selves through reflection and inquiry. *Teaching and Teacher Education, 22*, 100–119.

Gun, B. (2011). Quality self-reflection through reflection training. *ELT Journal, 65*(2), 126–135.

Hatton, N., & Smith, D. (1995). Reflection in teacher education: Towards definition and implementation. *Teaching and Teacher Education, 11*(1), 33–49.

Hyland, K. (2002). Genre: Language, context, and literacy. *Annual Review of Applied Linguistics, 22*, 113–135.

Jay, J. K., & Johnson, K. L. (2002). Capturing complexity: A typology of reflective practice for teacher education. *Teaching and Teacher Education, 18*(1), 73–85.

Killion, J. P., & Todnem, G. R. (1991). A process for personal theory building. *Educational Leadership, 48*(6), 14–16.

Korthagen, F. A. J. (2010). Teacher reflection: What it is and what it does. In E. G. Pultorak (Ed.), *The purposes, practices, and professionalism of teacher reflectivity: Insights for twenty-first-century teachers and students* (pp. 377–401). Rowman & Littlefield.

Larrivee, B. (2008). Meeting the challenge of preparing reflective practitioners. *New Educator, 4*(2), 87–106.

Leung, C. (2009). Second language teacher professionalism. In A. Burns & J. Richards (Eds.), *The Cambridge guide to second language teacher education* (pp. 49–58). Cambridge University Press.

McDonough, K. (2006). Action research and the professional development of graduate teaching assistants. *The Modern Language Journal, 90*(1), 33–47.

Micek, T. A. (2017). Completing edTPA: TESOL candidate performance and reflection. *Issues in Teacher Education, 26*(1), 85–99.

National Board for Professional Teaching Standards. (2010). *World Languages Standards* (2nd ed.). NBPTS.

Okraski, C. V., & Kissau, S. P. (2018). Impact of content-specific seminars on candidate edTPA preparation and performance. *Foreign Language Annals, 51*, 685–705.

Quinn, L., Pultorak, E., Young, M., & McCarthy, J. (2010). Purposes and practices of reflectivity in teacher development. In E. G. Pultorak (Ed.), *The purposes, practices, and professionalism of teacher reflectivity: Insights for twenty-first-century teachers and students* (pp. 25–43). Rowman & Littlefield Education.

Reiman, A. (1999). The evolution of the social role-taking and guided reflection framework in teacher education: Recent theory and quantitative synthesis of research. *Teaching and Teacher Education, 15*, 597–612.

Richards, J. C. (1990). Beyond training: Approaches to teacher education in language teaching. *The Language Teacher, 14*(2), 3–8.

Rodgers, C. (2002). Seeing student learning: Teacher change and the role of reflection. Voices inside schools. *Harvard Educational Review, 72*(2), 230–253.

SCALE – Stanford Center for Assessment, Learning, & Equity. (2019a). *edTPA Making good choices: Candidate support resource*. Board of Trustees of the Leland Stanford Junior University.

SCALE – Stanford Center for Assessment, Learning, & Equity. (2019b). *edTPA Educative assessment and meaningful report*. Board of Trustees of the Leland Stanford Junior University/Pearson Education.

SCALE – Stanford Center for Assessment, Learning, & Equity. (2019c). *edTPA English as an additional language assessment handbook*. Board of Trustees of the Leland Stanford Junior University.

Schön, D. (1983). *The reflective practitioner*. Basic Books.

Schön, D. (1987). *Educating the reflective practitioner: Toward a new design for teaching and learning in the professions*. Jossey-Bass.

Swales, J. M. (1990). *Genre analysis: English in academic and research settings*. Cambridge University Press.

Swales, J. M. (2004). *Research genres: Explorations and applications*. Cambridge University Press.

Troyan, F. J., & Kaplan, C. S. (2015). The functions of reflection in high-stakes assessment of world language teacher candidates. *Foreign Language Annals, 48*(3), 372–393.

Tsui. (2007). Complexities of identity formation: A narrative inquiry of an EFL teacher. *TESOL Quarterly, 41*, 657–680.

Urzúa, A., & Vásquez, C. (2008). Reflection and professional identity in teachers' future-oriented discourse. *Teaching and Teacher Education, 24*(7), 1935–1946.

Van Manen, M. (1977). Linking ways of knowing with ways of being practical. *Curriculum Inquiry, 6*, 205–228.

Ward, J. R., & McCotter, S. S. (2004). Reflection as a visible outcome for preservice teachers. *Teaching and Teacher Education, 20*(3), 243–257.

Zeichner, K., & Liston, D. (1987). Teaching student teachers to reflect. *Harvard Educational Review, 57*(1), 23–49.

Zeichner, K., & Liu, K. (2010). *A critical analysis of reflection as a goal for teacher education*.

Alfredo Urzúa is Associate Professor of Applied Linguistics at San Diego State University. He has an MA degree in TESL/Applied Linguistics from the University of California at Los Angeles and a Ph.D. in Applied Linguistics from Northern Arizona University. His teaching focuses on second language teaching pedagogy, teacher education, and bilingualism, and his main research interests include teacher development, identity construction, and reflective discourse. He has extensive experience coordinating different types of language programs in the US and in Mexico. Contact: aurzua@sdsu.edu

Nancy Drescher is a full Professor in the Teaching English to Speakers of Other Languages at Minnesota State University, Mankato. She has a Ph.D. in Applied Linguistics from Northern Arizona University. Her teaching focuses on English language teaching, teacher education, sociolinguistics, and literacy. Her main research interests include teacher development, educational policies, and reflection. She has taught English at the K-12 level in the United States and overseas and currently works primarily at the university level. Contact: nancy.drescher@mnsu.edu

Applying Peer Rubric Feedback in Foreign Language Teacher Education: Fostering Pre-service Teachers' Oral Feedback Skills Through Facilitating Reflective Moments

Olivia Rütti-Joy

1 Introduction

The competencies that foreign language (L2) teachers require to successfully meet the needs of their profession are broadly discussed (Thonhauser, 2019). International frameworks and policy documents such as the European Profile for Language Teacher Education (Kelly et al., 2004), the European Portfolio for Student Teachers of Languages (Newby et al., 2007), The European Profiling Grid (North et al., 2013), and Towards a Common European Framework of Reference for Language Teachers (ECML, 2017) constitute large-scale attempts to identify and outline the required professional expertise of L2 teachers. Among the many competencies listed, the ability to provide meaningful, constructive, and actionable feedback is a skill that features repeatedly, especially with reference to its importance for successful teaching and learning. Indeed, feedback as an essential component of assessment (Black & William, 1998) is considered one of the most highly prized interventions in teaching and learning (Hattie, 2009; Hattie & Timperley, 2007;

O. Rütti-Joy (✉)
Department of Multilingualism and Foreign Language Education, Université de Fribourg, Fribourg, Switzerland
e-mail: olivia.ruetti-joy@unifr.ch

Kluger & DeNisi, 1996). In particular, formative feedback embedded in formative assessment has shown to improve student outcomes, academic performance, self-regulated learning, and self-efficacy (Black & William, 1998; Panadero & Jönsson, 2013). As teachers play a central role when it comes to facilitating feedback opportunities and enabling learners to actively seek, critically reflect on and constructively engage with feedback, it is essential for teachers to develop comprehensive feedback skills. This study addresses the oral linguistic and practical skills that pre-service teachers need to develop to become professional social agents in their (future) vocation. It investigates to what extent reflective interventions in formative, multi-stage assessment may be conducive to developing these competencies as they are defined in a specifically developed framework of reference for L2 teachers (cf. Kuster et al., 2014) in the Swiss L2 teacher education context.

2 Theoretical Background

2.1 Teachers' Feedback Skills

Traditionally, feedback is considered a didactic intervention with the goal to improve learning outcomes where information is transmitted from a feedback provider (usually a teacher) to a feedback receiver (mostly a learner). This traditional feedback paradigm places information processing, planning, and decision-making at its core and focuses mainly on the content and the (unidirectional) delivery of information (Ajjawi & Boud, 2017). The traditional paradigm is, however, criticized for conceptualizing feedback as a static, monologic, and information-centered process encompassing hierarchical roles between the teacher and student, and for mostly ignoring student agency (Ajjawi & Boud, 2017; Ajjawi & Regehr, 2019). Such concerns led to further advancements in feedback research with a stronger focus on all feedback participants.

The contemporary feedback paradigm views feedback from a socio-constructivist, holistic, and process-oriented angle (Carless, 2015). Accordingly, students as autonomous and active social agents are at the center of the feedback process, make sense of the received information from various sources, and use feedback to improve their subsequent work or learning strategies (Carless & Boud, 2018). Feedback is thereby a multidirectional, iterative, interactional, and student-centered process where its meaning is socially constructed through dialogic and reciprocal negotiation (Carless, 2006; Carless et al., 2011; Higgins et al., 2002). For feedback to be effective, among a range of other factors, students are required to be able to "read, interpret, and use feedback" (Sutton, 2012, p. 31). These dispositions are also termed "student uptake" (Carless, 2006; Carless et al., 2011).

Feedback literacy, a concept that has emerged out of the contemporary feedback paradigm, is understood as a prerequisite for student uptake (Carless & Boud, 2018; Sutton, 2012). While feedback literacy is now considered to be comprised of both student feedback literacy and teacher feedback literacy (TFL) (Carless et al., 2011), the concept initially focused on learners only. From this perspective, student feedback literacy encompasses the competencies that students need in order to actively seek, generate, use, and make sense of feedback information to improve their learning outcomes as well as to develop capacities in making academic evaluative judgements (Carless & Boud, 2018; Hoo et al., 2021; Molloy et al., 2020; Sutton, 2012). A broadening of this concept resulted from Sutton's (2012) work to include the feedback literacy of teachers. It was not until Carless and Boud's seminal 2018 article, however, that TFL started to be investigated on a greater scale both conceptually and empirically. It is now understood as a set of situated practices that include a range of competencies in relation to teachers' encounters with students and teachers' reflection and planning of feedback processes (Esterhazy et al., 2021). For instance, Carless and Winstone (2020) conceptualized TFL as a teacher's "knowledge, expertise and dispositions to design feedback processes in ways which enable student uptake of feedback" (p. 4).

Underpinning this concept is a move towards the socio-constructivist idea that feedback is most effective when all participants share equal responsibilities within the feedback process (Carless & Boud, 2018; Carless et al., 2011; Carless & Winstone, 2020; Winstone et al., 2017). More recent work defines TFL to include a teacher's ability to work with colleagues to establish innovative and student-centered feedback methods (Winstone & Carless, 2019), to design and manage assessment conditions and feedback processes that nurture student uptake and student feedback literacy (Carless, 2020a, 2020b; Carless & Boud, 2018; Carless & Winstone, 2020), and to create conditions that are conducive to students' engagement with feedback (Chong, 2021; Winstone et al., 2017).

For feedback processes to be successful and to ensure that students engage with feedback productively, therefore, there is a strong need for teachers to develop TFL (Carless & Winstone, 2020). However, regardless of the sophistication of students' and teachers' feedback literacies, it is essential that all agents involved have the communicative skills to participate in a co-constructive dialogue. This requirement is especially relevant for feedback interactions in the L2 classroom. The way an L2 teacher linguistically frames a feedback conversation is a deciding factor for students' understanding of the conversation's content. In other words, L2 teachers need to be able to express themselves within the feedback process clearly and comprehensibly. Thus, teachers' communicative skills may not only facilitate feedback, but may even be partly responsible for its success (Rütti-Joy, 2022).

For instance, research has shown that learners find feedback most effective when the comments are usable i.e. understandable, detailed, tactful, and personalized (Dawson et al., 2019). Consequently, successful feedback demands specific (or specialized) communicative strategies and language competence by all feedback participants. For example, a teacher must have the ability to adapt their linguistic expression to the cognitive level and language competence of their target audience (Rütti-Joy, 2022). The nature of such specific communicative strategies and linguistic skills aligns with the concept of Teacher Language Competence (TLC) (Burke, 2015; Elder & Kim, 2014). TLC suggests that effective, action-oriented and target-audience appropriate L2 teaching not only requires high general L2 proficiency (cf. Cullen, 1998) but also an additional set of profession-related language competencies (Bleichenbacher et al., 2014a; Bleichenbacher et al., 2019; Burke, 2015; Elder, 2001; Legutke, 2012; Loder-Büchel, 2014).

While a number of researchers have attempted to define and conceptualize TLC (Doff & Klippel, 2007; Elder, 2001; Elder & Kim, 2014; Freeman, 2017; Freeman et al., 2015; Kissau & Algozzine, 2017; Richards et al., 2013; Sokolova, 2012; Wipperfürth, 2009; Wulf, 2001), the available construct definitions remain vague (Rütti-Joy, 2022). One of the most comprehensive attempts is found in the profession-related language competence profiles (PRLCP) and the corresponding analytic profession-related language competence assessment rubric (PRLC-R) (Kuster et al., 2014). Both instruments were developed based on an extensive needs analysis (Long, 2005) in the Swiss L2 teaching and learning context (Kuster et al., 2014). The PRLCP describe L2 teachers' specific language requirements according to a range of profession-specific communicative skills which are operationalized in a collection of can-do descriptors in five areas of activity, including, among others, competencies like "assessing, giving feedback and advising." The PRLC-R is an analytic rubric of linguistic and indigenous criteria with the purpose to foster and assess the TLC as conceptualized in the profiles. Indigenous criteria assess non-linguistic, action-oriented, real-world aspects of a language production with a focus on the appropriate completion of an authentic task (McNamara, 1996). Addressee-specificity, which is a teacher's ability to adapt their expression to the cognitive and linguistic proficiency of their addressees, is a central component of feedback and constitutes an all-encompassing factor for the evaluation of profession-related language skills such as feedback competence (Doff & Klippel, 2007; Wipperfürth, 2009; Wulf, 2001). This aspect of TLC is incorporated in the PRLC-R as an indigenous assessment criterion. According to the developers, a combined use of the PRLCP and PRLC-R thus allows to specifically foster, profile, and evaluate L2 TLC and consequently linguistic aspects of TFL. While there are no uniform institutionalized standards across Switzerland regarding TLC, the PRLCP serves as an overall framework of reference for Swiss L2 teacher education and L2 teacher professional development (EDK, 2017; Kuster et al., 2014; swissuniversities, 2015). Thus, these tools are also intended to serve the development of language-related aspects of L2 feedback and TFL in appropriate didactic and reflection-oriented interventions.

2.2 Developing L2 Oral Feedback Competence

Engaging in effective feedback conversations requires L2 teachers to acquire language skills and practical skills such as TFL, which are highly specific to the teaching profession (Bleichenbacher et al., 2014b). These skills are not simply acquired through exposure. Instead, they need to deliberately be developed, for instance through the application of reflective tools, practice, and specific tasks (Ryan et al., 2021). In L2 teacher education, pre-service teachers need to develop both their student feedback literacy (as they are still learners themselves and regularly engage with feedback as part of their studies) *and* their TFL in preparation for their future professional teaching practice. However, the conceptualizations of TLC, student feedback literacy and TFL are still in their infancies (Chong, 2021), and little empirical research has been conducted to investigate the development of TLC (Rütti-Joy, 2022) and TFL (Ryan et al., 2021).

Despite the lack of empirical evidence, there are some research findings suggesting that promoting self-awareness via self-assessment, feedback, rubrics, and exemplars, and engaging with multi-stage assignments with reflective components may assist the development of student feedback literacy (Hoo et al., 2021). Multi-stage assignments are a common form of assessment for learning (AfL) praised for their positive effects on student learning. Indeed, students seem to learn best when they complete scaffolded multi-stage assignments (Carless & Boud, 2018; Sutton, 2012), serve as assessors, and provide rubric-based peer feedback (Dawson, 2017).

If learners receive appropriate training in the application of rubrics, rubrics can positively influence student achievement (Panadero & Jönsson, 2013) because they generally play a significant role at clarifying learning targets (Smit & Birri, 2014) and making assessment criteria transparent. Rubrics can also aid peer- and self-assessment during a learning process, improve students' self-efficacy, reduce anxiety, and foster self-regulation (Panadero et al., 2016; Panadero & Jönsson, 2013; Saddler & Andrade, 2004). Multi-stage assessments such as portfolios often include rubrics and are known to be particularly beneficial (Burch, 1997) because they promote learning through progress-tracking and analyzing work at different points in time (Bearman et al., 2020; Smit & Birri, 2014).

Research has also shown that such teaching interventions may not only foster student feedback literacy but also the development of learners' general oral L2 skills (Bower et al., 2011; Cabrera-Solano, 2020; Castañeda & Rodríguez-González, 2011; De Grez et al., 2009; Gómez Sará, 2016; Hung & Huang, 2015; Kennedy & Lees, 2016; Lao-Un & Khampusaen, 2018; Murillo-Zamoranoa & Montanero, 2018; Yeh et al., 2019). It is thus possible that such interventions are transferable to a language for specific purpose context to foster oral TLC and oral TFL. The PRLCP and PRLC-R have been designed with the purpose of fostering and assessing TLC including teachers' language-related feedback competences. However, the application, usability, and effectiveness of the instruments in (L2) teacher education has not yet been researched, and the effects of their practical implementation are unknown.

The present paper seeks to address this gap by empirically investigating the systematic implementation of the PRLC-R as a reflective tool for peer feedback in L2 teacher education and its potential effects on the development of pre-service teachers' oral L2 feedback skills. By means of a quasi-experimental pre-post design, this study seeks to answer the following research question:

> How do qualitative, language-specific aspects of pre-service English teachers' oral feedback in the target language (English) provided to lower secondary school students develop under the administration of a profession-related, reflective assessment rubric and systematic feedback training?

3 Research Method

This research was conducted at a Swiss university of teacher education that specifically aligns its curriculum with the PRLCP (EDK, 2017; swissuniversities, 2015). The language teacher education BA-MA curriculum contains the Bachelor (BA) E-Portfolio, a multi-stage AfL assignment equivalent to a bachelor's thesis devised over the course of one academic year, which provided the setting for the intervention study. The purpose of the BA E-Portfolio is to foster pre-service L2 teachers' oral L2 feedback skills as a partial competence of TLC as conceptualized in the PRLCP. It requires students to complete three iterations of the following steps: (1) devising and video-recording a microteaching sequence, (2) providing (dialogic) peer feedback on their peers' microteaching sequences in a face-to-face discussion immediately after the respective microteaching sequence (cf. Ajjawi and Boud 2017; Carless et al., 2011), and (3) reflecting on and optimizing their microteaching sequence based on the received feedback.

3.1 Participants and Data Collection

The participants of the research study constituted the university's 2017–2022 student cohort (n = 50, 32% male, 68% female) who completed their BA E-Portfolio starting in March 2019 and ending in March 2020. The participants subsumed two types of learners: students with a focus on language and historical subjects who aspired to attain a Master of Arts (MA) teaching degree (phil I, n = 40), and students with a mathematics and science focus who aspired to attain a Master of Science (MSc) teaching degree plus the teaching certification in one L2 (phil II, n = 10). The experimental-control-group pre-post design encompassed a pre-test (March 2019), the completion of the BA E-portfolio as the intervention itself, and a post-test (March 2020, see test description below).

For the intervention, the research participants were allocated to three comparison groups of the following conditions: an experimental group E who used the PRLC-R to provide rubric-based peer feedback (phil I students, n = 21), a control group C1 who did not receive any predefined assessment criteria for their peer feedback (phil I students, n = 19), and a second control group C0 who did not complete the BA E-Portfolio but partook in the pre- and post-test (phil II students, n = 10). PRLC-R thus constituted the intervention treatment. After the pre-test, the E and C1 groups participated in a one-off, hands-on feedback and rubric training session where they were familiarized with best-practice principles of successful feedback (cf. Hattie & Timperley, 2007). The E group received additional training in the application of the PRLC-R criteria through rating sample microteaching video sequences, comparing their ratings and settling on a consensus rating in a plenary discussion (cf. Panadero & Jönsson, 2013).

By giving and receiving feedback from a peer in dialogic feedback conversations during each cycle of the BA E-Portfolio intervention, the participants trained their feedback and advising skills in the target language. Based on the conceptual framework of teacher and student feedback literacy (Carless, 2020a, 2020b; Carless & Boud, 2018; Carless et al., 2011; Chong, 2021), the participants fulfilled a double role. On the one hand, through completing the BA E-Portfolio and undergoing a series of purposeful reflective tasks, they participated in an activity that aimed to foster the development of student feedback literacy, communicative competence, and evaluative judgment. On the other hand, the participants' iterative participation in dialogic peer feedback sought to mitigate the limitations of feedback based on the unidirectional transmission of information and to reconcile feedback-providers' and feedback-recipients' potentially differing understandings of feedback. This also allowed the participants to train their reflective skills and language analytical ability to promote student comprehension, feedback uptake, and TFL (Shintani & Ellis, 2015).

3.2 Research Instruments

The analytic assessment rubric PRLC-R as the complementing assessment tool of the PRLCP constituted the main research instrument of the present study. It was designed to specifically facilitate the teaching, learning, and formative and summative assessment of L2 teachers' TLC. Like most assessment rubrics used in education, the PRLC-R is comprised of performance levels, performance level descriptors, and evaluation criteria (Dawson, 2017) that help make learning goals explicit and evaluation processes transparent (Brookhart, 2013; Brookhart & Chen, 2015). The PRLC-R contains the scales (1) general: task completion, (2) listening, (3) reading, (4) qualitative characteristics of speaking including (4a) spoken language production and (4b) spoken language interaction, and (5) qualitative characteristics of writing.

The performance levels for each dimension include a pre-entry level (0), an entry-level (1), an intermediate-level (2), and a professional-level (3). Table 3.1 below illustrates the individual assessment criteria of the scale "qualitative characteristics of speaking":

In the present study, the above scale served as an assessment rubric and reflective tool to foster and assess the partial competences of area of activity 3: Assessing, giving feedback, and advising. Specifically, the PRLC-R scale constituted the treatment component that facilitated targeted peer feedback practice. With the research interest being on oral L2 feedback skills, and due to there not being any known tests that enable collecting data on this particular construct from the PRLCP, I designed an online-administered, near-authentic, competence-oriented performance test that elicits constructed responses in form of test-taker performances. The test instrument's purpose was to measure oral L2 feedback skills i.e. TLC via the online learning management system Moodle. The test aligns with an action-oriented approach (Council of Europe, 2020) and seeks to support the active use of language. The performance test is based on the contextualized PRLCP and PRLC-R and was developed according to a rigorous and iterative process (ALTE, 2018, 2020; Bachman & Dambök, 2018; Bachman & Palmer, 1996; Douglas, 2000,

Table 3.1 Assessment criteria of the PRLC-R scale "Production: Qualitative characteristics of speaking" (cf. Rütti-Joy, 2022, translation by the author)

Performance level	0	1	2	2*	3
Vocabulary	Their word choice is consistently inappropriate in relation to a given context	Their word choice is repeatedly inappropriate in relation to a given context	Their word choice is mostly appropriate in relation to a given context		Their word choice is appropriate and precise in relation to a given context
	0	1	2	2*	3
Accuracy	High frequency of grammar mistakes significantly impedes comprehension so that it remains unclear throughout what they want to express	They frequently make grammar mistakes. It is sometimes unclear what they want to express	They occasionally make grammar mistakes. It is mostly clear what they want to express		They rarely or never make noticeable grammar mistakes
	0	1	2	2*	3
Pronunciation	Their pronunciation and intonation are unintelligible and unclear, which severely limits comprehension throughout	They repeatedly mispronounce or mis-emphasize words, which can lead to comprehension problems	They rarely mispronounce or mis-emphasize words. It is mostly clear what they want to express		Their pronunciation and intonation are intelligible, clear and precise (even if they speak with a foreign accent)
	0	1	2	2*	3
Fluency	Linguistic insecurities restrict them to such an extent that no fluency can be achieved	They speak slowly due to linguistic insecurities and/or pause frequently to search for expressions or restart	They speak with noticeable variety in speech rate and/or occasional pauses due to linguistic insecurities		They rarely or never pause because of linguistic uncertainty
	0	1	2	2*	3

(continued)

Table 3.1 (continued)

Performance level	0	1	2	2*	3
Cohesion & coherence	They consistently express themselves incoherently and unclearly. Used linguistic linking devices are inappropriate	They occasionally express themselves incoherently and unclearly. They link their utterances with only few linguistic means, some of which are inappropriate	They express themselves in a mostly coherent and structured way. They link their utterances with a limited number of appropriate linguistic devices		They consistently express themselves in a coherent and clearly structured manner. They link their utterances flexibly and confidently with precise and appropriate linguistic devices
	0	1	2	2*	3
Addressee-specificity	They fail to adapt the language to the learners to enable their comprehension	They somewhat succeed in adapting the language to the learners to enable their comprehension	They moderately succeed in adapting the language to the learners to enable their comprehension		They completely succeed in adapting the language to the learners to enable their comprehension
	0	1	2	2*	3

2010; Harsch, 2016; McNamara, 1996). The test construct was taken from the PRLCP area of activity 3 and constitutes the following:

In the target language, the teacher is able to…

3.7 comment on the performance of a class.
3.8 conduct a dialogue that serves to assess a learner's ability.
3.9 give oral feedback on a learner's performance.
3.12 hold an advisory talk with learners with the aim of fostering their skills in a personalized manner.

The test tasks constructively align with the PRLC-R performance level descriptors from the above scale "qualitative characteristics of speaking" (see Table 3.1). As performance assessment is characterized through the close relationship of the test tasks to the *real-world* (McNamara, 1996), the present test replicates prototypical situations that test takers encounter in their professional lives (Bachman & Palmer, 1996; Caspari et al., 2016; Douglas, 2010). Integrated and integrative test tasks with stimuli such as video- and photo-vignettes (Campbell, 1996; Goldman et al., 2007; Hughes & Huby, 2002) and genuine text-material provide such a near-authentic communicative context in the present test. For the former, I filmed relevant classroom scenarios with lower-secondary school students that correspond to the test construct. Embedded in specific test task instructions, the videos display prototypical situations from the *first-person-perspective* to prompt test takers to *spontaneously* and *intuitively* respond to the test tasks. For the latter, I embedded genuine written assignments from lower-secondary L2 learners in the test tasks. The task instructions prompted the participants to respond to those stimuli in the target language English, adapt their L2 expression to a predefined target level audience, and voice-record and save their oral task responses in the Moodle test tasks directly. Among others, tasks included the test takers to provide PRLC-R-criterion-referenced oral feedback to a learner's input, oral presentation, or written performance, to provide oral feedback to a group of learners on their overall behavior, or to conduct feedback conversations with learners.

4 Analyses

To draw inferences from the observed test taker performance on their underlying competencies and identify possible treatment effects, I first conducted an expert rating of each recorded test response against the PRLC-R and thereby ensured constructive alignment (Bachman & Palmer, 1996; Caspari et al., 2016; Douglas, 2000, 2010). Following a comprehensive rater training, four raters evaluated 40% of all language productions double-blind.

After the completion of the rating process, interrater reliability (IRR) was determined by computing Krippendorff's α. In addition, as there is no prior research available on the implementation and functioning of the PRLC-R in an L2 assessment context, rater bias and interaction analyses were conducted by means of a multifaceted Rasch analysis (MFRA and partial credit model (PCM)) to identify differential rater behavior and rater variability with reference to rating criteria and test tasks. To compare the pre- and post-test results based on the expert ratings to investigate intervention effects, I then conducted a competence comparison by means of a PCM. First, I calculated an overall within and between-group competence comparison at and between t0 and t1 across the test takers' overall pre- and post-test performance. Second, a repetition of the same calculation across all treatment groups per individual rating criterion at and between t0 and t1 served to investigate competence differences in specific areas of performance. Finally, I compared the competencies of each individual treatment group and per individual rating criterion at and between t0 and t1. A one-dimensional model was computed using person IDs and treating the research participants at t1 as different persons to the research participants at t0. The data from the C1 at t0 served as the overall reference point to determine possible treatment effects. For increased transparency of the interaction model with reference to the group comparisons, estimated means by means of weighted likelihood estimation (WLE, no adjustment for multiple testing, cf. Warm, 1989) were calculated.

5   Results

The IRR calculations reveal an observed mean α level for four raters (R1, R2, R3 and R4; 5000 iterations) of $\alpha = 0.338$ at a confidence interval of 0.257 and 0.415. According to Landis and Koch's (1977) recommendations for IRR value interpretation (indexes below 0 indicate no, between 0 and 0.20 slight, 0.21 and 0.40 fair, 0.41 and 0.60 moderate, 0.61 and 0.80 substantial, and 0.81 and 1 near-perfect agreement), the computed mean α value of 0.338 reveals fair rater agreement. The results of the MFRA bias and interaction analyses reveal that the raters differed strongly with reference to the severity and leniency with which they judged participants' L2 speech performances. In other words, raters applied the PRLC-R inconsistently in relation to criteria, tasks, and test takers.

Even though the α value of 0.338 can be interpreted as fair, the quality and usability of the data for measuring and pre-post-treatment effects was compromised. Nevertheless, it is important to treat these findings with caution as there is substantial research evidence that raters are subject to many systematic biases (Winke et al., 2013) that even the most comprehensive quality assurance measures cannot fully mitigate—especially when it comes to assessing elusive constructs such as TLC (Eckes, 2005, 2011; McNamara, 1996). At the same time, both the IRR and interaction analysis results highlight an urgent need for further research and optimization of the rating criteria of the PRLC-R. The differential rater functioning was controlled by means of an MFRA (PCM) for the subsequent competence comparison calculations. The results of the overall competence difference between groups at t0 and between groups at t1 show that they all performed overall at a similar competence level both at t0 and t1 respectively.

When investigating the measured competences at t1 between the comparison groups with reference to the individual rating criteria, the criterion *accuracy* stands out: group C1 outperformed group C0 and group E at t0 ($p = .0327*$ and $p = .0587*$, respectively), however not at t1. In other words, while the control group C1 performed slightly better in *accuracy* at t0, the difference between E and C0 and C1 disappeared at t1. This finding could mean that either the E and C0 group improved, or C1 worsened during the intervention. While these findings indicate slight competence differences *between* the treatment groups at t0 and t1, no statistically significant competence development from t0 to t1 *within* the groups can be observed, as shown below (Table 3.2):

The pre-post competence comparison per individual criterion across all groups led to the same results. Indeed, no statistically significant difference becomes apparent apart from the criterion *content* (see Table 3.3). It is plausible that there was a memory effect with reference to test tasks, or that the treatment led to a learning effect regarding providing feedback or solving such a specific type of test task.

Further, the pre-post competence measurement comparisons between groups per individual criterion show that C0 as the only treatment group improved with reference to *content*. Because C0 did not receive any treatment but completed the pre- and post-test only, this is an unexpected result. No *p* value adjustment for multiple comparison testing was performed. The few significant *p* values thus need to be interpreted accordingly.

In summary, the treatment of the present study did not yield any statistically significant results with regard to competence development both between and within groups, and with reference to individual PRLC-R criteria. The answer to the research question is thus that no significant effects could be observed on pre-service English teachers' oral feedback skills when evaluated against the PRLC-R under the administration of the PRLC-R and systematic feedback training.

6 Discussion

While previous research on treatments that combine multi-stage assessment with (peer) feedback or other forms of reflective practice led to learning effects on learners' oral L2 skills (Bower et al., 2011; Cabrera-Solano, 2020; Castañeda & Rodríguez-González, 2011; De Grez et al., 2009; Gómez Sará, 2016; Hung & Huang, 2015; Kennedy & Lees, 2016; Lao-Un & Khampusaen, 2018; Murillo-Zamoranoa & Montanero, 2018; Yeh et al., 2019), the present intervention did not.

Table 3.2 Overall pre-post competence comparison between groups (WLEs)

Treatment group	Estimate	SE	df	t.ratio	*p*.value
C1	−0.0792	0.0787	38.3	−1.007	0.3204
C0	0.0409	0.115	38.3	0.355	0.7247
E	0.010	0.0845	38.3	0.122	0.9037

Table 3.3 Pre-post competence comparison across groups per criterion (WLEs)

Criterion	Estimate	SE	df	t.ratio	p.value
Content	−1	0.473	38.3	−2.120	0.0406*
Vocabulary	−0.12	0.269	38.3	−0.444	0.6596
Accuracy	−0.0545	0.195	38.3	−0.279	0.7816
Pronunciation	0.156	0.267	38.3	0.582	0.5638
Fluency	−0.0671	0.149	38.3	−0.452	0.6539
Coherence & Cohesion	−0.425	0.339	38.3	−1.252	0.2183
Addressee-Specificity	0.169	0.242	38.3	0.698	0.4891

Reasons for this may include that the effectiveness of portfolios on learning achievement depends on a range of factors (Gläser-Zikuda et al., 2020). For example, learners generally share a low level of acceptance of portfolios because they consider them as cumbersome, irrelevant to their own needs and interests, and as lacking objective evaluation (Gläser-Zikuda et al., 2020).

In addition, learners' knowledge on how to effectively engage with portfolios can strongly influence their effectiveness respectively, as students' ability to do so is a precondition for releasing the assignment's full potential (Ntuli et al., 2009). A possible explanation for why the intervention did not result in any observable competence development may thus be that the participants potentially had a critical attitude towards the portfolio task or that they lacked the necessary skills and knowledge to reach learning success. Other possible reasons for the lack of treatment effects may be that the treatment itself, i.e. the rubric-based iterative peer feedback practice, was insufficient or that the treatment context was not suitable. It may be that training TLC with peers in a teacher education course may not be as effective as receiving real-world target language use (TLU) domain exposure in the actual L2 classroom. Follow-up replication studies that implement similar interventions in the context of pre-service teachers' practical placements or that encompass more intensive feedback and reflective and oral TLC practice in the relevant real-world TLU context and more rigorous feedback training constitute a promising avenue for further research.

Another possible reason for why the participants did not improve language-specific aspects of their feedback-related L2 TLC might encompass a mistrust of the received peer feedback. It is a stable finding that learners at any age prefer their educators' feedback over their peers,' and that they are more likely to act on the former rather than the latter (Nelson & Carson, 1998). The participants may thus not have exploited the received feedback's full potential. Furthermore, participants' potentially low level of student feedback literacy may have compromised the effectiveness of the treatment, as low student feedback literacy reduces learners' abilities to recognize valuable feedback by their peers (Leki, 1990; Stanley, 1992) and thus to revise their work accordingly (Connor & Asenavag, 1994; Liu & Sadler, 2003). Finally, the participants' peer feedback itself may have been of low quality or unusable. Imprecise feedback may counteract the benefits of peer feedback (Leki, 1990; Lockhart & Ng, 1993; Mendonca & Johnson, 1994; Min, 2016; Tsui & Ng, 2000) and thus prevent possible learning effects.

Overall, and even though the implemented treatment did not show any statistically significant results, it would not do the study justice to claim that systematically incorporating the PRLC-R in the BA E-Portfolio task did not lead to any positive results or learning insights. Including the PRLC-R as a tool for assessment, peer feedback, and reflection contributed to better structuring the overall assignment, to providing guidance to the students throughout the process, and to offering a more stable and research-and development-informed basis for students' peer feedback in a learning context that is more closely related to the TLU domain. Furthermore, the study revealed highly valuable insights on the functioning and usability of the PRLC-R in an L2 assessment context in L2 teacher education.

6.1 Limitations and Further Research

Limitations of the present research study include, among others, the relatively small sample size, the validity concerns of both the PRLCP and PRLC-R instruments, as well as validity concerns of the pre- and post-test that was developed for the purpose of this study. The validity concerns in relation to the instruments alone pose a strong call for further research into the use and effects of these tools, especially in light of their recommended use in Swiss teacher education and for future TLC certification by policy makers and official Swiss stakeholders (EDK, 2017; swissuniversities, 2015).

First, for instance, further refinement and development of the PRLCP and PRLC-R is urgently needed in order to differentiate a better clear-cut TLC construct, higher instrument validity and more evidence with reference to the usability and functioning of their application in teacher education. Insights gained from further investigations on pre-service teachers' TLC development can then be used to a) further develop the PRLCP and b) design teaching interventions and learning materials to promote the development of pre- and in-service teachers' L2 TLC and TFL (Rütti-Joy, 2022). Second, further research on the applicability, usefulness, and appropriateness of implementing the PRLC-R in formative and summative assessment of TLC and TFL is indispensable, such as for instance validity, reliability, and usability studies of the assessment criteria (Rütti-Joy, 2022). Third, the PRLC-R's potential affordances in formative AfL in L2 teacher education, for instance with a focus on rubrics and/or exemplars, needs further research in order to uncover the processes underlying the development of feedback-related language skills and TFL. Finally, the available PRLCP and PRLC-R instruments, as well as the already existing teaching and assessment designs, call for creativity and innovation when it comes to their application, as they certainly provide a conducive basis for enabling the kind of reflection necessary for teacher development.

7 Conclusion

Investigating the development of pre-service teachers' oral L2 feedback skills and TFL is central to the improvement of feedback effectiveness in the L2 classroom. This study sought to research the effectiveness of a reflection-oriented teaching intervention that was based on instruments that were developed specifically for this purpose. By devising a teaching design based on the PRLCP and PRLC-R and thereby focusing on the application of the PRLC-R as a reflective tool, the results of this study suggest that, while rubric peer feedback may contribute to raising awareness of TLC requirements and TFL, stronger interventions are necessary to foster actual competence development in this area.

References

Ajjawi, R., & Boud, D. (2017). Researching feedback dialogue: An interactional analysis approach. *Assessment & Evaluation in Higher Education, 42*(2), 252–265. https://doi.org/10.1080/02602938.2015.1102863

Ajjawi, R., & Regehr, G. (2019). When I say... feedback. *Medical Education, 53*, 652–654. https://doi.org/10.1111/medu.13746

ALTE. (2018). *Guidelines for the development of Language for Specific Purposes tests. A supplement to the manual for language test development and examining.* Association of Language Testers in Europe.

ALTE. (2020). *ALTE principles of good practice.* Cambridge: Association of Language Testers in Europe.

Bachman, L. F., & Damböck, B. (2018). *Language assessment for classroom teachers.* Oxford University Press.

Bachman, L. F., & Palmer, A. S. (1996). *Language testing in practice.* Oxford University Press.

Bearman, M., Boud, D., & Ajjawi, R. (2020). New directions for assessment in a digital world. In M. Bearman, P. Dawson, R. Ajjawi, J. Tai, & D. Boud (Eds.), *Re-imagining* university assessment in a digital world. The enabling power of assessment (Vol. 7, pp. 7–18). Springer. https://doi.org/10.1007/978-3-030-41956-1_2

Black, P. J., & William, D. (1998). Assessment in classroom learning. *Assessment in Education: Principles, Policy, & Practice, 81*(1), 7–74.

Bleichenbacher, L., Kuster, W., Egli Cuenat, M., Klee, P., Roderer, T., Benvegnen, R., Schweitzer, P., Stocks, G., Kappler, D., & Tramèr-Rudolphe, M.-H. (2014a). *Berufsspezifische Sprachkompetenzprofile für Lehrpersonen für Fremdsprachen: Schlussbericht zu den Projektetappen 3 und 4: 2012–2014.* http://extranet.phsg.ch/Portaldata/1/Resources/forschung_und_entwicklung/fachdidaktik_sprachen/kp/Sprachkompetenzprofile__Schlussbericht_2014_Website.pdf

Bleichenbacher, L., Kuster, W., Egli Cuenat, M., Klee, P., Roderer, T., Benvegnen, R., Schweitzer, P., Stoks, G., Kappler, D., & Tramèr-Rudolphe, M.-H. (2014b). *Berufsspezifische Sprachkompetenzprofile für Lehrpersonen für Fremdsprachen: Schlussbericht zu den Projektetappen 3 und 4: 2012–2014.* https://www.phsg.ch/forschung/projekte/berufsspezifische-sprachkompetenzprofile-fuer-lehrpersonen-fuer-fremdsprachen

Bleichenbacher, L., Kuster, W., Heinzmann, S., Hilbe, R., & Annen, M. (2019). *Entwicklung sprachenübergreifender curricularer Elemente für die Ausbildung von Sprachenlehrpersonen Sek I. Zweite, überarbeitete Auflage.* https://www.phsg.ch/sites/default/files/cms/Forschung/Institute/Institut-Fachdidaktik-Sprachen/CV/ESCEAS_Bleichenbacher_et_al_2019.pdf

Bower, M., Cavanagh, M., Moloney, R., & Dao, M. (2011). Developing communication competence using an online video reflection system: Pre-service teachers' experiences. *Asia-Pacific Journal of Teacher Education, 39*(4), 311–326. https://doi.org/10.1080/1359866X.2011.614685

Brookhart, S. M. (2013). *How to create and use rubrics for formative assessment and grading.* Association for Supervision & Curriculum Development (ASCD).

Brookhart, S. M., & Chen, F. (2015). The quality and effectiveness of descriptive rubrics. *Educational Review, 67*(3), 1–26. https://doi.org/10.1080/00131911.2014.929565

Burch, C. B. (1997). Creating a two-tiered portfolio rubric. *The English Journal, 86*(1), 55–58.

Burke, B. M. (2015). Language proficiency testing for teachers. In C. A. Chapelle (Ed.), *The encyclopedia of applied linguistics.* Wiley-Blackwell.

Cabrera-Solano, P. (2020). The use of digital portfolios to enhance English as a foreign language speaking skills in higher education. *International Journal of Emerging Technologies in Learning, 15*(24), 159–176. https://doi.org/10.3991/ijet.v15i24.15103

Campbell, P. B. (1996). How would I handle that? Using vignettes to promote good math and science education. [Brochure]. In *American Association for the Advancement of Science.* Washington, DC.

Carless, D. (2006). Differing perceptions in the feedback process. *Studies in Higher Education, 31*(2), 219–233. https://doi.org/10.1080/03075070600572132

Carless, D. (2015). *Excellence in university assessment.* Routledge.

Carless, D. (2020a). Double duty, shared responsibilities and feedback literacy. *Perspectives on Medical Education, 9*, 199–200. https://doi.org/10.1007/s40037-020-00599-9

Carless, D. (2020b). From teacher transmission of information to student feedback literacy: Activating the learner role in feedback processes. *Active Learning in Higher Education.* https://doi.org/10.1177/1469787420945845.

Carless, D., & Boud, D. (2018). The development of student feedback literacy: Enabling uptake of feedback. *Assessment & Evaluation in Higher Education, 43*(8), 1315–1325. https://doi.org/10.1080/02602938.2018.1463354

Carless, D., Salter, D., Yang, M., & Lam, J. (2011). Developing sustainable feedback practices. *Studies in Higher Education, 36*(4), 395–407. https://doi.org/10.1080/03075071003642449

Carless, D., & Winstone, N. (2020). Teacher feedback literacy and its interplay with student feedback literacy. *Teaching in Higher Education.* https://doi.org/10.1080/13562517.2020.1782372.

Caspari, D., Klippel, F., Legutke, M., & Schramm, K. (2016). *Forschungsmethoden in der Fremdsprachendidaktik. Ein Handbuch.* Narr Francke Attempto.

Castañeda, M., & Rodríguez-González, E. (2011). L2 speaking self-ability perceptions through multiple video speech drafts. *Hispania, 94*(3), 483–501. https://doi.org/10.1353/hpn.2011.0066

Chong, S. W. (2021). Reconsidering student feedback literacy from an ecological perspective. *Assessment & Evaluation in Higher Education, 46*(1), 92–104. https://doi.org/10.1080/02602938.2020.1730765

Connor, U., & Asenavage, K. (1994). Peer response groups in ESL writing classes: How much impact on revision? *Journal of Second Language Writing, 3*, 257–276.

Council of Europe. (2020). *Common European framework of reference for languages: Learning, teaching, assessment – Companion volume.* Council of Europe Publishing. www.coe.int/lang-cefr.

Cullen, R. (1998). Teacher talk and the classroom context. *ELT Journal, 52*(3), 179–187. https://doi.org/10.1093/elt/52.3.179

Dawson, P. (2017). Assessment rubrics: Towards clearer and more replicable design, research and practice. *Assessment & Evaluation in Higher Education, 42*(3), 347–360. https://doi.org/10.1080/02602938.2015.1111294

Dawson, P., Henderson, M., Mahoney, P., Phillips, M., Ryan, T., Boud, D., & Molloy, E. (2019). What makes for effective feedback: Staff and student perspectives. *Assessment & Evaluation in Higher Education, 44*(1), 25–36. https://doi.org/10.1080/02602938.2018.1467877

De Grez, L., Valcke, M., & Roozen, I. (2009). The impact of an innovative instructional intervention on the acquisition of oral presentation skills in higher education. *Computers & Education, 53*, 112–120. https://doi.org/10.1016/j.compedu.2009.01.005

Doff, S., & Klippel, F. (2007). *Englisch Didaktik. Praxishandbuch für die Sekundarstufe I und II.* Cornelsen Verlag Scriptor.

Douglas, D. (2000). *Assessing language for specific pruposes.* Cambridge University Press.

Douglas, D. (2010). *Understanding language testing.* Hodder Education.

Eckes, T. (2005). Examining rater effects in TestDaF writing and speaking performance assessments: A many-facet Rasch analysis. *Language Assessment Quarterly: An International Journal, 2*(3), 197–221. https://doi.org/10.1207/s15434311laq0203_2

Eckes, T. (2011). Facetten der Genauigkeit: Zur Reliabilität der Beurteilung fremdsprachlicher Leistungen [Facets of accuracy: On the reliability of foreign-language performance assessments]. *Deutsch als Fremdsprache, 48*, 195–204.

ECML. (2017). *Towards a Common European framework of reference for language teachers: Frameworks, standards and instruments.* European Centre for Modern Languages.

EDK. (2017). *Empfehlungen zum Fremdsprachenunterricht (Landessprachen und Englisch) in der obligatorischen Schule.* Retrieved from https://edudoc.ch/record/128697/files/empfehlungen_sprachenunterricht_d.pdf

Elder, C. (2001). Assessing the language proficiency of teachers: Are there any border controls? *Language Testing, 18*(2), 149–170.

Elder, C., & Kim, S. H. O. (2014). Assessing teachers' language proficiency. In A. J. Kunnan (Ed.), *The companion to language assessment* (1st ed.). Wiley. https://doi.org/10.1002/9781118411360.wbcla138

Esterhazy, R., de Lange, T., & Damşa, C. (2021). Performing teacher feedback literacy in peer mentoring meetings. *Assessment & Evaluation in Higher Education.* https://doi.org/10.1080/02602938.2021.1980768.

Freeman, D. (2017). The case for teachers' classroom English proficiency. *RELC Journal, 48*(1), 31–52. https://doi.org/10.1177/0033688217691073

Freeman, D., Katz, A., Gomez, P. G., & Burns, A. (2015). English-for-teaching. Rethinking teacher proficiency in the classroom. *ELT Journal, 69*(2), 129–139.

Gläser-Zikuda, M., Feder, L., & Hofmann, F. (2020). Portfolioarbeit in der Lehrerinnen- und Lehrerbildung. In C. Cramer, J. König, M. Rothland, & S. Blömeke (Eds.), *Handbuch Lehrerinnen- und Lehrerbildung* (pp. 706–712). Klinkhardt. https://doi.org/10.35468/hblb2020-085

Goldman, R., Pea, R., Barron, B., & Derry, S. J. (2007). In R. Goldman, R. Pea, B. Barron, & S. J. Derry (Eds.), *Video research in the learning sciences.* Lawrence Erlbaum.

Gómez Sará, M. M. (2016). The influence of peer assessment and the use of corpus for the development of speaking skills in in-service teachers. *HOW Journal, 32*(1), 103–128. https://doi.org/10.19183/how.23.1.142

Harsch, C. (2016). Testen. In D. Caspari, F. Klippel, M. Legutke, & K. Schramm (Eds.), *Forschungsmethoden in der Fremdsprachendidaktik. Ein Handbuch* (pp. 204–217). Narr.

Hattie, J. (2009). *Visible learning. A synthesis of over 800 meta-analyses relating to achievement.* Routledge.

Hattie, J., & Timperley, H. (2007). The power of feedback. *Review of Educational Research, 77*(1), 81–112.

Higgins, R., Hartley, P., & Skelton, A. (2002). The conscientious consumer: Reconsidering the role of assessment feedback in student learning. *Studies in Higher Education, 27*(1), 53–64. https://doi.org/10.1080/03075070120099368

Hoo, H.-T., Deneen, C., & Boud, D. (2021). Developing student feedback literacy through self and peer assessment interventions. *Assessment & Evaluation in Higher Education.* https://doi.org/10.1080/02602938.2021.1925871.

Hughes, R., & Huby, M. (2002). The application of vignettes in social and nursing research. *Journal of Advanced Nursing, 37*, 382–386.

Hung, S. T. A., & Huang, H. T. D. (2015). Video blogging and English presentation performance: A pilot study. *Psychological Reports, 117*(2), 614–630.

Kelly, M., Grenfell, M., Allan, R., Kriza, C., & McEvoy, W. (2004). *European profile for language teacher education: A frame of reference*. European Commission Brussels.

Kennedy, A. S., & Lees, A. T. (2016). Preparing undergraduate pre-service teachers through direct and video-based performance feedback and tiered supports in early head start. *Early Childhood Education Journal, 44*, 369–379. https://doi.org/10.1007/s10643-015-0725-2

Kissau, S., & Algozzine, B. (2017). Effective foreign language teaching: Broadening the concept of content knowledge. *Foreign Language Annals, 50*(1), 114–134. https://doi.org/10.1111/flan.12250

Kluger, A. N., & DeNisi, A. (1996). The effects of feedback interventions on performance: A historical review, a meta-analysis, and a preliminary feedback intervention theory. *Psychological Bulletin, 119*, 254–284.

Kuster, W., Klee, P., Egli Cuenat, M., Roderer, T., Forster-Vosicki, B., Zappatore, D., Kappler, D., Stoks, G., & Lenz, P. (2014). *Berufsspezifisches Sprachkompetenzprofil für Fremdsprachenlehrpersonen der Primarstufe und der Sekundarstufe I.*. https://www.phsg.ch/forschung/projekte/berufsspezifische-sprachkompetenzprofile-fuer--lehrpersonen-fuer-fremdsprachen.

Landis, J., & Koch, G. (1977). The measurement of observer agreement for categorical data. *Biometrics, 33*(1), 159–174. https://doi.org/10.2307/2529310

Lao-Un, J., & Khampusaen, D. (2018). *Using electronic portfolio to promote English speaking ability of EFL undergraduate students* ICETE 2018: 20th International Conference on Education, Teaching and E-learning, Tokyo, Japan.

Legutke, M. K. (2012). Fort- und Weiterbildung von Lehrkräften für Deutsch als Fremdsprache. In H.-J. Krumm, C. Fandrych, B. Hufeisen, & C. Riemer (Eds.), *Handbuch Deutsch als Fremd- und Zweitsprache* (pp. 1351–1357). Walter de Gruyter.

Leki, I. (1990). Coaching from the margins: Issues in written response. In B. Kroll (Ed.), *Second language writing* (pp. 57–68). Cambridge University Press.

Liu, J., & Sadler, R. W. (2003). The effect and affect of peer review in electronic versus traditional modes on L2 writing. *Journal of English for Academic Purposes, 2*, 193–227.

Lockhart, C., & Ng, P. (1993). How useful is peer response? *Perspectives, 5*(1), 17–29.

Loder-Büchel, L. (2014). *Association between young learners' English language performance and teacher proficiency and experience with English*. [Université de Fribourg]. Fribourg.

Long, M. (2005). *Needs analysis in second language learning*. Cambridge University Press.

McNamara, T. (1996). *Measuring second language performance*. Longman.

Mendonca, C. O., & Johnson, K. E. (1994). Peer review negotiations: revision activities in ESL writing instruction. *TESOL Quarterly, 28*(4), 745–769.

Min, H.-T. (2016). Effect of teacher modeling and feedback on EFL students' peer review skills in peer review training. *Journal of Second Language Writing, 31*(31), 43–57. https://doi.org/10.1016/j.jslw.2016.01.004

Molloy, E., Boud, D., & Henderson, M. (2020). Developing a learning-centred framework for feedback literacy. *Assessment & Evaluation in Higher Education, 45*(4), 527–540. https://doi.org/10.1080/02602938.2019.1667955

Murillo-Zamoranoa, L. R., & Montanero, M. (2018). Oral presentations in higher education: A comparison of the impact of peer and teacher feedback. *Assessment and Evaluation in Higher Education, 43*(1), 138–150. https://doi.org/10.1080/02602938.2017.1303032

Nelson, G., & Carson, J. G. (1998). ESL students' perceptions of effectiveness in peer response groups. *Journal of Second Language Writing, 7*, 113–131.

Newby, D., Allan, R., Fenner, A.-B., Jones, B., Komorowska, H., & Soghikyan, K. (2007). *Europäisches Portfolio für Lehrpersonen in Ausbildung (PEPELF/EPOSA/EPOSTL)*. European Centre for Modern Languages (ECML). https://epostl2.ecml.at/Resources/tabid/505/language/de-DE/Default.aspx

North, B., Mateva, G., & Rossner, R. (2013). *European Profiling Grid (EPG)*. European Commission. https://egrid.epg-project.eu/

Ntuli, E., Keengwe, J., & Kyei-Blankson, L. (2009). Electronic portfolios in teacher education: A case study of early childhood teacher candidates. *Early Childhood Education Journal, 37*(2), 121–126.

Panadero, E., Gavin, B., & Strijbos, J.-W. (2016). The future of student self-assessment: A review of known unknowns and potential directions. *Educational Psychology Review, 28*(4), 803–830.

Panadero, E., & Jönsson, A. (2013). The use of scoring rubrics for formative assessment purposes revisited: A review. *Educational Research Review, 9*, 129–144. https://doi.org/10.1016/j.edurev.2013.01.002

Richards, H., Conway, C., Roskvist, A., & Harvey, S. (2013). Foreign language teachers' language proficiency and their language teaching practice. *Language Learning Journal, 41*(2), 231–246. https://doi.org/10.1080/09571736.2012.707676

Rütti-Joy, O. (2022). *Fostering and assessing pre-service English teachers' oral teacher language competence through an assessment rubric and peer feedback: An LSP approach* Université de Fribourg]. Fribourg.

Ryan, T., Henderson, M., Ryan, K., & Kennedy, G. (2021). Identifying the components of effective learner-centred feedback information. *Teaching in Higher Education*. https://doi.org/10.1080/13562517.2021.1913723.

Saddler, B., & Andrade, H. (2004). The writing rubric. *Educational Leadership, 62*(2), 48–52.

Shintani, N., & Ellis, R. (2015). Does language analytical ability mediate the effect of written feedback on grammatical accuracy in second language writing? *System, 49*, 110–119.

Smit, R., & Birri, T. (2014). Assuring the quality of standards-oriented classroom assessment with rubrics for complex competencies. *Studies in Educational Evaluation, 43*(5–13).

Sokolova, N. (2012). Teacher language competence description: Towards a new framework of evaluation. *Quality of Higher Education, 9*, 75–97. https://doi.org/10.7220/2345-0258.9.3

Stanley, J. (1992). Coaching student writers to be effective peer evaluators. *Journal of Second Language Writing, 1*(3), 217–233.

Sutton, P. (2012). Conceptualizing feedback literacy: Knowing, being, and acting. *Innovations in Education and Teaching International, 49*(1), 31–40. https://doi.org/10.1080/14703297.2012.647781

swissuniversities. (2015). *Empfehlungen zur Nutzung der berufsspezifischen Sprachkompetenzprofile für Lehrpersonen der Primarstufe und Sekundarstufe I im Rahmen der Aus- und Weiterbildung*. Retrieved from https://www.swissuniversities.ch/fileadmin/swissuniversities/Dokumente/Kammern/Kammer_PH/Empf/EmpfehlungenAGFS_de.pdf

Thonhauser, I. (2019). Welche fachdidaktische Kompetenz brauchen Lehrende? Einige Antworten im Blick auf die Textarbeit im Fremdsprachenunterricht. In E. Peyer, T. Studer, & I. Thonhauser (Eds.), *IDT 2017, Band 1: Hauptvorträge* (pp. 163–174). Erich Schmidt Verlag.

Tsui, A. B. M., & Ng, M. (2000). Do secondary L2 writers benefit from peer comments? *Journal of Second Language Learning, 9*(2), 147–170. https://mite.edu.hku.hk/f/acadstaff/399/Do_Secondary_L2_Writers_Benefit_from_Peer_Comments.pdf

Warm, T. A. (1989). Weighted likelihood estimation of ability in item response theory. *Psychometrika, 54*(3), 427–450. https://doi.org/10.1007/BF02294627

Winke, P., Gass, S., & Myford, C. (2013). Raters' L2 background as a potential source of bias in rating oral performance. *Language Testing, 30*(2), 231–252.

Winstone, N. E., & Carless, D. (2019). *Designing effective feedback processes in higher education: A learning-focused approach* (1st ed.). Routledge. https://doi.org/10.4324/9781351115940

Winstone, N. E., Nash, R. A., Parker, M., & Rowntree, J. (2017). Supporting learners' agentic engagement with feedback: A systematic review and a taxonomy of recipience processes. *Educational Psychologist, 52*(1), 17–37.

Wipperfürth, M. (2009). Welche Kompetenzstandards brauchen professionelle Fremdsprachenlehrer und-lehrerinnen? *ForumSprache, Ausgabe 2/2009.*

Wulf, H. (2001). *Communicative teacher talk – Vorschläge zu einer effektiven Lehrersprache.* Max Hueber.

Yeh, H.-C., Tseng, S.-S., & Chen, Y.-S. (2019). Using online peer feedback through blogs to promote speaking performance. *Educational Technology & Society, 22*(1), 1–14.

Olivia Rütti-Joy is a post-doc researcher at the Université de Fribourg and the research assistant of the rector of the St.Gallen University of Teacher Education in Switzerland. Her background is in English and Media Studies (BA), English Literature (MA) and in English language teaching at both upper secondary school and tertiary level (post-graduate teaching diplomas) in Europe and New Zealand. She received her PhD in applied linguistics from the Université de Fribourg. Her research interests are in foreign language teaching and learning, language testing, LSP testing, teacher education, language aptitude, collaborative feedback processes, and educational assessment. Contact: olivia.ruetti-joy@unifr.ch

4

Developing J-POSTL Elementary for English Language Teacher Education in Japan: Challenges and Opportunities

Fumiko Kurihara, Takane Yamaguchi, Sakiko Yoneda, Eri Osada, and Rie Adachi

F. Kurihara (✉)
Faculty of Commerce, Chuo University, Hachioji, Tokyo, Japan
e-mail: fkuri.21w@g.chuo-u.ac.jp

T. Yamaguchi
Department of Teacher Education, Shumei University, Yachiyo, Chiba, Japan

S. Yoneda
Department of English Language Education, College of Humanities, Tamagawa University, Machida, Tokyo, Japan
e-mail: yoneda_s@lit.tamagawa.ac.jp

E. Osada
Department of Elementary Education, Faculty of Human Development, Kokugakuin University, Yokohama, Japan
e-mail: osada-e@kokugakuin.ac.jp

R. Adachi
Department of Child Development, School of Education, Sugiyama Jogakuen University, Nagoya, Japan

© The Author(s), under exclusive license to Springer-Verlag GmbH, DE, part of Springer Nature 2024
P. Voerkel et al. (eds.), *Tools, Techniques and Strategies for Reflective Second & Foreign Language Teacher Education*,
https://doi.org/10.1007/978-3-662-68741-3_4

1 English Language Education in Japan

1.1 English Education Policies and Guidelines Post 2000

As globalization continued to progress at a rapid rate in the late twentieth century, the need to raise Japanese students with sound English communicative skills appeared in a number of government reports. For example, the Prime Minister's Commission on Japan's Goals in the twenty-first Century (2000) proposed that Japanese people acquire a working knowledge of English as the international lingua franca, while also stating that it is imperative for Japanese people to use English as a tool to obtain information, express ideas, make deals, and work collaboratively in a globalized world. This report also highlighted the necessity of drastic changes in English education and the teacher training system. In 2003, the Ministry of Education, Culture, Sports, Science and Technology (hereafter MEXT) announced an Action Plan to Cultivate "Japanese with English Abilities" to address these issues. In the document, the education minister emphasized the importance of improving English teachers' ability to teach English and creating better curricula to foster Japanese people's communication competence in English.

As part of the Action Plan, concrete achievement goals were set for junior high school (hereafter JHS) and senior high school (hereafter SHS) students using EIKEN—a Japanese domestic test of English proficiency. In addition, it was argued that teachers were expected to acquire sufficient English teaching skills to conduct lessons in English in a communicative and interactive way. In fact, MEXT requested education boards nation-wide to offer compulsory training to all the in-service JHS and SHS English language teachers within five years from 2003 to 2008. Although these specific plans were not without criticisms (Okuno, 2007), it was clear that English language teachers were urged to improve their competence to teach English so that their students could gain sufficient English ability to be able to communicate effectively in various global contexts.

1.2 Developing a Portfolio for English Teachers in Japan

In Japan, MEXT determines curriculum content and broad national curriculum standards for all schools, from kindergarten through to senior high school. The national curriculum, also referred to as Courses of Study, is generally revised once every 10 years. However, there were no benchmarks of didactic competencies that language teachers should strive to attain. In August 2008, some members of the special interest group on English language education (hereafter SIG-ELE) at the Japan Association of College English Teachers (JACET) first learned about the European Portfolio for Student Teachers of Languages (hereafter EPOSTL), developed by Newby et al. (2007). The EPOSTL is a reflection tool for language teachers and builds on the Common European Framework of Reference for Languages (CEFR) (Council of Europe, 2001) as well as the European Language Portfolio (ELP). It was first published in English, and subsequently translated into more than 20 languages. The SIG-ELE members saw the potential of the portfolio as a suitable tool to improve didactic competencies of English language teachers in Japan. While can-do descriptors for linguistic competencies similar to those used in CEFR had already been developed for students at the time, teaching practices in Japan still remained teacher-centered in many classrooms. Thus, the SIG-ELE members were convinced that principles, such as learner-centered teaching, reflective and autonomous learning, and the development of intercultural competence should be incorporated into teacher development in Japan. The SIG-ELE began contextualizing the Japanese Portfolio for Student Teachers of Languages (hereafter J-POSTL) and commenced the process of adapting the EPOSTL into Japanese educational settings after receiving copyright permission in 2014. It was hoped that this portfolio with its selection of self-assessment descriptors (hereafter SADs) would provide both pre- and in-service teachers in Japan with guidelines on communicative language teaching and a roadmap to become autonomous teachers who can critically reflect on and improve their teaching practice throughout their careers. Furthermore, the SIG-ELE members anticipated that the use of the J-POSTL would lead to greater consistency among English teachers, and act as a kind of quality assurance for English language education throughout Japan. In addition, selected SADs are expected to help pre-service teachers reflect deeply on their own growing competencies through experiences including elementary school teacher education programs and teaching practicum, which in turn will help them become reflective practitioners (Yoshizumi, 2018; Yoneda, 2021; Tanaka et al., 2022).

There are three main sections in the J-POSTL. The "personal statement" section helps students reflect on experiences related to language learning and teaching, the "self-assessment" section consists of can-do descriptors, which facilitate reflection and self-assessment. The "dossier" section provides opportunities for monitoring progress and recording examples of work relevant to teaching, including English learning outcomes and demonstration lesson plans. This three-section structure allows students to confirm their own beliefs as teachers, reflect on performance based on their own practice, and at the same time, objectively confirm and demonstrate their own efforts among peers through presentations and demonstrations.

1.3 Issues Related to Adapting the EPOSTL to the Japanese Educational Setting

Introducing the EPOSTL to the Japanese educational context required considerable modifications. One of the European language policies aims to encourage the mobility of people to contribute to peace and harmony of society across Europe. On the other hand, as the MEXT action plan (2003) states, students in Japan are encouraged to learn English as a lingua franca so that they can contribute to the development of Japan in a globalized world. Subsequently, the J-POSTL was recognized as a systematic trial in a non-European context by EPOSTL authors, and given greater copyright flexibility. This allowed the SIG-ELE to adapt the portfolio to the Japanese educational context, and thus make it more user-friendly and accessible and less time-intensive for users (Hisamura, 2014, 2016).

The SIG-ELE spent approximately five years conducting surveys and validating various aspects of the Japanese version of the portfolio and published the J-POSTL in 2014 (JACET SIG on ELE, 2014). Throughout this adaptation process, three main changes occurred. First, while the original EPOSTL has 195 SADs, some could not be adapted to the Japanese context and were removed. Second, some terms were modified to suit the Japanese setting. Lastly, the term "(other/another) language(s)" was replaced with "English" in certain cases, as English is the dominant foreign language taught in Japan. This is a significant difference from the European foreign language education context, where the emphasis is on promoting plurilingualism and pluriculturalism. Examples of these three adaptations are shown in Table 4.1.

The J-POSTL containing 180 SADs is currently in use as a reflection tool for the professional development of both in- and pre-service secondary English teach-

Table 4.1 Examples of differences in J-POSTL and EPOSTL

Type of adaptation	Original EPOSTL SADs	J-POSTL SADs
Elimination	I can help learners to use the European Language Portfolio.	Eliminated
Modification	I can evaluate and select various activities to help learners to identify and use typical features of spoken language (informal language, fillers, etc.)	I can evaluate and select meaningful speaking and interactional activities to help learners to use typical features of spoken language (fillers, nodding, etc.).
Replacement	I can take into account differing motivations for learning another language.	I can take into account differing motivations for learning English.

ers. It has been utilized in 31 teacher training programs in universities in Japan over the past eight years, accounting for about 10% of all such programs in the country.

2 Developing the J-POSTL Elementary

In 2013, the MEXT announced the English Education Reform Plan Corresponding to Globalization (MEXT, 2013). This plan included the aim of making foreign language classes for fifth and sixth grade students in elementary schools mandatory from 2020. As a result, elementary school (hereafter ES) teachers, who basically teach all subjects, would also be responsible for teaching English and assessing their students' skills. In addition, foreign language activity classes for third and fourth grade students were also set to become compulsory.

In line with this decision to implement compulsory English education in elementary schools, core curricula were established both for ES and JHS teacher education programs. However, the ES teacher education program requires only two English focused courses while the JHS and SHS teacher education programs require 14 English focused courses. This means that ES pre-service teachers need to equip themselves with the necessary knowledge and skills for teaching English in a much shorter time while also acquiring knowledge and skills to teach other subjects. With a view to supporting pre-service and in-service ES teachers and providing necessary didactic competencies and opportunities for reflection throughout their teaching careers, the SIG-ELE felt that the existing J-POSTL should be adapted to the ES context. Thus, the development of the J-POSTL Elementary commenced.

2.1 J-POSTL Elementary Development Stages

The entire process of developing the J-POSTL elementary took place in five stages as follows:

Stage 1 (2016–2017): Creation of a list of potential SADs for the ES version of the J-POSTL i.e. J-POSTL Elementary.
> Process: A project team was formed within the SIG, and its members held group interviews on the SADs of the J-POSTL three times in Tokyo and twice in Nagoya, inviting several experienced elementary school teachers and English support staff as participants each time. As a result, a list of SADs was prepared for the next stage.

Stage 2 (2017): Identification of 167 descriptors as a draft of SADs for J-POSTL Elementary.

> Process: A committee consisting of six participants from the group interviews and one elementary English education specialist was organized, and together with the project team members spent two days in June and July 2017 to discuss and create the draft for a total of 15 hours (Jimbo et al., 2018).

Stage 3 (2018): Selection of 93 descriptors as potential SADs for pre-service teacher education.

> Process: A survey using the draft of SADs for J-POSTL Elementary was conducted from January to August 2018 among academics of primary and secondary teacher training programs at universities throughout Japan. The results indicate that 93 descriptors were deemed appropriate for pre-service teacher education (Yamaguchi et al., 2019).

Stage 4 (2018): Development of a competence matrix or a difficulty scale for 74 SADs intended for in-service English teachers.

> Process: A national survey was conducted among in-service ES teachers from October to December 2018, using 74 SADs, which were not selected in Stage 3. The difficulty scale was developed from the survey results (Nakayama & Yamaguchi, 2020).

Stage 5 (2018–2020): Specification of 70 SADs for pre-service teacher education and a study on the use of the preliminary version of J-POSTL Elementary for pre-service teacher education.

> Process: A total of 530 students enrolled in ES teacher training programs at 13 universities participated in the study over four semesters. They used the trial version of the J-POSTL Elementary with 93 SADs which had been selected at stage 3. The study was conducted to determine SAD suitability for pre-service teachers and to investigate their perceptions using the trial version of the J-POSTL Elementary. The students were asked to self-assess their confidence on the SADs using a five-point Likert scale (1. Not confident, 2. Not very confident, 3. Can't decide, 4. Somewhat confident, 5. Confident) at the beginning and end of a semester. They were also asked to complete a questionnaire on their use of a "personal statement" section, a "self-assessment" section and a "dossier" section in the J-POSTL Elementary. The data were analyzed statistically (Yamaguchi (2022a; Yamaguchi & Yoneda, 2020) and 42 SADs were chosen as suitable SADs for pre-service teacher education. Furthermore, an editors' meeting was held with teacher trainers in charge of English methodology courses for elementary education,

and another 28 SADs were added to the list of SADs to form a set of skills, knowledge, and competencies that pre-service teachers should develop before graduation. Finally, a total of 70 SADs were identified for pre-service teacher education.

Yoneda (2022a) also analyzed the data obtained from the study at Stage 5 using the KJ method (Kawakita, 2017). This method was developed by a Japanese ethnologist, Jiro Kawakita, and is often used to reach a consensus on establishing priorities of subjective data in a group. This method was applied for the qualitative analysis of this research using the following procedure: First, the respondents' sentences were segmented thematically, then similar segments were collected as a group, and subsequently, group priorities were established. The results indicate that participants consider the J-POSTL Elementary to be useful for understanding the didactic competencies necessary for teachers, and for reflecting on their learning and progress related to pre-service teacher education by visualizing their progress clearly. However, the results also indicate that participants felt that the self-assessment section had too many SADs. In fact, many expressed concerns that some SADs looked similar or the same. In addition, most participants pointed out that they did not engage in enough discussions with other pre-service teachers or teacher educators. The study suggests that teacher educators have a key role in utilizing the portfolio, creating a system that would enable pre-service teachers to make more use of the portfolios through systematic efforts, such as using them in the classroom regularly through discussions with their teachers or peers.

The J-POSTL Elementary was launched in March 2021. Like the J-POSTL, the J-POSTL Elementary consists of three main sections: a personal statement, a self-assessment, and a dossier. The aim of the J-POSTL Elementary is four-fold (JACET SIG-ELE, 2021, p. 4):

- to encourage pre-service teachers to reflect on the didactic knowledge and skills necessary to teach English at elementary schools in Japan,
- to help pre-service teachers to assess their own didactic competencies,
- to enable pre-service teachers to monitor their progress and to record their teaching experiences during their teacher education degree,
- to promote discussion between pre-service teachers, and between pre-service teachers and their teacher educator

3   Comparison Between the Positions of J-POSTL and J-POSTL Elementary SADs for In-service Teachers on a Competence Matrix

This section highlights the study (Kurihara & Hisamura, 2021) presented at AILA in 2021 as a focal point of the studies associated with the development of J-POSTL Elementary.

3.1   Introduction

The J-POSTL and J-POSTL Elementary are designed for both pre-service and in-service teachers. As such, some SADs only become fully applicable once users commence their teaching careers, while others are appropriate for more experienced teachers. During the process of developing J-POSTL and J-POSTL Elementary, national surveys were conducted among in-service JHS/SHS teachers and ES teachers to categorize the descriptors at appropriate levels for use at certain career stages. A total of 5658 in-service JHS/SHS teachers participated in the survey for J-POSTL (see Hisamura, 2014) and a total of 583 in-service ES teachers participated in the survey (see Stage 4 in the previous section) for J-POSTL Elementary (Nakayama & Yamaguchi, 2020). The participants were asked to judge whether each descriptor includes pedagogical competencies necessary for English teachers in secondary or elementary schools on a 5-point Likert scale (5. necessary, 4. somewhat necessary, 3. indecisive, 2. not very necessary, 1. not necessary). Based on the results of the two surveys, a competence matrix was developed for all the SADs in the J-POSTL and the J-POSTL Elementary respectively. The SADs were classified into five levels in terms of their difficulty as follows.

- Level 1: Preservice.
- Level 2: Novice (1–2 years of teaching experience).
- Level 3: Apprentice (3–5 years of teaching experience).
- Level 4: Practitioner (6–10 years of teaching experience).
- Level 5: Expert (more than 10 years of teaching experience).

Thus, the matrix shows benchmarks of skills and competencies to be achieved at different stages of the teaching profession. However, ES and JHS/SHS teachers are likely to see certain skills and competencies as more essential than others. This study aims to ascertain any differences in how SADs common to both the J-POSTL and J-POSTL Elementary were classified in the Competence Matrix so that we could gain some insight into the differences in the didactic competencies ES and JHS/SHS teachers need to acquire at different stages of their teaching career. There were three research questions in the study.

1. Are there any SADs that are classified differently by two or more stages on the Competence Matrix?
2. If so, in what areas of teaching are they categorized?
3. What are the pedagogical implications of teaching English at elementary schools?

3.2 Method

Out of 180 SADs in J-POSTL, nearly 10% of them are used without any modifications in J-POSTL Elementary, and a little over 70% of them were adapted with some modifications to wording or terminology to suit the context of teaching English at elementary schools. Thus, a total of 144 SADs were identical or nearly the same in J-POSTL and J-POSTL Elementary. For each SAD, the difficulty level on the Competence Matrix shown in J-POSTL and in J-POSTL Elementary was compared to find how they were classified differently in terms of their difficulty scale.

3.3 Findings

The results indicate that 107 SADs fell into the same or slightly different difficulty level by only one level on the competence matrix. An example is shown in Table 4.2.

This suggests that both ES and JHS/SHS teachers consider this SAD to be a fundamental didactic competence that should be acquired during "pre-service" teacher training.

Table 4.2 SAD classified into the same group on the competence matrix

SAD	J-POSTL-E	J-POSTL
I can take into account learners' knowledge of Japanese and make use of it when teaching a foreign language.	Pre-service	Pre-service

Table 4.3 SAD classified into the different group on the competence matrix

SAD	J-POSTL-E	J-POSTL
I can design ICT materials and activities appropriate for my learners.	Novice	Practitioner

Table 4.4 The didactic competencies classified as more fundamental by ES teachers

	Area of didactic competencies	Number of SADs	SAD example
1	ICT and digital materials	4	I can design ICT materials and activities appropriate for my children.
2	Culture	5	I can assess the child's ability to respond to and act appropriately in encounters with different cultures.
3	Lesson planning/setting goals/extra-curricular activities	5	I can help to organize exchanges in cooperation with relevant resource persons and institutions.
4	Conducting interactive lessons	8	I can keep and maximize the attention of children during a lesson.
5	Assessment	4	I can assign grades using procedures which are reliable and transparent.

However, out of the 144 SADs in the J-POSTL and the J-POSTL Elementary, 37 SADs (26%) fell into different classifications in the competence matrix by more than one level. For example, the following SAD was a benchmark for "practitioner" in the J-POSTL, but "novice" in the J-POSTL Elementary, which indicates that it was perceived as a more fundamental didactic competence by ES teachers (Table 4.3).

The results show how ES and JHS/SHS teachers differ in prioritizing the didactic competencies that they need to acquire. Out of the 37 SADs, 26 SADs are regarded as more fundamental core competence by ES teachers than JHS/SHS teachers. Table 4.4 shows the number of SADs classified into each competence area with an example of SADs.

A total of 11 SADs are regarded as more fundamental core competences by JHS/SHS teachers than ES teachers. Table 4.5 shows the number of SADs classified into each competence area with an example of SADs.

Table 4.5 The didactic competences classified as more fundamental by JHS/SHS teachers

	Area of didactic competence	Number of SADs	SAD example
1	Reading	3	I can help learners to develop different strategies to cope with difficult or unknown vocabulary in a text.
2	Vocabulary and grammar instruction	4	I can plan activities that link grammar and vocabulary with communication.
3	Independent learning / learning strategies	4	I can assist learners in choosing tasks and activities according to their individual needs and interests.

3.4 Discussion

In this section, the results of the didactic competencies classified as more fundamental by ES teachers will be discussed.

Firstly, there is a greater emphasis on using ICT in elementary schools. This seems to be motivated by a number of factors such as the current Course of Study (MEXT, 2018), which encourages teachers to use ICT, and the government-initiated Global and Innovation Gateway for All (GIGA) school program (MEXT, 2019), which ensures that each student is given a tablet or a computer and that schools have high-speed internet access. Thus, educators are expected to teach learners how to master digital tools and learn online, and in fact, newly introduced government-authorized English textbooks for ES are equipped with extensive digital content and materials.

Secondly, SADs related to teaching culture are considered more fundamental competencies by ES teachers than JHS and SHS teachers. This suggests that ES teachers in particular appear to recognize the significance of building a solid intercultural understanding foundation in learners, including fostering positive attitudes and developing skills to communicate with people from diverse cultural backgrounds.

Thirdly, the ability to plan lessons, set clear learning goals, and organize exchanges is classified as a fundamental core competence by ES teachers, suggesting that ES teachers should be able to give clear learning goals to learners and create effective lesson plans. Also, it is important for the teachers to maximize the opportunities to increase motivation to learn English or to raise their intercultural awareness through out-of-class activities.

Fourthly, the competence of conducting interactive lessons with special attention to individual children is considered more fundamental among ES teachers. Building mutual understanding and trust with learners and creating a learner-centered classroom environment is a priority challenge, and ES teachers are expected to gain these competencies at an earlier stage of their teaching career.

Finally, the ability to assess a child properly is considered a more fundamental competence for ES teachers. Assessment of younger learners is complex, and teachers are required to pay special attention to the physical, linguistic, cognitive, and mental development of individual learners and differences in the learning process.

3.5 Implications

This study suggests that there are distinctive differences in how elementary and secondary school teachers prioritize core competencies. Ensuring the smooth and effective transition from elementary to secondary English education is essential, and teachers, especially those who have no experience of teaching at elementary schools should acknowledge these differences before planning and conducting lessons. Teacher educators also need to consider these differences when designing curricula for elementary and secondary teacher education programs.

4 The J-POSTL Elementary in Action

Since the release of the preliminary version, the J-POSTL Elementary has been used by teacher educators in 17 universities in Japan. This section provides several examples of how the J-POSTL Elementary has been used in different educational contexts based on a collection of 13 studies by 12 teachers edited by Yoneda et al. (2022). The purposes of this collection are to:

- clarify the idea, purpose, and significance of the J-POSTL as a reflection tool,
- align the instructional content with the Courses of Study for elementary schools and the Core Curriculum,
- develop guidelines for its use in accordance with the requirements of the teaching curriculum, and
- compile specific practices from diverse universities, and to provide them to users as instructional manuals.

While the J-POSTL Elementary consists of three main parts (see Sect. 2), teachers utilize them differently. However, the SAD section is probably considered to be the most useful part for students in pre-service teacher training programs. Section 4 provides several examples of distinctive instructional practices that highlight both the value and versatility of the J-POSTL Elementary.

4.1 Using J-POSTL Elementary in Teaching Methodology Courses

Of the 13 studies mentioned above, nine were conducted in English teaching methodology courses. Due to the spread of COVID-19, most universities conducted classes online in 2020. Since English teaching methodology courses are generally conducted in a practical manner, and often include demonstration classes, most instructors experienced some challenges in teaching these classes. However, each teacher made an effort to introduce the J-POSTL Elementary effectively to improve pre-service teacher motivation in an online learning environment. The studies conducted by the four teacher trainers are summarized as follows:

Osada (2022) introduced the J-POSTL Elementary to her students online in 2020. She encouraged them to self-assess their didactic competencies during the foreign language methodology course for elementary education. The students self-rated their didactic competencies at the beginning and at the end of the course using 94 SADs. Their average score on the Likert scale increased, and many students commented that using the SADs was beneficial because it allowed them to grasp their current skills, understand necessary competence in terms of teaching and evaluating young learners, and visualize their own growth throughout the course. Osada concluded that most students could understand how to reflect on their competencies from different viewpoints.

Nakayama (2022) used the portfolio in two classes, English Teaching Methodology Course 1 and English Teaching Methodology Course 2. In Methodology Course 1, she designed the class with a focus on the SADs in the J-POSTL Elementary, and to deepen the students' understanding of each SAD gradually through several stages. As a result, students' self-rated values on many SADs increased significantly by the final class. In addition, from the comments in their final reports, it was observed that students used the J-POSTL Elementary as a growth indicator, and as a perspective tool for reflecting on practice. Methodology Course 2 aimed to deepen students' understanding of the teaching of the four macro skills (reading/listening/speaking/writing). The four skills were taught in eight lessons, and the class was introduced to the SADs related to each skill. After students discussed their lesson plans in groups, their comments indicated that they were able to relate their learning and practical experience to the SADs, and their understanding of the competencies outlined in the SADs increased.

Adachi (2022) instructed her students to freely choose several SADs to be aware of when preparing lesson plans in an English teaching methodology course for ES education. After students practiced their demonstration lesson, she first provided them with opportunities for cooperative peer discussion. Next, students were encouraged to write reflections from three perspectives:

- Keep (what they would like to continue),
- Problem (what they regretted or what they want to change) and
- Try (what they challenge next).

She directed students to write these reflections based on their own experiences and the peer discussions. She analyzed the students' reflection comments and as a result, she found that they were able to reflect on their mock teaching practices from a more objective perspective (Adachi, 2023).

Benthien (2022) introduced the J-POSTL Elementary in Elementary Education English Content (EEEC) and Elementary Education English Methodology (EEEM) courses. Both courses comprise students of different specializations and varying English levels who may or may not become elementary school teachers. In the EEEC course, the students were encouraged to complete the personal statement section at home and a discussion of their past L2 experiences was conducted in class time. However, due to a lack of time at the beginning of the semester, a detailed explanation of the J-POSTL Elementary itself could not be provided, and the full potential of the personal statement section could not be achieved by all students. Thus, she suggests that careful integration of the portfolio is essential. In the EEEM class, selected J-POSTL Elementary SADs that matched course contents were given to students. The use of the J-POSTL SADs was evaluated positively by the pre-service teachers at the end of the semester, with SADs functioning as a roadmap, a goal-setting device, and a tool for reflection in combination with the practical content of the course.

4.2 Using J-POSTL Elementary in Different Educational Contexts

The remaining four studies show how the J-POSTL Elementary could be used in different teaching contexts.

Iwanaka (2022) used the J-POSTL Elementary in an elective English course consisting of 15 classes offered at the Department of Education at a private university. In the first class, he used the personal statement section to help students reflect on their past experiences and questions related to teaching at the beginning of their teacher education. The following classes made use of the dossier section where students could track their progress and record work relevant to their teacher education such as teaching plans of their mock classes. At the same time, he helped the students become familiar with all the SADs through discussions. In the final class, he had the students read all the SADs again. Most students reported that they had learned what competencies and skills are required for teaching ES English.

Yamaguchi (2022b) implemented the J-POSTL Elementary in a foreign language teaching support program. This is a unique program where pre-service teachers observe foreign language classes or support ES teachers at nearby elementary schools. The program is not mandatory, and students participate on a voluntary basis. Students were asked to reflect on their experiences and discuss these using SADs in the J-POSTL Elementary. Although students were not asked to rate their competence on each SAD, referring to the SADs in the J-POSTL Elementary allowed the pre-service teachers to report on their experiences in detail using insights gained from this section of the J-POSTL Elementary.

Yoneda (2022b) focused on three students who used the portfolio and had a two-week teaching practicum in elementary schools. The students had used the J-POSTL Elementary over the past year in different courses, including seminar and English teaching methodology courses. Although these experiences helped the students set clear goals in their teaching practicum, they found designing classes in unfamiliar situations like modules and special activities challenging. This raised the issue of cultivating more practical skills, and the ability to reflect through practice. She concluded that using the J-POSTL Elementary has a dual purpose. First, it helps students deepen their understanding of SADs and gain a wider perspective on foreign language teaching. Second, it enables educators to identify new instructional goals.

Kashimoto (2022) implemented the J-POSTL Elementary before and after a teaching practicum. She asked students to discuss the meaning of several SADs in her class, and subsequently extracted 30 SADs based on their opinions and feedback. After the students finished their teaching practicum, they were asked to share their ideas and opinions about the chosen 30 SADs again. She concluded that they could improve their teaching skills and gain a broader perspective in teaching foreign languages to children through this experience.

5 Future Directions

As indicated in the studies of the J-POSTL Elementary in use, it can be a useful tool for pre-service teachers to reflect on their past experiences of learning English, assess their didactic competencies before and after their micro-teaching and teaching practicum experiences, and become aware of their growth in the competencies that they have achieved through their experiences. In addition, it can provide a specific focus for discussions that the students engage with their peers and enable them to gain an overall understanding of required competencies. The J-POSTL Elementary SADs in particular provide points for reflection and encourage pre-service teachers to gain a deeper understanding of what skills and competencies are expected to be developed throughout their future teaching career. Nevertheless, it should be noted that effective mediation and usage support led by course instructors need to take place because the pre-service teachers may feel overwhelmed by the number of SADs, leading to a loss of motivation to apply them to practice. However, with adequate intervention from instructors and peers, it is anticipated that pre-service teachers will be able to use the J-POSTL Elementary effectively and acquire the skills to become reflective and autonomous practitioners.

In addition, awareness of distinctive differences in priorities for core competencies between ES and JHS/SHS teachers is crucial. University teachers in charge of pre-service teacher training for both ES and JHS/SHS need to take these differences into consideration and adjust their courses accordingly.

The SIG-ELE members involved in the development of the J-POSTL Elementary hope that it will be used not only in teacher training courses but that its usage will also spread among in-service teachers. This use would provide ample opportunities for reflection and build a common foundation among teachers. Nevertheless, further research needs to be conducted to investigate the effective implementation of the J-POSTL Elementary across different educational contexts.

Acknowledgments This paper was supported in part by a Grant-in-Aid for Scientific Research (B) from the Japan Society for the Promotion of Science, "Systematization of Portfolio as a Reflection Tool and Development of a Guide for Its Application" (Project No. 19H01288, Leader: Professor Emeritus Hisatake Jimbo). We would like to express our special thanks to Professor Emeritus Ken Hisamura who initiated the portfolio project and guided us throughout the development and the use of J-POSTL Elementary. We are also grateful to Professor Gaby Benthien, who provided insightful comments on the earlier manuscripts as well as editorial assistance. Last but not least, we would like to extend our sincere gratitude to all the students, teachers, and teacher educators who participated in the studies.

References

Adachi, R. (2022). J-POSTL Elementary to KPT 3 kanten niyoru seisatsu (J-POSTL Elementary and reflection using KPT perspectives). In Yoneda, S., Yamaguchi, T., & Osada, E. (Eds.), *J-POSTL Elementary: Kyoshoku Katei ni okeru Katsuyo Jissen* (Using J-POSTL Elementary in pre-service teacher education). JACET SIG on ELE, 82–91.

Adachi, R. (2023). Shogakko gaikokugo shidoho jugyo niokeru J-POSTL Elementary no donyu to KPT no 3 kanten niyoru rifurekushon niyoru rishusei no shidoishiki eno koka (Effects on student teachers' teaching attitudes by introduction of J-POSTL elementary and reflection on the three perspectives of KPT in an elementary foreign language teaching methodology class). *Journal of the School of Education, Sugiyama Jogakuen University, 16*, 143–152. https://doi.org/10.20557/00003538

Benthien, G. (2022). Integrating the J-POSTL elementary into English-focused classes for pre-service teachers: Challenges and benefits. In Yoneda, S., Yamaguchi, T., & Osada, E. (Eds.), *J-POSTL Elementary: Kyoshoku Katei ni okeru Katsuyo Jissen* (Using J-POSTL Elementary in pre-service teacher education). JACET SIG on ELE, 102–112.

Council of Europe. (2001). *Common European framework of reference for languages: learning, teaching, assessment*. Cambridge University Press.

Hisamura, K. (2014). J-POSTL: Specification of descriptors and strategies for implementation. *Language Teacher Education, 1*(2), 5–25. http://www.waseda.jp/assoc-jacetenedu/VOL1NO2.pdf

Hisamura, K. (2016). Exploring the transportability of the rationale and principles behind the J-POSTL to a Japanese educational context. *Language Teacher Education, 3*(2), 1–25. https://www.waseda.jp/assoc-jacetenedu/VOL3NO2.pdf

Iwanaka, T. (2022). Jiko hyoka kijyutsu bun o mochiita hanashiai katsudo: Jyukosei no seisatsu ryoku kojo no kokoromi(Discussion activities using self-assessment descriptors: An attempt to improve students' reflective skills). In Yoneda, S., Yamaguchi, T., & Osada, E. (Eds.), *J-POSTL Elementary: Kyoshoku Katei ni okeru Katsuyo Jissen* (Using J-POSTL Elementary in pre-service teacher education). JACET SIG on ELE, 15–24.

JACET SIG on English Language Education. (2014). *Gengo Kyoshi no Portfolio* (Japanese Portfolio for Student Teachers of Languages: J-POSTL).

JACET SIG on English Language Education. (2021). *Shogakko Eigo Shidosha no Portfolio* (J-POSTL for Elementary-school Teacher Education: J-POSTL Elementary).

Jimbo, H., Hisamura, K., Sakai, S., Adachi, R., Osada, E., Kurihara, F., Kiyota, Y., & Nakayama, N. (Eds.). (2018). J-POSTL Shogakko eigo shido sha hen: Jikohyoka kijutsubun soan (J-POSTL Elementary: Preliminary version for in-service teachers). *Language Teacher Education, 5*(1), 174–180.

Kashimoto, Y. (2022). Kyoiku jisshu zengo ni okeru katsuyo rei: Zemi sei o taisho toshita jissen (A case study on using J-POSTL Elementary for student teachers: Focusing on the seminar students before and after their teaching practicum). In Yoneda, S., Yamaguchi, T., & Osada, E. (Eds.), *J-POSTL Elementary: Kyoshoku Katei ni okeru Katsuyo Jissen* (Using J-POSTL Elementary in pre-service teacher education). JACET SIG on ELE, 133–141.

Kawakita, J. (2017). *Hasso-ho*. Kaiban (revised edition). Tokyo: Chuko Shinsho.

Kurihara, F., & Hisamura, K. (2021). Distinctive differences in priorities for core competences between secondary and elementary school EFL teachers. *Language Teacher Education, 8*(2), 24–41. http://www.waseda.jp/assoc-jacetenedu/VOL8NO2.pdf

Ministry of Education, Culture, Sports, Science, and Technology. (2003). "Eigo ga tsukaeru nihonjin" ikusei no tameno kodo keikaku (Action plan to cultivate Japanese with English abilities). https://www.mext.go.jp/b_menu/shingi/chukyo/chukyo3/004/siryo/04031601/005.pdf

Ministry of Education, Culture, Sports, Science, and Technology. (2013). English education reform plan corresponding to globalization. https://www.mext.go.jp/en/news/topics/detail/__icsFiles/afieldfile/2014/01/23/1343591_1.pdf

Ministry of Education, Culture, Sports, Science, and Technology. (2018). Shogakko gakushu shido yoryo (Course of Study for elementary school).

Ministry of Education, Culture, Sports, Science, and Technology. (2019). GIGA (Global and innovation gateway for all) school koso ni tsuite (Regarding the GIGA school program).

Nakayama, N. (2022). Jikohyoka kijutsubun ni taisuru rikai o fukameru tameni: "gaikokugo no shido ho" ni okeru katsuyo (Using the portfolio in a foreign language methodology course: To foster learners' understanding of self-assessment descriptors). In Yoneda, S., Yamaguchi, T., & Osada, E. (Eds.), *J-POSTL Elementary: Kyoshoku Katei ni okeru Katsuyo Jissen* (Using J-POSTL Elementary in pre-service teacher education). JACET SIG on ELE, 45–52.

Nakayama, N., & Yamaguchi, T. (2020). Elementary school teachers' perceptions on the qualities and competencies of English language instructors: Results of a national survey on the descriptors of the J-POSTL Elementary. *Language Teacher Education, 7*(2), 5–27. http://www.waseda.jp/assoc-jacetenedu/VOL7NO2.pdf

Newby, D., Allan, R., Fenner, A.-B., Jones, B., Komorowska, H., & Soghikyan, K. (2007). *European Portfolio for Student Teachers of Languages. A reflection tool for language teacher education*. Strasbourg, France/Graz, Austria: Council of Europe Publishing. Retrieved from: http://www.ecml.at/epostl

Okuno, H. (2007). A critical discussion on the action plan to cultivate "Japanese with English Abilities". *The Journal of Asia TEFL, 4*(4), 133–158. https://citeseerx.ist.psu.edu/document?repid=rep1&type=pdf&doi=fad880e33e9ff9cf3866f4e330c24628d7145856

Osada, E. (2022). Shidosha to kyoshoku rishu sha no hashiwatashi toshiteno J-POSTL Elementary (Using J-POSTL Elementary as collaborative work between pre-service teachers and their instructors). In Yoneda, S., Yamaguchi, T., & Osada, E. (Eds.), *J-POSTL Elementary: Kyoshoku Katei ni okeru Katsuyo Jissen* (Using J-POSTL Elementary in pre-service teacher education). JACET SIG on ELE, 35–44.

Tanaka, T., Minami, Y., & Takagi, A. (2022). The potential of teachers' collaborative reflection in English language teaching: In light of theories and problems of teacher reflection and reflective practice. *Language Teacher Education, 9*(2), 13–30. https://www.waseda.jp/assoc-jacetenedu/VOL9NO2.pdf

The Prime Minister's Commission on Japan's Goals in the 21st Century. (2000). *The Frontier within: Individual Empowerment and Better Governance in the New Millennium*. https://www.kantei.go.jp/jp/21century/report/pdfs/index.html

Yamaguchi, T. (2022a). Shogakko deno gaikokugo shidosha o yosei suru tameno kyoshoku katei ni okeru jikohyoka kijutsubun eno jikohyoka no henka (Changes in perceptions for self-assessment descriptors of pre-service elementary school teachers in teacher training programs). *Language Teacher Education, 9*(1), 20–40.

Yamaguchi, T. (2022b). Kogi to gaikokugo shien katsudo deno J-POSTL Elementary no shiyo ho (Using J-POSTL Elementary in a lecture and foreign language support activities). In Yoneda, S., Yamaguchi, T., & Osada, E. (Eds.), *J-POSTL Elementary: Kyoshoku Katei ni okeru Katsuyo Jissen* (Using J-POSTL Elementary in pre-service teacher education). JACET SIG on ELE, 113–122.

Yamaguchi, T., Osada, E., Hisamura, K., & Benthien, G. (2019). Japanese portfolio for elementary English educators: Specifying self-assessment descriptors for student teachers. *Language Teacher Education, 6*(2), 37–64. http://www.waseda.jp/assoc-jacetenedu/VOL6NO2.pdf

Yamaguchi, T., & Yoneda, S. (2020). Qualities and abilities related to English language teaching required of elementary school teachers projected from a pre-service teacher survey. *Language Teacher Education, 7*(2), 18–52. http://www.waseda.jp/assoc-jacetenedu/VOL7NO2.pdf

Yoneda, S. (2021). Students' growth and learning in elementary English teacher pre-service education. *Language Teacher Education, 8*(2), 62–76. http://www.waseda.jp/assoc-jacetenedu/VOL8NO2.pdf

Yoneda, S. (2022a). J-POSTL Elementary kaihatsu no tame no keinen chosa ni okeru shitsumonshi chosa no shitsuteki bunseki kekka hokoku (Questionnaire Analysis of the Two-year "J-POSTL Elementary" Survey). *Language Teacher Education, 9*(1), 103–119.

Yoneda, S. (2022b). Shogakko kyoiku jisshu ni okeru katsuyo jirei: J-POSTL Elementary o chokishiyo shita gakusei no rei (A case study on using J-POSTL Elementary in teaching practicum: A longitudinal study). In Yoneda, S., Yamaguchi, T., & Osada, E. (Eds.), *J-POSTL Elementary: Kyoshoku Katei ni okeru Katsuyo Jissen* (Using J-POSTL Elementary in pre-service teacher education). JACET SIG on ELE, 123–132.

Yoneda, S., Yamaguchi, T., & Osada, E. (Eds.). (2022). *J-POSTL Elementary: Kyoshoku Katei ni okeru Katsuyo Jissen* (Using JPOSTL Elementary in pre-service teacher education).. JACET SIG on ELE.

Yoshizumi, K. (2018). Investigating student teachers' reflection on micro teaching using Japanese Portfolio for Student Teachers of Languages (J-POSTL). *Language Teacher Education, 5*(2), 1–21. http://www.waseda.jp/assoc-jacetenedu/VOL5NO2.pdf

Fumiko Kurihara is a professor in the Faculty of Commerce at Chuo University, Japan. She received her MA from Georgetown University, and PhD from International Christian University, and has been teaching English as a foreign language at Japanese universities for more than 25 years. She is currently the chair of the English Language Education Special Interest Group in the Japan Association of College English Teachers (JACET) and an editorial board member of the SIG's journal, *Language Teacher Education*. Her research interests include the development of learners' intercultural competence and mediation skills through foreign language learning. Contact: fkuri.21w@g.chuo-u.ac.jp

Takane Yamaguchi is a lecturer in the Faculty of Teacher Education Department at Shumei University in Japan. He received an MA in language education from Waseda University, Japan in 1999. He has been teaching English as a foreign language at universities for more than 20 years and has been involved in training pre-service teachers of English in primary and secondary education for the past five years. His research interests include teacher education and computer-assisted language learning. He is currently the president of the Kanto Chapter of the Japan Association of College English Teachers (JACET). Contact: takane46@gmail.com

Sakiko Yoneda is a professor in the Department of English Language Education, College of Humanities at Tamagawa University, Japan. She received her MEd from Yokohama National University, MA in Linguistics from San Jose State University, and PhD from Kanazawa University, Japan. She has taught from kindergarten through graduate school in Japan. Her research interests include bilingualism in Japanese children, teaching English in elementary schools in Japan, training pre-service teachers of English, and cultural exchanges such as COIL between Japanese pre-service teachers and American children. Contact: yoneda_s@lit.tamagawa.ac.jp

Eri Osada is an associate professor in the Department of Elementary Education in the Faculty of Human Development, Kokugakuin University, Japan. She has taught English in elementary schools and obtained an MA in linguistics from Sophia University, Japan. She mainly teaches primary school EFL methodology in addition to English linguistics and communication courses, while also being involved in in-service teacher training. Her research interests include teacher education, lesson study, and language teacher cognition. Contact: osada-e@kokugakuin.ac.jp

Rie Adachi, PhD, is a professor in the School of Education at Sugiyama Jogakuen University, Japan and also teaches English teaching methodology at Aichi University. Her main research interests are intercultural receptive attitudes of Japanese people, motivation of Japanese children, and the development of a global mindset in Japanese students. She is also currently interested in introducing CLIL-based programs into Japanese education. She has published extensively in the areas of motivation for language learning, intercultural communication attitudes and foreign language education. Contact: macchacake91011@gmail.com

Tools of Action Research in Undergraduate Teacher Education: Experiences from Brazil

Paul Voerkel

1 About the Need for Well-Trained Teachers

Comprehensive learning processes have shaped the coexistence and social development of humankind from the very beginning, and today—in the face of global crises such as the Covid pandemic, armed conflicts, and ecological challenges—they appear more important than ever. Quality education is therefore one of the United Nations' development goals (cf. Holzbaur, 2020) and is recognized as strategically important in many countries.

For the quality and efficiency of education, a crucial point of impact lies with the teachers (cf. Legutke & Schart, 2016, 9), which is one of the reasons why it is important that they are well trained and can act professionally. This training is relevant, not least of all because there is an acute shortage of teachers: To achieve the goal of high-quality school education worldwide and across subjects, some 70 million teachers would need to be recruited by 2030 (cf. UNESCO, 2021, 84). As the numbers show, the global shortage of teachers affects all countries, both in the Global North and the Global South, and cuts across all subjects and levels of education, which is one factor that contributes to government and civil society agencies increasingly speaking of an education emergency (cf. OECD, 2003).

As in other subjects, the shortage has had a profound effect in the area of German as a Foreign Language (GFL) and the lack of well-trained teachers is a

---

P. Voerkel (✉)
Schmalkalden University of Applied Sciences, Schmalkalden, Germany

© The Author(s), under exclusive license to Springer-Verlag GmbH, DE, part of Springer Nature 2024
P. Voerkel et al. (eds.), *Tools, Techniques and Strategies for Reflective Second & Foreign Language Teacher Education*,
https://doi.org/10.1007/978-3-662-68741-3_5

problem that is repeatedly pointed out, both in reports from the German-speaking world and from other contexts. (cf. Auswärtiges Amt, 2020, 7f.). This shortage is seen in Europe, where the German language has long played an important role due to intensive economic relations and geographical proximity, but it can also be felt worldwide. In this sense, Chaves and Soethe (2020, 36f.) report that there are 41,400,000 pupils enrolled in the Brazilian school system, while only 80,000 (less than 0.2%) of them have access to German lessons. This is somehow surprising because the south of the country in particular was strongly influenced by German-speaking immigration (in the 1920s, there is evidence of almost 1000 German-run schools in the three southern states alone) and up to five million Brazilians refer to German ancestors, which is also expressed in a generally high regard for the German language and culture (cf. Voerkel, 2017, 17–29; Ammon, 2018, 373; Voerkel, 2021, 193). One reason for the rather low offering of German, especially in the school sector, is the lack of teachers: there are about 800 German teachers at the approximately 350 schools that offer German nationwide, but only about 140 of these are employed in the public-school network (compared to aproximately 70,000 teachers of English).

The lack of teachers is certainly not the only reason why German cannot be offered to a greater extent in schools or in the education system in general, but it is a decisive one. For this reason, there has been increasing conversation about how the training and further education of German teachers can be strengthened. The lecturers of German departments that train German teachers at 17 Brazilian universities, as well as various German intermediary organizations, are involved in this ongoing conversation (cf. Voerkel, 2017). One focus of their concern is how to strengthen teacher education at the micro, meso, and macro levels, and especially through focused research. In the joint discussions, it has become clear how important the practical relevance of reflection already is during teacher training, and that reflective, research-based learning can at the same time contribute to a professionalization and strengthening of the teachers (cf. Legutke & Schart, 2016). Additionally, there is a lack of broader studies on how research and reflection can be implemented in practice.

This is where this chapter comes in, by describing a project on Action Research (AR) in the context of higher education. In order to facilitate a fundamental understanding of the project, I will first describe some of the main characteristics of Research-Based Learning (RBL) and AR (Sect. 2). Still, the main part of the chapter is used for the presentation and contextualization of the project and the follow-up survey (Sect. 3), the results of which are summarized in a separate section (4). The chapter ends with some considerations on the possibilities of sensibly using tools of AR in the university context (Sect. 5).

2 Research-Based Learning and Action Research

The foundations of RBL go back to John Dewey and his work in the 1930s (cf. Frey, 2012, 36f.). Since then, the approach has steadily evolved and has also played a role in teacher education and foreign language didactics for some time (cf. Feldmeier, 2014, 258f.). Within academic practice in Germany, the corresponding ideas have prevailed since the 2000s and have thus found their way into university didactics on the one hand (cf. Basten et al., 2020) but have also become established in the field of GFL with the concept of Action Research (cf. Altrichter & Posch, 2007; Saunders et al., 2020) on the other. Underlying both approaches is the idea that researchers and subjects jointly try to clarify and solve the problems and issues under investigation, and stakeholders are made active participants in the research process. As one of the characteristics, the boundary between everyday activities and research becomes fluid, in consequence the subject-object model of research, in which researchers look at their research subject from the outside, is replaced by a subject-subject model, in which the participants (in this case the teachers) themselves actively participate in the research process (cf. Feldmeier, 2014, 257).

Since RBL and AR form the basis of the teacher education project presented in this chapter and the subsequent evaluation, the most important characteristics are presented in the following sections and supplemented with an example from continuing education in GFL.

2.1 Research-Based Learning

RBL is a compelling format for teacher education which has become increasingly popular in higher education didactics (and, thus, also in foreign language didactics) since the turn of the millennium, and which is strongly based on the idea of intertwining theory and practice via projects of joint planning, experimentation, and reflection (cf. Aguado, 2015, 303f.; Lehmann, 2018, 17). In recent years, RBL has been described not only theoretically but also as a practical approach to teacher education (e.g. Mieg & Lehmann, 2017, or Basten et al., 2020) and can be summarized as follows:

> Research-based learning is distinguished from other forms of learning by the fact that learners (co-)design, experience and reflect on the process of a research project, which is aimed at gaining knowledge that is also of interest to third parties, in its essential phases—from the development of questions and hypotheses to the choice and

execution of methods to the examination and presentation of results in independent work or in active collaboration in an overarching project.[1] (Huber, 2009, 11)

The potential of Research-based Learning in foreign language teaching is therefore based not least on the fact that the active involvement of foreign language students can minimize the "practice shock" (Legutke & Schart, 2016, 29) between university education and acting as a teacher. RBL promotes basic observation, understanding, and research skills, all of which are important for university students' future work as language teachers (cf. Aguado, 2015, 300–302). These skills need to be transferred into a suitable setting, where AR, for example, can play a significant role.

2.2 Action Research

AR can ultimately be seen as a way to implement and guide RBL through the use of scaffolding of questions and reflection. This concept—also known as teacher research (cf. Schart & Legutke, 2012, 186)—has existed since the 1940s but has only become established in the German-speaking world in the last twelve years or so (cf. Benitt, 2015, 66–68).

The AR approach can be said to be a type of research conducted by professional agents (e.g., teachers) directly in their practice setting. The goal of AR is to research an intervention to improve practice. In doing so, an iterative cycle of action, research, and reflection emerges. This cycle yields both progress in knowledge with regard to theory and progress in development with regard to practice (Altrichter & Posch, 2007, 27) and for this reason is often described as a spiral. AR differs from everyday practice—which often includes phases of trial and error, observation, and reflection—in its systematic nature, the documentation of the process, and the dissemination of the results (cf. Boeckmann, 2016, 592).

In Germany, AR is often seen in connection with teacher action and is, therefore, mainly mentioned in the framework of teacher education and teaching. For this reason, one of the most common definitions of the approach also refers to the school context, where it is consistently described as a method for both exploring and changing classroom practice, with the added feature that the research is conducted by practitioners who, in turn, are investigating their own practice. Altrichter & Posch summarize these aspects of AR as follows: "Action Research is the

---

[1] This quote, like all other direct quotes in this chapter, has been translated into English by the author.

systematic study of professional situations conducted by teachers themselves with the intention of improving them" (Altrichter & Posch, 2007, 13).

In addition to a look at Germany, where AR is known mainly in the academic milieu and is discussed more theoretically or as an educational approach, it is also worthwhile to consider the Brazilian perspective. AR is known here as "Pesquisa Ação" and refers more to social realities and emancipation (cf. Franco-Santoro, 2005). In this sense, it is seen as an approach that is taught to students from undergraduate level onwards, so that they become familiar with suitable tools for advancing society and positively influencing their social environment. In the university context, there are dedicated theory-practice programs for this purpose, which go by the acronyms PIBIC (Programa Institucional de Bolsas de Iniciação Científica—for research) and PIBID (Programa Institucional de Bolsa de Iniciação à Docência—specifically for teaching experiences), include a small scholarship and allow young professionals to get in touch with research themselves (cf. Voerkel et al., 2022b). If we take a look at the research literature on AR in Brazil, we can see that the relevance of AR in higher education is constantly increasing, but only about ¼ of it refers to the researchers' own actions (cf. Molina, 2007). What we can observe here is a gap between the different approaches to AR that needs to be closed if the language teacher training follows the aim to unite theory, practice, and the individual experience of the students in a sensitive way.

2.3 On the Implementation of Action Research in the GFL Context

We have seen that in Germany, in Brazil, and in different parts of the world, the paradigm of the teacher-researcher reverberates in different methodological possibilities such as exploratory practice or AR. There are different views about how this aspiration can best be implemented and strengthened, both in the initial training and later professional development of language teachers. An example of how these ideas are being put into practice in the area of GFL is the Deutsch Lehren Lernen program (henceforth DLL, which we can translate into English as "Learning to teach German"), where AR appears as a central methodology so that investigation processes about pedagogical practices can be carried out.[2] Moreover, DLL promotes the necessary space for these practices to be questioned, reflected upon,

---

[2] A profound overview of the concept, structure and implementation of the program can be found in the 2023/2 issue of "Kontexte", an international open-access journal on the professionalization of GFL teachers. Link: https://kontexte-journal.org

discussed, and constantly rethought. The conceptualization of the material explicitly states:

> In order to train teachers in the best possible and most practical way, DLL uses methods of action or teacher research. This means that, in addition to acquiring subject-specific didactic knowledge, teachers in their DLL continuing education or professional development program are continuously encouraged to observe their own and other people's teaching, to recognize new possibilities for action, and to try these out in their teaching. In this way, theoretical knowledge acquisition and research-based and reflective experiential learning complement each other. (Legutke & Rotberg, 2018)

The DLL program was designed by the Goethe-Institut and developed in partnership with lecturers and researchers from different German universities. This partnership corresponds, then, to its inception to the most current methodological insights in GFL didactics and is also reflected in the comprehensive preliminary studies and carefully thought-out accompanying research. The result of the developments was finally a methodically and didactically well-planned program offer with three special features: numerous teaching documentations, practice exploration projects (PEPs) to be created specifically on the basis of teaching experience, and a cooperative approach of joint elaboration and reflection of contents (cf. Legutke & Rotberg, 2018; Mohr & Schart, 2016).

Since the launch of the program in 2012, it has been used by the Goethe-Institut itself for internal training of its teaching staff. In addition, DLL is also available to the general public in individual modules according to the specific interests and needs of each context (cf. Voerkel et al., 2022a). At present, 50 universities around the world integrate modules from the DLL series into their classes, such as didactics or German language teaching methodology. Due to the partnership with the Goethe-Institut, the modules offered by the universities are made available on the institutional platform, so that all students have access to the entire material, i.e., texts, assignments, and videos, and can interact with other participants and with the teachers throughout the course (cf. Legutke, 2023, 7).

The widespread use of the program, and especially the explicit reference to the theory-practice connection, has led to a closer look at certain elements and consideration of whether the practice explorations, in particular, can be usefully embedded in university education. This is how the research project came about, which is described in more detail in the following section.

3 From Theory to Action: The Research Project

The academic discussion continuously points out the high relevance that practice orientation plays for the educational process, especially for the training of future teachers. This is not different in German teacher training in Brazil, where two things apport additional complexity to the general situation: First, students often have to learn the target language German from the very beginning during their four to five years of study, and second, there is no transitional period between university and the start of work as a teacher, such as an accompanied traineeship. In discussions with colleagues as well as in an examination of the literature, we find therefore numerous references to the fact that practical elements and reflection should be an essential part of teacher training and, thus, be integrated in university curricula and practice (cf. Santos et al., 2019; Gondar & Ferreira, 2020). These claims led to the teaching and research project realized in the context of German teacher training in Brazil, and that will be explained in more detail next.

3.1 Motivation and Project Design

When I was a guest lecturer in Brazil for several years, I had the opportunity to speak with numerous peers and observe in practice the challenges of teacher education in GFL. In this way, I could see that embedding moments of reflection in the didactic seminars was a relevant concern for both students and colleagues. This gave rise to the idea of exploring the possibilities in teacher training in more detail and initiating a project to that end, which ultimately included two essential parts and ran over a longer period of time.

The research question that initially arose when starting the project was the following: Is it possible to use AR already in the undergraduate training of German teachers to structure lesson planning and reflection? And if so, what should be considered success? To this end, I organized three semester courses in didactics at my Brazilian host universities over a three-year period (2017 to 2019), in which AR, among other topics, played a central role. At the core of these courses were project phases in which the students' own teaching behavior was examined and reflected upon using embedded guiding questions, which in turn were inspired by specifications from the DLL program. How the courses were ultimately implemented and accepted by students is described in the next subsection (Sect. 3.2).

My time as a guest lecturer in Brazil ended in an unexpected way and sooner than intended due to the Pandemic so that I could not continue this kind of didactic seminar for the time being. At the same time, I asked myself about the sense and success of the approach I had chosen. Based on this motivation, I decided to plan and implement a second part of the project: a study on the effects of the courses offered so far. For this purpose, two guiding questions were drafted:

1. Does incorporating Practice Exploration Projects (PEPs) into a didactic seminar prove useful for student teachers, even if PEPs are conducted only once?
2. Are consequences for perceptions of teaching, lesson planning, and for one's own teaching behavior still perceptible several years later?

This second part of the project was planned and implemented in 2021. It soon became clear that a useful way to gain insights into the students' learning process and the consequences of engaging with AR could be to survey the participants. To this end, several guiding questions were first formulated and discussed collaboratively with a small group of experts. Students who had participated in the seminars between 2017 and 2019 were then contacted and asked if they would be willing to share their experiences in an interview. After reviewing the feedback, students were again contacted, asked to provide written informed consent, and group interviews were arranged and conducted. These group interviews were recorded, transcribed, and then analyzed. More details about this second part of the project can be found in the next but one section of this chapter (Sect. 3.3) as well as in Voerkel and Scribelk (2022).

3.2 The Course Offer

At the core of the project presented here were the courses offered between 2017 and 2019 as part of two Brazilian German degree programs. They will, therefore, be described in more detail below.

The didactics courses were held at two important public universities: the Federal University of Rio de Janeiro (UFRJ) and the State University of Rio de Janeiro (UERJ). The 2017 course at UFRJ was offered as an elective, whereas the 2018 and 2019 courses were embedded in the curricular didactics' seminars *Prática de Ensino* and *Metodologia*. Each course was attended by 6 to 10 participants, all of them enrolled as German-Portuguese double majors (undergraduate) and realizing the second part of their studies at the time of the course, summing up a total of 22 participants.

Before the semester started, the students had to be aware of some course details. A prerequisite for participation was access to teaching, either by being a teacher themselves or through class observation. Then, they had to cope with German as a language of instruction (although during the discussions a model of "pragmatic multilingualism "was adopted, which means that Portuguese and English were equally accepted in class). An important detail was that the students were expected to participate actively in class and to elaborate a Practice Exploration Project (PEP) as part of the coursework.

Students were not alone in developing the PEPs, but were given close guidance. On the one hand, this was done by first introducing the background of AR and presenting the DLL education program in this context. A particular focus was placed in this setting on the guiding questions that orient the explorations in the preparation of the PEPs in DLL. In the program, these serve to structure and document (as a follow-up) one's own classroom explorations, which in turn form the basis for collegial exchange and conversations with peers.

The five lead questions can be summarized and translated as follows:

1. What is the main question in my own Practice Exploration Project (PEP)?
2. How is the PEP question connected to the course content, and what is my personal motivation to work on it?
3. How has the PEP project been realized?
4. What are the main results of the data collection?
5. How can I evaluate the results of the PEP, and what are possible consequences for my further professional development?

The guiding questions were announced to the students and discussed with them in detail before they planned their own practice explorations so they knew the expectations related to their own classroom observations. The topics of the PEPs were then developed on this basis, discussed with each other in class, modified if necessary, and sharpened. As a result, the research questions emerged that students explored in their PEPs. The questions were quite diverse and were each oriented towards the (teaching) reality of the students, as the following examples show:

- Why is the use of apps and their technologies a benefit in the learning of children aged 5 and 6?
- How can ludic activities underline the process in foreign language teaching for children?
- How could my student better memorize the declinations of adjectives in German?

- How can the close analysis of a German song help a student to improve his or her language skills? What specific points can be improved through this practice?

It was particularly exciting to see how the PEPs were implemented and the lessons learned documented through writing. To describe their explorations, students followed the questions fairly closely, writing an average of 3 pages. The choice of language was optional, and most chose their L1 (Portuguese for the majority). The language was, therefore, not a particular difficulty, but rather the content was on focus.

It is particularly interesting to look at PEPs in some detail because they are described in the research literature as a key challenge of the DLL program (cf. Mohr & Schart, 2016). On the one hand, this is due to the text type, which is quite new and therefore not routine for the students, and on the other hand, to the fundamental need for abstraction and reflection. Against this background, the students' experiences in writing the PEPs can be summarized as follows:

- A first major hurdle was to formulate a suitable research question. To support this process, time was given several times in the seminar for queries and exchange between the students, so that after the first third of the semester everyone had phrased an appropriate question.
- A next challenge was to summarize the topic and approach in a coherent and concise way. When asked, the students confirmed that they found it difficult to abstract the essential contents and to write a concise text (with consideration of academic standards).
- It was also by no means as easy as expected to make the connection between theory and practice. To do this, the students had to identify the most important ideas from several proposed specialist texts and relate these to their approach during the exploration.
- Perhaps the most difficult part of the PEP was the final reflection. For this, students had to take a step back, reflect on what they did during the project phase, and most importantly, see if they could identify a connection to their teaching practice. Especially in answering the fifth question, the one about reflection, the students' elaborations differed significantly from each other, both in scope and in depth.

In the last part of the seminar, students had the opportunity to present their PEPs to the group and discuss them with their peers. This was particularly fruitful as they were able to assess each other's teaching situation quite well and give constructive feedback. The written elaborations of the PEPs themselves were reviewed by me as the seminar leader and given detailed feedback.

In summary, it can be said that the seminar was initially oriented towards content-related (methodological-didactic) issues, but also very decidedly took into account the students' own experiences. The engagement with the academic discourse in the target language, German, was promoted by the verbal input in the seminar sessions as well as by the reading of the subject texts and the discussion about them (whereby a pragmatic multilingualism was generally used in the seminar). But engagement with basic academic skills was also practiced extensively, such as through the use and awareness of reading strategies, writing activities, critical-constructive questioning, and repeated summaries by students of their own observations and actions.

3.3 Analyzing the Course

The generally positive outcome of the course offering was evident from the direct feedback received from participants. At the same time, it was unclear whether the seminar had any impact on the way students perceive or implement language teaching themselves. For this reason, an investigation was to be carried out with some distance, in which the participants were interrogated.

The investigation process was exciting for several reasons. On the one hand, the time lag should be mentioned, because at the time of the survey the course had taken place between two and four years earlier. On the other hand, the situation had changed fundamentally for most of them, as they had now completed their studies. They were, therefore, now able to assess and justify their opinion from the perspective of a teacher with a broad classroom experience.

In order to obtain feedback on the course and to support it with data, it was decided to conduct interviews with former participants.

In preparation for the interviews, guiding questions were formulated that related to the main content of the course and were intended to provide a stimulus for the interviewees' contributions. There were five questions involved:

- What characterizes a "good German teacher"?
- How important is "Research-Based Learning" for teachers?
- What is "Action Research", and how important is this approach for teachers?
- Which tools of AR are known? And are these considered useful?
- Are there any suggestions for an appropriate design of German teacher training courses?

Since the basic opinion of the former participants was at stake, but this should be influenced as little as possible, the decision was made in favor of narrative interviews. For a good use of resources, but also to reinforce main statements and effects, the interviews were conducted in pairs: two interviewers (one person with L1 German and the other with L1 Portuguese) each interviewed two former participants.

In order to find interview subjects, all former students who had attended the course were contacted by email and asked if they would be willing to be interviewed. Out of 22 people, 12 agreed and signed the declaration of consent and data protection respectively. In the end, six pairs could be formed and interviewed in this way. The interviews were conducted in July 2021 and recorded using the Zoom video conferencing tool. The participants were left to decide whether they wanted to give their answers in German or Portuguese, with 10 people answering in Portuguese and 2 people answering in German. On average, the interviews lasted about 40 minutes, so that with six interviews a total of 242 minutes of audio material was collected.

All interviews then went through a multi-stage transcription process. They were first transcribed using mechanical transcription software ("Happy Scribe") and then further edited. In the process, all personality-related data were anonymized, and the transcripts were standardized in terms of minimal transcription (cf. Mayring, 2015).

In order to be able to compare the text passages and assign them to the respective interviews, the speakers were given a code. "TN" stands for "participant" ("Teilnehmer" in German), the number indicates the number of the interview and "A" or "B" represent the two interviewees who took part in the interview. In the further course of the text, for example the combination "TN2A" will appear after a specific quote, which means that it is a direct utterance of the first speaker from the second interview (and translated into English specifically for this paper).

For analyzing the data, the software "MAXQDA" was used. For this purpose, in a first step a coding system was established in order to highlight the information given to the respective questions (cf. Kuckartz, 2016). The analysis itself was then realized using inductive-deductive criteria, which was, on the one hand, a coding for the five main questions, and on the other hand, new information contained in the specific answers. The following section keeps up with the main results and findings brought by the answers of the participants.

4 Main Findings

The second part of the project can be described as accompanying and impact research, which refers to the seminar offer. The guiding questions here are whether active participation in the seminar has had an effect on beliefs, awareness, and actions as a teacher. In this regard, the results are derived from the main statements of the interviewed former student teachers (n = 12) and are presented below oriented to the guiding questions of the interviews.

4.1 What Determines a "Good German Teacher"?

What makes a "good teacher" seems at first to be a very subjective question. At the same time, the answer is anything but trivial. By stating what they themselves see as good and important skills and abilities in teachers, teachers simultaneously reveal their convictions about what they themselves perceive, strive for in a particular way, and, if applicable, also implement.

In the seminar we had dealt with the characteristics of "good foreign language teachers", discussed the difficulty of such concepts on the basis of certain texts (e.g., Meyer, 2004), and got to know alternative views (e.g., Schart & Legutke, 2012). Of course, opinion about teaching behavior among students is not only influenced by one course—nevertheless, the question has been asked in order to capture some of the subjective theories of the respondents.

In the responses, 50% of the participants stated that they consider good foreign language skills on the part of teachers to be particularly important, and 50% placed didactic skills in first place. In addition, other aspects were mentioned in the statements, such as a confident handling of teaching culture, patience, learner orientation, adaptability, and empathy. What is exciting here is the division into two equal halves between the reference to (subject) content, namely language, and to its mediation. This ties in with various discussions in the Brazilian context, such as the question of a sufficient level of language that can be achieved during studies and the institutional division between philology and educational sciences (cf. Friesen Blume, 2011; Voerkel, 2017, 285–291). In this context, the clear statement of one of the interviewees appears interesting, according to which there can hardly be any meaningful learning successes without suitable mediation: "Didactic knowledge should not be missing. I think it's no use if you only know the language, but you lack appropriate strategies to deal with the group of learners." (TN3B) This quote underlines the high relevance of having the appropriate strategies for dealing with language in the classroom as a teacher (cf. Krumm, 2012).

4.2 Importance of "Research-Based Learning" for Teachers

The preoccupation with this question stems from the discussion of what role research should play in the teaching profession: Opinions that prefer training based on strongly prescribed content contrast with those that are constructivist in nature and emphasize the free process of constructing when teaching. In the area of GFL, voices are growing stronger that emphasize extensive engagement with research in the area of teacher education, especially as it relates to lifelong learning. This is also where the proposals from approaches such as RBL and AR, which are anchored in concrete programs in the discipline, come in.

The belief that research is important for teachers is confirmed by 50% of the respondents, while 25% explicitly refer to the goal of AR, namely, to improve one's own teaching. An interesting point is that several participants mentioned the radical changes their teaching underwent due to the worldwide pandemic in the last years and that clearly showed the necessity to adapt to new circumstances. In this glance, research skills are seen as useful and connected with the fact that teaching includes the need for lifelong learning, as the following quote shows:

> This pandemic, this whole situation served to make some teachers aware of…, I mean teachers who were only using the same formula always, the same activities always, it made them see that they need, regardless of their age, that you need to continue researching and studying about the subject, that is, about education or teaching… (TN3B).

Another interesting point that was raised is about the nature of research. Do teachers have the need (and the resources) to realize high-stakes research? A quote made by one of the participants sums it up in an interesting way: "I think it's also about looking at what level of research the teacher needs to do" (TN5B). We have here the need to consider both the aims and the feasibility of research.

4.3 Knowledge and Relevance of Action Research

The next question was directly related to the given seminar, as it specifically asked for a description of AR as well as its relevance. The responses here were relatively broad and showed that a clear definition of AR could no longer be automatically recalled by respondents, and that they instead recalled specific aspects that they could relay. Eventually, 42% of respondents said that AR can help them try out new things and check whether they work in a given situation. An important aspect here is that it is permitted to commit errors and AR might be a way to introduce a positive way of dealing with mistakes (TN1A). Furthermore, 17% of participants felt that AR was a good way to bring theory and practice together, that it could improve their own teaching practice, and that it was a good opportunity for both in-depth observation and reflection. The following quote sums up the opinions expressed about AR well and adds another aspect, namely that AR can help to see students more comprehensively and thus support them better: "So it's always about improving the process, improving the teaching, being more responsive to the student as a person and supporting them better" (TN2A).

4.4 Utility and Impact of Action Research

This question related to how useful the respondents perceived the AR to be and what influence it had on their actions. This aspect of the research is exciting insofar as the participants were all practicing teachers and could thus link the previously learned theoretical concept directly to everyday teaching. It is clear that the answers may not have been entirely neutral: Respondents knew that the common denominator of the interview was attendance at the seminar, and that there was a particular focus on AR. Consequently, the general statement made by all respondents (being that AR is extremely useful) is not very meaningful when taken on its own. At the same time, they had no reason to package their opinions into desirable answers and were free to express themselves, and the points raised become exciting when it comes to concrete examples.

One-third of respondents said AR can help them better observe and assess themselves. Further answers highlighted the impulse for reflection as well as the possibility to automate a close look at teaching to a certain extent. At the same time, challenges were also mentioned that AR brings with it: It is a complex concept and can mainly be implemented if the learners are ready for it. Another voice emphasized the great opportunity AR represents for the student-teacher relationship, as it makes students feel more like they are taken seriously and accepted: "Because learners also want to be heard, that's a concern. […] This kind of project maybe connects us more with the students" (TN3A).

4.5 Potential for Innovation in Degree Programs

The last question was no longer even directly about specific techniques or tools, but about aspects that respondents would identify as opportunities for innovation or improvement in German studies programs. With the end of their studies and their entry into the working world a relatively short time ago, they were able to provide relevant information here.

In first place, and explicitly mentioned by 42% of the respondents, was the demand for more practical references and experiences during university studies. In second place, and still mentioned by a quarter of respondents, is the desire for greater variety in teaching forms and formats. Specific examples here related to online teaching (which is hardly surprising in the second year of the pandemic) and showed that there is still a great need for innovation here. Furthermore, several of the respondents each mentioned that they would suggest earlier exposure to didactic issues (which are usually treated in Brazilian teacher training during the second part of the undergraduate study cycle) and that the level of dealing with the target language should be even more of a focus during the study times. A special emphasis was set on the potentials opened through the third mission project, especially for teaching experience, and is reflected by the quote from one of the former students: "If it wasn't for LICOM and these extracurricular projects, I think then we would finish university without having taught classes once" (TN6C).

4.6 Summing up the Experience with AR

It may seem that the second part of the project, the interviews with former students, brought rather general and, thus, few concrete results. This impression is possibly created because the statements of the interviewees can only be partially reproduced due to the format of this article. In order to better understand how extensive and varied the participants' statements on AR ultimately turned out to be, the code system that forms the basis for the analysis of the interviews is shown below. The first column represents the three main categories (relevance of AR, definitions & concepts, benefits of AR) and the codes associated with them. The second column shows which respondents' statements contained the codes, and the third column (arranged in descending order) displays the total number of mentions. Since the statements are the results of narrative interviews, it is possible to deduce which aspects are particularly important to the interviewees with regard to the topic of AR.

Undoubtedly, the results could be analyzed in more detail and the codes could also be focused or merged in one direction or another depending on the interest of the findings. In any case, some main statements can be summarized with a view to the table (Table 5.1).

Regarding the relevance of AR, it can be said that all stakeholders agreed in some way that the concept was important and useful. In five of the twelve responses, this statement was made explicitly, and another two added that the importance lay primarily in the possibility of a good complement to theory and practice.

In the impulse to define or describe AR, the respondents first mentioned the fact that it could be used to try out new methods and tools in a protected setting, that research can be combined with one's own professional actions, that it is a specific and controlled procedure, and that AR thus represents an instrument for lifelong learning. It becomes clear that the participants, with some distance, can no longer give a precise, firmly established definition of the concept, but that they inherently master very well the main contents and concerns of AR.

A fundamental understanding becomes particularly clear when asking about possible outcomes and positive benefits of AR. Here, the respondents first cite the high potential to improve teaching and dynamics in class. In second place is the ability of AR to help them better "read" classroom events and the classroom situation, which is a particularly important aspect of high teaching skills according to Shulman (1987). A divided third place in the number of mentions is taken by one's own perception as a teacher and of the teaching forms, as well as the fact that with AR one can meaningfully embed theory and subject knowledge in one's own teaching practice. It is also important to emphasize the possibility of using AR to optimize the planning and organization of one's own lessons and to sustainably improve the classroom climate and the relationships between teachers and students (the latter point is essential in Hattie's famous meta study published in 2009).

Of course, teaching and learning are complex processes that are influenced by many factors. Concrete theories, approaches, and tools can only map the dynamics of teaching in small excerpts and, above all, are no guarantee for the success of teaching. At the same time, it is very clear via the responses that emerged during the interview that reflective approaches such as AR are perceived by students as an important support and can help them to rethink and improve their own teaching.

Table 5.1 Code system as a basis for the analysis of the interviews

Aspect	Mentioned by	Nr.
Relevance of AR		
AR is important	TN1A, TN1B, TN2A, TN3A, TN5A	5
AR is a link between theory and practice	TN2B, TN5A	2
Definitions & Concepts		
Try out new methods and tools	TN1A, TN1B, TN3B	5
Combine research with own practice	TN3A, TN3B, TN4A	3
Uses structured + cyclic procedures	TN2A, TN4A	2
Tool for lifelong learning	TN5B, TN6A	2
Trial and error	TN1A	1
Goal: improve own teaching competencies & skills	TN3A	1
Make people reflect	TN6A	1
Benefits of AR		
Improve teaching and dynamics in class	TN1A, TN2A, TN3A, TN3A, TN3B, TN4A, TN5A, TN5B, TN6C	13
Helps to "read" classroom situations	TN1A, TN1B, TN2A, TN3A, TN5A, TN5B, TN6B	8
Self-assessment as a teacher & teaching practice	TN1A, TN1B, TN3A, TN3B	7
Adapt theory to a specific context	TN1A, TN1B, TN3A, TN3B, TN4A, TN5A, TN5B	7
Know the students better	TN1A, TN3B, TN5B	5
Improve planning & classroom organization	TN1A, TN2B, TN3B, TN5A	4
Identify problems in class & find solutions	TN4A	3
Know to use new research tools	TN1B, TN2B, TN5B	3
Improve teacher personality	TN3A, TN3B, TN5A	3
Improve general reflection	TN4A, TN6C	3
Possibility to justify teacher behavior	TN2B, TN5A	2
Establish improvement as a routine	TN3A, TN6A	2
Be able to try out new things	TN2B, TN3A	2
Get more knowledge	TN3B	1
Change perspectives & points of view	TN5A	1
Receive (structured) feedback from learners	TN3B	1
Improve relationship between learners & teachers	TN3A	1

5 Conclusion

Both the course offerings in Brazil and the follow-up study were extremely stimulating and revealed students' beliefs about teaching and learning as well as their own beliefs as teachers. The initial results of the survey can also be located in this area. In the words of the participants, language knowledge & skills and didactic competences are considered to be of central importance for good teaching. The respondents are also aware of the importance of "research-based learning" (especially in times of the pandemic) and connect the approach to lifelong learning. They know about the high relevance of professional and personal development and connect it with the scaffolding offered by AR. Another interesting point is that in several statements, the respondents gave very positive feedback towards collaborative work and the inspiring discussions held in class—in the end, learning is a social process (cf. Mohr & Schart, 2016, 296). They are open to collaborative techniques and collaborative work and demand it even more for their own education, just as they emphasize the high relevance of practical experience accompanying their studies.

As far as Action Research (as a reflection tool) is concerned, it can be summarized here that the former students achieve little concrete knowledge about the concept, but recognize the high relevance of AR. In the answers we can state, that the respondents remembered more details from the contents and contexts from the seminar more accurately, the higher their language skills in German (the language of instruction) had been during the common semester. Still, all interviewees agreed with the idea that the impulses they had gained from AR during the seminar have had a great impact on their perception of their teaching (especially in the fields of observation and reflection).

From these opinions, some implications can be drawn for further engagement with AR in teaching and higher education contexts. For example, we can see that it would be quite desirable to run a complete cycle of AR to sustain results. At the same time, it became clear that even a few subject lessons or impulses can be enough to draw attention and awareness to teacher action – even if it is clear that awareness alone does not automatically mean a change in action. However, in order to achieve lasting results through AR, at least curricular integration is necessary, as well as close supervision, place for exchange and shared experience, and a sufficient time frame. While much research and data collection are still needed, the results of this study do indicate that AR may be considered as an appropriate tool for promoting reflection in foreign language teacher education.

References

Aguado, K. (2015). Forschendes Lernen und Lehren als Strategie zur Professionalisierung von Fremdsprachenlehrerinnen und -lehrern. In S. Hoffmann & A. Stork (Eds.), *Lernerorientierte Fremdsprachenforschung und -didaktik* (pp. 297–307). Narr.

Altrichter, H., & Posch, P. (2007). *Lehrerinnen und Lehrer erforschen ihren Unterricht. Unterrichtsentwicklung und Unterrichtsevaluation durch Aktionsforschung*. Klinkhardt.

Ammon, U. (2018). *Die Stellung der deutschen Sprache in der Welt*. De Gruyter.

Auswärtiges Amt. (2020). *Deutsch als Fremdsprache weltweit. Erhebung 2020*. Berlin: Auswärtiges Amt. https://www.goethe.de/de/spr/eng/dlz.html

Basten, M., Mertens, C., Schöning, A., & Wolf, E. (Eds.). (2020). *Forschendes Lernen in der Lehrer/innenbildung. Implikationen für Wissenschaft und Praxis*. Waxmann.

Benitt, N. (2015). *Becoming a (better) language teacher. Classroom action research and teacher learning*. Narr.

Boeckmann, K.-B. (2016). Aktionsforschung. In E. Burwitz-Melzer et al. (Eds.), *Handbuch Fremdsprachenunterricht* (pp. 592–597). A. Francke.

Chaves, G., & Soethe, P. (2020). Alemão no Brasil: Demanda evidente, oferta viável? In R. Bohunovsky et al. (Eds.), *Ensinar alemão no Brasil. Percursos e procedimentos* (pp. 31–51). Editora UFPR.

Feldmeier, A. (2014). Besondere Forschungsansätze: Aktionsforschung. In J. Settinieri et al. (Eds.), *Empirische Forschungsmethoden für Deutsch als Fremd- und Zweitsprache* (pp. 255–267). Paderborn.

Frey, K. (2012). *Die Projektmethode. Der Weg zum bildenden Tun*. Beltz.

Franco-Santoro, A. M. (2005). Pedagogia da pesquisa-ação. *Educação e pesquisa, 31*(3/2005), 483–502.

Friesen Blume, R. (2011). Prática como Componente Curricular – Desafio e oportunidade na formação universitária de professores de alemão no Brasil. In R. Bohunovsky et al. (Eds.), *Ensinar alemão no Brasil. Contextos e Conteúdos* (pp. 53–68). Editora UFPR.

Gondar, A., & Ferreira, M. (2020). Herausforderungen der Professionsbildung angehender DaF-Lehrerinnen und -Lehrer in Rio de Janeiro: Bestandsaufnahme auf der Grundlage subjektiver Theorien und Aussichten für die Forschung. *InfoDaF, 47*(5), 491–506. https://doi.org/10.1515/infodaf-2020-0095

Hattie, J. (2009). *Visible learning. A synthesis of over 800 meta-analyses relating to achievement*. Routledge.

Holzbaur, U. (2020). *Nachhaltige Entwicklung. Der Weg in eine lebenswerte Zukunft*. Wiesbaden: Springer. https://link.springer.com/book/10.1007/978-3-658-29991-0

Huber, L. (2009). Warum Forschendes Lernen nötig und möglich ist. In L. Huber et al. (Eds.), *Forschendes Lernen im Studium. Aktuelle Konzepte und Erfahrungen* (pp. 9–35). Universitätsverlag Webler.

Krumm, H.-J. (2012). Veränderungen im Bereich des Lehrens und Lernens von Fremdsprachen und deren Konsequenzen für die Ausbildung von Fremdsprachenlehrerinnen und -lehrern: Überlegungen aus europäischer Perspektive. In I. Feld-Knapp (Ed.), *Beruf und Berufung. Fremdsprachenlehrer in Ungarn* (pp. 53–73). Eötvös-József-Collegium.

Kuckartz, U. (2016). *Qualitative Inhaltsanalyse. Methoden, Praxis, Computerunterstützung*. Beltz Juventa.

Legutke, M. K. (2023). Deutsch Lehren Lernen – eine Einführung. *KONTEXTE: Internationales Journal Zur Professionalisierung in Deutsch Als Fremdsprache, 1*(2), 6–21. https://doi.org/10.24403/jp.1335303

Legutke, M., & Rotberg, S. (2018). Deutsch Lehren Lernen (DLL) – das weltweite Fort- und Weiterbildungsangebot des Goethe-Instituts. *Info-DaF, 45*(5), 605–634. https://www.degruyter.com/document/doi/10.1515/infodaf-2018-0082/html

Legutke, M., & Schart, M. (Eds.). (2016). *Fremdsprachendidaktische Professionsforschung: Brennpunkt Lehrerbildung*. Narr.

Lehmann, J. (2018). Überblick. In J. Lehmann & H. Mieg (Eds.), *Forschendes Lernen. Ein Praxisbuch* (pp. 12–17). Fachhochschule Potsdam.

Mayring, P. (2015). *Qualitative Inhaltsanalyse. Grundlagen und Techniken*. Beltz Juventa.

Meyer, H. (2004). *Was ist guter Unterricht?* Cornelsen.

Mieg, H., & Lehmann, J. (2017). *Forschendes Lernen. Wie die Lehre in Universität und Fachhochschule erneuert werden kann*. Campus Verlag.

Mohr, I., & Schart, M. (2016). Praxiserkundungsprojekte und ihre Wirksamkeit in der Lehrerfort- und Weiterbildung. In M. Legutke & M. Schart (Eds.), *Fremdsprachendidaktische Professionsforschung: Brennpunkt Lehrerbildung* (pp. 291–322). Tübingen.

Molina, R. (2007). *A pesquisa-ação/investigação-ação no Brasil. Mapeamento da produção (1966–2002) e os indicadores internos da pesquisa-ação colaborativa*. São Paulo: Universidade de São Paulo (Dissertation).

Organisation for Economic Co-operation and Development – OECD. (2003). *Education at a glance*. OECD.

Santos, Y., Kleinbing, H., Scribelk, L., & Voerkel, P. (2019). Platz zum Denken!? – Praxis und Reflexion als entscheidende Impulse in der brasilianischen Deutschlehrerausbildung. *Pandaemonium Germanicum, 22*(36/2019), 178–206. https://www.revistas.usp.br/pg/article/view/151436/148319

Saunders, C., Gess, C., & Lehmann, M. (2020). Forschendes Lernen im Lehramt. Entwicklung eines Instruments zur Erfassung von Überzeugungen zur forschend-reflexiven Lehrpraxis. In C. Wulf et al. (Eds.), *Forschendes Lernen. Theorie, Empirie, Praxis* (pp. 171–185). Springer VS.

Schart, M., & Legutke, M. (2012). *Lehrkompetenz und Unterrichtsgestaltung*. Klett-Langenscheidt.

Shulman, L. S. (1987). Knowledge and Teaching: Foundations of the New Reform. *Harvard Educational Review, 57*, 1–22.

United Nations Educational, Scientific and Cultural Organization – UNESCO. (2021). *Reimagining our futures together. A new social contract for education. Report from the international commission on the futures of education*. UNESCO.

Voerkel, P. (2017). *Deutsch als Chance: Ausbildung, Qualifikation und Verbleib von Absolventen brasilianischer Deutschstudiengänge*. ThULB. https://www.db-thueringen.de/receive/dbt_mods_00033644

Voerkel, P. (2021). Zu Entstehung und Entwicklung der Deutschstudiengänge in Brasilien. In P. Voerkel et al. (Eds.), *Germanistik in Lateinamerika. Entwicklungen und Tendenzen* (pp. 191–218). Universitätsverlag.

Voerkel, P., Ferreira, M., & Silva, R. (2022a). A formação de professores de línguas, o programa "Aprender a Ensinar Alemão" e o ensino remoto: Desafios e possibilidades.

In: Redel, E. et al. (Eds.), *Ensino e aprendizagem de línguas em contexto pandêmico: práticas, desafios e novos caminhos* (pp. 131–152). São Carlos: Pedro & João Editores.

Voerkel, P., Santos, M., & Veríssimo, M. (2022b). Brazil. In H. Mieg et al. (Eds.), *Cambridge handbook on undergraduate research* (pp. 472–479). Cambridge University Press.

Voerkel, P., & Scribelk, L. (2022). Aktionsforschung im Hochschulkontext? Überlegungen zu einer stärkeren Praxisorientierung von Deutschstudiengängen am Beispiel Brasiliens. In: Auteri, L. et al. (Eds.), *Wege der Germanistik in transkultureller Perspektive*. Akten des XIV. Kongresses der Internationalen Vereinigung für Germanistik – IVG (Bd. 3) (pp. 719–729). Bern: Peter Lang.

Paul Voerkel is a passionate language teacher. He studied German as a Foreign Language, History, Hispanic Studies and Educational Sciences at the University of Leipzig (Germany) and received his PhD on teacher education in Brazil from Jena University (Germany). Since 2007, he has been active at various universities in Germany, Ecuador and Brazil, among others as an invited DAAD lecturer. After several years as a Research Assistant in the Department of German as a Foreign Language at the University of Jena (Germany), he currently works as head of the Department of Studies and International Relations at Schmalkalden University of Applied Sciences (Germany). His research interests include teacher education, methodology-didactics, cultural studies, and language policy. Contact: paul.voerkel@gmail.com

6

Developing a Critical Reflection Stance Towards Language Teaching Practice: European Portfolio for Student Teachers of Languages and Reflective Tasks in Language Education

Larisa Kasumagić-Kafedžić and Selma Đuliman

1 Teacher Education at the Department of English (University of Sarajevo)

Since its foundation in 1949, the University of Sarajevo has embraced a myriad of different scientific and artistic fields, and we can say without exaggeration that different individuals educated at this university have greatly contributed to the social, scientific, and artistic development of not only our country, but beyond. Also, in all these years of the functioning and development of our university, we can observe a struggle of sorts to find a suitable and rightful place for pedagogical disciplines. As if set between the worlds of science, arts, and language learning, pedagogical disciplines are everywhere and nowhere. Even university lecturers often fail to recognize the importance of the tools necessary to transmit the highly abstract notions to the future practitioners, irrespective of the field they are coming from. Also, many teacher trainers, to a significant extent, also fail to recognize the skills necessary to

---

L. Kasumagić-Kafedžić (✉) · S. Đuliman
English Department, University of Sarajevo, Faculty of Philosophy,
Sarajevo, Bosnia and Herzegovina
e-mail: larisa.kasumagic@ff.unsa.ba; selma.djuliman@ff.unsa.ba

© The Author(s), under exclusive license to Springer-Verlag GmbH, DE, part of Springer Nature 2024
P. Voerkel et al. (eds.), *Tools, Techniques and Strategies for Reflective Second & Foreign Language Teacher Education*,
https://doi.org/10.1007/978-3-662-68741-3_6

introduce the most recent findings in pedagogy that would enable future teachers to enter the classroom and engage learners in a productive acquisition of knowledge.

Although the University of Sarajevo has faced a number of difficulties, significant progress can also be observed in that respect. In 2005, the University of Sarajevo introduced the Bologna reform (Komšić et al., 2010), which entailed a complete change of the curricular paradigm. From a distance of almost 18 years, one conclusion we can draw is that the efforts have been significant, but also that there is a lot more work to be done. By that, we primarily mean the possibilities of improvement of the curricular model at the English Language and Literature Department at the Faculty of Philosophy, University of Sarajevo, where we teach.

The department is one of the oldest at the University of Sarajevo and consists of two chairs—the chair for language and the chair for literature. In the years preceding the Bologna reform, the approach to both teaching and learning can be characterized by a strict division between the fields of linguistics and literature, history, and theory. Many subjects were taught in a highly traditional manner, where the focus was on memorizing, for example, grammatical rules or sections of novels, without an open possibility of practical implementation of the rules on contemporary texts, and without a possibility of reflection on certain novels, poems, etc. Such was a rather harsh, traditional university classroom, in which teaching methodology did exist as a subject, but was never given the necessary importance, which, we are convinced, caused irreparable damage to many students who later became teachers of English as a foreign language.

Still, the Bologna reform was recognized at the department as a unique opportunity to transform the curriculum to an extent that it is today fully comparable with many departments of foreign language and literature worldwide. That said, the place and importance of teacher training has been not only recognized, but also placed in a curricular context that would allow both university practitioners and future teachers of English as a foreign language the development necessary in the contemporary classroom. The previous rigid model has been transformed so that at the undergraduate level the English language teaching methodology and Introduction to Practice are introduced in the 5th and 6th semesters (the University of Sarajevo operates on the 3+2 model), while a comprehensive program of English Language Teaching Methodology is introduced at the postgraduate level.

The postgraduate level is characterized by elective subjects, encompassing both the field of literature and linguistics, with the aim of using the wider, previously rather compartmentalized knowledge, in classrooms. And this is the very place that we see as an achievement, but also the place that needs true improvement. Namely, the department is very open to, but we daresay, is still learning about, the potentials of true inter- and multi-disciplinary cooperation. Although the subjects introduced at the postgraduate English language methodology program can be used as means to integrate knowledge and practices from different fields that the future teachers will be able to use in the EFL classroom, we are of the opinion that we still need to fully grasp and apply those notions. It is only recently that we began to see the merger of such fields in articles published in some journals and conference proceedings, as well as in some initiated projects, etc. Also, we are yet to see the introduction of a true interdisciplinary program at the doctoral level.

Still, efforts are being made and small steps taken in that respect. To that end, we will present in this paper an interdisciplinary practice we have initiated at the postgraduate level of studies where we present a "pure linguistic" theory to future EFL teachers in a manner that is useful to them in a professional context. This is one of the attempts at liberating theoretical linguistics from the chains being perceived as unavailable and intimidating to many. We will also present the examples of innovation introduced to language pedagogy courses at the teacher education program, where greater emphasis has been placed on classroom interaction, learner autonomy, reflection, and practice. This is a step which marked the need for making further efforts in recognizing the inevitability and necessity of interdisciplinary and multidisciplinary approaches in university curricula, especially regarding the English Language and Literature Department.

2 Theoretical Foundations: Reflective Pedagogies in Language Education

A lot of research (e.g., Pine, 2009; Newby, 2012; Liu, 2020; Lam, 2018; Korthagen & Nuijten, 2022; Huang, 2021; Ryan, 2015) draws on different case studies that point to numerous benefits of reflective approaches in language education and teacher development. One reason for that is that teachers do not find adequate responses in following conventional approaches as a way to address the multiple problems and complex challenges of today's world and their specific language classroom contexts. Reflective teaching has been offered as a response to the proposal for a substitute for the concept of language teaching method in the current pedagogical trends of "post-method era" that is a practice-driven construct which calls into question the traditional conceptualization of teachers as a channel of received knowledge (Kumaravadivelu, 1994, 2003, cited in Fat'hi & Behzadpour, 2011). In those traditional approaches to teacher education which "view teachers as passive recipients of transmitted knowledge rather than active participants in the construction of meaning and which do not take into account the thinking or decision-making of teachers" (Crandall, 2000, p. 35), the post-method era proposes a more active role for teachers where they "have to act as mediators between theory and practice, between the domain of disciplinary research and pedagogy" (Widdowson, 1990, p. 22). As Kumaravadivelu (2001) pointed out, no pedagogy is politically neutral, but is always a politically charged process embedded in the realization, comprehension, and awareness of specificities of local conditions. It is within such pedagogy that teachers are entrusted with "observing their teaching acts, evaluating their outcomes, identifying problems, finding solutions, and trying them out to see once again what works and what does not" (p. 539). "Reflection has become an integral part of teacher education" (Jay & Johnson, 2002, p. 73), and as Tabachnik and Zeichner (2002) put it, "there is not a single teacher educator who would say that he or she is not concerned about preparing teachers who are reflective" (p. 13) (in Fat'hi & Behzadpour, 2011).

Language education in the European context of different traditions and practices has greatly relied on the work of the Council of Europe, which has played a major role in language teaching methodology and research throughout Europe (Trim, 2007, cited in Newby, 2012). At the beginning of the twenty-first century, the Common European Framework of Reference (CEFR) emphasized its "action-oriented" view of language use that enables authentic human communication. Additionally, an important "sister instrument," the European Language Portfolio, reinforced the reflective mode of language learning advocated in the CEFR (Newby, 2012), which opened the doors for learners to use tools, strategies, and skills of self-assessment and reflection in order to provide evidence of their linguistic, pedagogic, and cultural competencies and experiences. As Cunningham (2001) explains, "constructivism views learning as an active process where learners reflect upon their current and past knowledge and experiences to generate new ideas and concepts" (p. 2). As a consequence, "a shift to a constructivist perspective of teaching and teacher learning makes teachers a primary source of knowledge about teaching" (Crandall, 2000, p. 35), and this, in turn, has created the possibilities for democratic approaches of teaching, which advocate for more reflective, more egalitarian, more inclusive, and more critical approaches in language education.

2.1 Reflective Teaching Tools: Case Studies from University Classrooms

In many teacher education institutions, the integration of reflective tools into the university classrooms and university programs requires the development, design, and implementation of a pedagogical framework that is founded on theoretical concepts that bind together theory, practice, and reflection on the learning. The case studies presented below illustrate a high potential for initiating and facilitating the learning process in language pedagogy courses as well as in linguistics courses that are integral to the teacher education program where reflection, reframing, role-playing, and negotiating meaning support the development of linguistic and pedagogical competences of prospective teachers of English.

2.2 Case Study in English Language Teacher Education: EPOSTL in Teaching Practice

EPOSTL—the *European Portfolio for Student Teachers of Languages* (Newby et al., 2007)—is a portfolio of professional competencies for teacher education, which encourages students to: (1) reflect on didactic knowledge and skills integral for language learning and teaching, (2) monitor and record their professional development progress, and (3) record their experiences and reflections on teaching languages. The use of the EPOSTL tool in language teaching pedagogy courses is generally seen as a very positive measure in different European countries and different teaching and learning contexts (Newby, 2012). The students use this document to reflect on their own linguistic and didactic competencies following around 200 descriptors (language and culture-specific, pedagogical, and organizational) critical for teaching foreign languages in a locally specific but also a globally changing world. The main focus of the EPOSTL is self-assessment, reflection, awareness-raising, focused observation, and meaningful discussion, which are all methodically guided in the process of learning through carefully selected "I can" statements that support student teachers of languages as well as teacher educators to recognize the continuous life-long learning nature of both "learning a language" and "learning to teach a language" (Fig. 6.1).

The tool also supports the prospective teachers of foreign language in planning and assessing their own professional development by keeping a record of their teaching experiences provided for them as in-class simulations (particular activities, lesson segments, or whole lessons), in-class observations (student-teacher/peer observation and teacher observation), or in-class and in-school practice teaching (micro-teaching experience as tandem/team teaching and independent teaching).

The use of reflective tools in language education provides multiple benefits at different levels of learning, and some of the major contributions of the EPOSTL in language education range from individual to institutional levels (Newby, 2012): between students and teacher educators (with greater emphasis on transparency of aims and didactic competencies of learners and teacher educators), at institutional

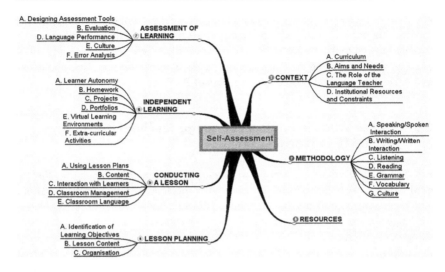

Fig. 6.1 Self-assessment as the main focus of the EPOSTL (areas of language, culture, and didactics in the reflection process: assessment of learning, autonomy, planning and implementing language class, context, methodology). From: European Portfolio for Student Teachers of Languages (Newby et al., 2007)

levels (with the harmonization of bottom-up and top-down curriculum planning), within institutions (having a more systematic approach in describing the competencies needed for language education and language teaching), and between universities and schools (with the capacity to bridge the gap and promote dialogue between university teacher educators and school teachers).

2.2.1 Self-Reflection Tasks: Reflection Papers and Poster Presentations in Teaching Practice

An important step in the professional growth of teachers is the teaching practice which students have as part of the following language pedagogy courses at the Teacher Education program of the English Department: Teaching Practice 1, Teaching Practice 2, and Interculturalism in English Language Didactics. The introduction of the EPOSTL to student teachers in our Department was made in 2010, but the development of a more systematic approach to integrating EPOSTL into the courses of the teacher education program has been a result of the conference for teachers "Using the European Portfolio for Student Teachers of Languages (EPOSTL)," implemented under the European Center for Modern Languages

(ECML) training and consultancy for member states, which was organized in 2017 at the English Department of the Faculty of Philosophy in Sarajevo, who acted as organizers and coordinators of the event. During the conference, the participants had an opportunity to learn about the EPOSTL document from the ECML experts and authors of the tool, as well as to critically reflect on the significance of the reflective pedagogies in language education and the application of the reflection tools in their own teaching and learning contexts, while referring their conclusion to the potential of the EPOSTL in supporting language teachers and teacher education in Bosnia and Herzegovina. The participants were engaged in discussions around the following questions: *What are the challenges of using EPOSTL in your professional development? (for in-service teachers); To what extent do you find the use of the EPOSTL useful in the development of your teacher's competencies? What were the rewards and challenges in using it? (for preservice teachers who used it)? How can EPOSTL contribute to the development of your teacher's competencies? Which segment of the EPOSTL do you find the most critical for student-teachers of languages? (for pre-service who did not use it previously).*

The main issue resulting from the conference was related to identifying specific areas of teaching practice at the Teacher Education Program that would help prospective teachers of English to become more self-reflective and more autonomous in the development of their teacher competencies. A small-scale action research project *Using EPOSTL as a self-reflection tool for improving pre-service and in-service teachers' competencies* was undertaken in the period 2016–2018, which focused on determining specific areas in the EPOSTL document that were used by student language teachers throughout their teacher preparation in several methodology courses. The teacher educator aimed for determining the most rewarding as well as the least rewarding practices in their teaching with the support of the EPOSTL tool as a self-reflection practice. More specifically, one of the main goals in the investigation was related to the selection of specific segments in the teaching practice of pre-service and in-service teachers, within the areas of *Methodology*, *Lesson planning*, and *Conducting a Lesson*, and by using the descriptors from the EPOSTL tool in the spirit of a self-reflective approach in order to identify the most critical segments for improvement.

As a result of those preparatory activities, the EPOSTL document has become more integral to the philosophy and teaching principles that underpin the development of practice teaching. During the period of 2018–2022, the EPOSTL has become a mandatory element of the courses in language pedagogy and practice teaching. In the period during the pandemic (2020–2021), the reflective pedagogy comprised a significant part of the teaching practice, although with the shift to virtual classrooms and online learning. In this period, around 30 students from the

Teacher Education program were involved in the reflection tasks as part of their course requirements.

In the *Teaching Practice 2* course, to facilitate the students' reflection on the "can-do" statements from the Portfolio, the students were asked to integrate them into the planning of their peer-teaching assignment. Each student was asked, with the help of the descriptors, to identify the skills they would like to focus on in their peer teaching. The following is the list with the tasks the students were invited to fulfill (adapted from Orlova, 2011):

1. *Select the area in the suggested topics of the EPOSTL (Methodology, Lesson Planning, and Conducting a Lesson) that you would like to focus on.*
2. *Look through the statements. Identify the skills you would like to practice and focus on.*
3. *If you think that the list is not inclusive of all the skills, expand on them. Note them down in your notes and reflections.*
4. *Articulate the goals and objectives (which is an integral part of the lesson plan). Prepare the materials.*
5. *Teach the lesson/or a sequence of a lesson (you will be video recorded).*
6. *The classmates will be invited to identify your primary focus in terms of the "can-do descriptors." Compare them with your evaluation and notes. Watch the video and analyze your teaching according to the descriptors (individually or with a partner).*
7. *The video is viewed with the instructor in the final reflection stage and critical reflection is developed in the discussion and analysis.*

In the Intercultural Workshop teaching assignment in the course *Interculturalism in English Language Didactics,* the students were asked to analyze the EPOSTL with the focus on the section on *Culture* within the "Methodology and Assessment of Learning" element of the document. They were required to identify the descriptors that they find the most challenging and those that they felt were the most important in their planning and teaching by focusing on 3–5 elements, which they include in their reflection log. After the completion of the planning and implementing the intercultural workshop, the students were invited to reflect on their performance in relation to the selected aspects, and they write the reflection paper by integrating responses to the following questions:

- *Was it easy or difficult to select a segment within the Culture section to focus on? Why/Why not? Were there some elements missing that you thought were critical in the planning stage and the actual teaching, but they were not*

integrated in the descriptors? Can you reflect on Competencies for Democratic Culture in connection to the descriptors in the Portfolio? Were the descriptors specific to our local culture/context? Were they relevant in connection to ICC as described in the CDC document (Competencies for Democratic Culture, Council of Europe, 2018)?
- *Was it easy to keep the selected aspects of teaching in mind while preparing/ conducting the teaching on intercultural communicative competences? Why/ Why not?*
- *After the workshop, was it easy to reflect on your performance in terms of the selected aspect(s) of teaching? Why/Why not?*
- *Comment on the experience of using self-reflection during your teaching practice. Did it require much extra effort? Did it affect the way you were planning the workshop? If yes, then how? If not, then why not? What have you learned from this experience? Would you like to use this method of self-reflection further, when already working as a teacher? Why/Why not?*

As the final assignment in the aforementioned teaching practice courses, students were required to write about specific challenges they faced in the context of teaching and learning remotely. Their final paper was aimed to be formulated within the larger theme of *Teaching English language and culture in the times of pandemic*, and they were supposed to use the EPOSTL document as the guidelines for the selection of the descriptors to lead them through the reflective process. They were required to frame their discussion in the course focused on practical experience of teaching by choosing some relevant theories and principles in educational science that informed their decisions in the planning stage and during the conducting of a lesson. Particular focus was put on the challenges, advantages and disadvantages of teaching online, and by referring to some good teaching practices in the selection of effective ICT tools and open educational resources that proved meaningful and effective in their practical teaching experience. The final assignments (reflection papers) were collected and analyzed in reference to the guiding questions (provided by the teacher educator), and the students' responses, insights, and reflections were grouped in major topics, which emerged as the most frequent and relevant.

(1) The difficulty of keeping the selected aspects of teaching in focus while preparing and conducting the lesson was commonly reflected upon. We can see a few examples of that focus in the following excerpts:

When I think of this self-reflection, I can say that it was a bit difficult to select segments to focus on, because all of the segments were really interesting and helped me to evaluate and reflect on my workshop. Since I am not an experienced teacher or moderator, it was a bit difficult to keep the selected aspects of teaching in my mind while preparing and conducting the workshop, but I did my best to fulfill everything that I planned and to follow these instructions as well.

(2) The importance of meticulous lesson planning and the complexities involved in the process of lesson drafting and implementation of different stages of the plans were also frequently mentioned in the students' reflection papers. Some of the students' voices supporting the recognition of this dimension in language education are presented in the following excerpt:

This self-reflection did not require a great deal of extra effort, but it surely affected the way I was preparing my workshop, because I would have probably forgotten many of these segments if I hadn't read about them before I started preparing the workshop. I easily forget about finishing off a lesson in a focused way or ensuring smooth transitions or timing the activities to reflect learners' attention spans etc., and the EPOSTL really helped me to stay focused and on the right track. This experience helped me to realize that lesson planning or any other planning is not an easy task, and it includes much more than just choosing and timing the activities. It raised my awareness about the importance of many different aspects of planning. I learned that my activities and materials should enhance the learners' intercultural awareness, that they should help learners to understand different value systems, that they should be coherent, balanced, varied, that I should be flexible, able to identify time needed for specific activities and topics, ensure smooth transitions, adjust my time schedule, take care of the learners and their interests and many other things as well.

(3) Recognizing the continuous process of learning in the teaching profession and the value of awareness raising, self-reflection, critical approach to reflection and lifelong learning were common topics in the students' deliberation:

When I start working as a teacher, I would really like to use this method of self-reflection and I am pretty sure I will use it. Teaching means lifelong learning and one of the best ways to learn is to detect one's own mistakes and flaws and try to correct them. Teaching means always striving to do better and be better.

This method of self-reflection might be even more useful in my future teaching career since there are many aspects which I have not had the chance to experience yet. In addition to all of the other things I learned and gained from this experience, I learned that being feedback-oriented and reflecting only made me a better teacher. This taught me that online classes do not need to replicate physical classroom classes and that there is a time and place for both in our education system. What makes a good online teacher? Is it how well they can utilize technology? Is it their ability to be engaging and encouraging in connection to social interaction in an online environment? I felt as if everything I had learned so far was ineffective and impractical for online teaching. However, reflecting on my own experience after the class, I came to the conclusion that all of the principles and qualities of an effective teacher still endure despite the circumstances under which they teach.

(4) The dilemmas and concerns about when and how to use mother language and how to adequately adjust teacher language to the level of student's competence was brought into the awareness through this reflection process and supported some students in becoming more confident about the decision they make in the classroom:

When it comes to the fourth section in the EPOSTL- Conducting a Lesson, I had the most difficulties with the segment Classroom Language. It was sometimes tricky to decide when it was appropriate to use the mother language and when not to or how to deal with some errors that students made. The facilitating factor was the fact that the students are actually advanced learners of English, and they did not have problems with using the target language in the activities or relating the target language to other languages.

Methodology is the second section in EPOSTL and the segments I had the most problems with were Vocabulary and Culture. Since I wanted the students to get familiar with certain language forms like food idioms, I had prepared a couple of activities related to these issues in particular. I had some doubts regarding this because I was afraid that these activities would be too boring or not challenging enough for the students. However, it turned out that they really enjoyed these activities and furthermore, they contributed with their own food idioms traced back from their L1.

(5) The values of self-reflection and the acknowledgement of teacher and student agency in the process of learning languages and cultures is a very important pillar in teacher preparation. Using reflection tools like EPOSTL enables students to appreciate and value the importance of community, growth, and process in teacher development, even in times of isolation and alienation that have been imposed during the pandemic. Such insights have been articulated through the following students' voices:

Speaking of the descriptors that I focused on, I can say that they were easy to select, because I am aware of what is personally important to me and also considering the feedback that I had previously received. Similarly, it was easy to reflect on my performance after the online lesson for the same reasons. Finally, I must say that I always find self-reflecting helpful. Although it does require a lot of additional effort, it ultimately affects the way I plan and conduct a lesson. Each time I conducted a lesson I learned something new after writing these reflections, and I integrated that knowledge into every succeeding experience. The same thing happened now with this online class, with additional reflections that I did on the lessons of my colleagues. To go back to the introductory part of this paper, I feel immensely proud of all of us because we managed to complete this process together and to learn from each other along the way. This is what an ideal future as a teacher looks like as well. Using tools for self-reflection such as the EPOSTL is imperative, as they help organize and evaluate the important components of our teaching, so we can reach a better understanding of ourselves as teachers and constantly improve. However, an opportunity to learn from each other is invaluable as well. Although the global pandemic forced us to self-isolate, we are fortunate enough to be able to remain a community, even while we are 2000 kilometers apart.

(6) Balancing the care for our students' wellbeing with the care for oneself and expanding the reflection on the teacher's emotional and physical wellbeing, especially during the pandemic, was a dominant topic for a lot of students. The acknowledgment of the need to be prepared to teach in the crisis situation of the scope like health crisis, or any other, even more extreme contexts, like poverty, wars, or social injustices, where student teachers need to be adequately prepared to know how to continue teaching despite the crisis, and how to efficiently teach controversial or sensitive topics in language classrooms were often voiced as very important perspectives.

Overall, my reflections on teaching English language and culture in the times of pandemic are positive. This experience had a positive impact on my self-confidence and made me re-discover my own potential as a teacher. The approaches that I support for teaching English language did not change, but only got adjusted to these new circumstances. Our students' well-being needs to be prioritized in every situation, but especially this one. This was not difficult to keep in mind while preparing and conducting the teaching. In fact, my problem was that I focused so much on prioritizing my students' well-being that I neglected my own. This is exactly what I find extremely important to be considered in the given global pandemic context but is unfortunately missing. Teacher burnout is always a risk, but it can be dangerous in this overwhelming situation. I find it necessary for teachers to have a tool to reflect on their own emotional and physical well-being.

Reflecting on my online teaching experience has been very eye-opening to me. To an extent, it was difficult to choose which descriptors to focus on because there is so much to a lesson that goes even beyond them. Some elements that I think are critical and should be integrated more in the descriptors are more aspects of intercultural learning that are related to the current context and designing materials. The descriptors were broad and not specific to our context. Something that is extremely important to be considered in the given context is that teaching and learning is going on amidst a crisis, which entirely changes the approach to teaching. The main challenge teachers are faced with is not teaching online but how to continue teaching during a crisis. This made me think about teachers who are dealing with these issues (and other daily issues such as war, poverty, injustice) and difficult situations and how we should be prepared to deal with this. Keeping the selected aspects in mind during planning and conducting the lesson was difficult because there is no way that everything can be ultimately taken into consideration. Teachers will inevitably have to sacrifice some aspects for others. Due to this, it was difficult for me to reflect on my lesson because not all of the aspects were static during the whole class, it tended to vary. Self-reflection is a strenuous but necessary experience. All the more, it even affected the way that I chose to plan my class because it provided some structure and guidance for what I wanted my class to focus on.

In addition to the task "reflection papers," the students were also invited to develop poster presentations that were used for final group reflections and discussion, and which were shared in the physical classrooms before the pandemic and through the Padlet platform in the virtual classrooms during the pandemic (Fig. 6.2: An example of the poster presentation and the students' final reflection).

In the preparation of their posters, the students were guided through the elements of the assignment using the following prompts in order to provide structure for the task:

- **Lesson observation (peer observation, teacher observation)**

- Technical information: school, grade, age group, number of students, interaction in the classroom, didactic tools, materials, teaching unit, teaching module, online and open-source materials, and tools. Pedagogically strong and weak points of the lesson reflective of the class observations you have completed as part of the school visits and observations.
- **Self-assessment of the lesson teaching**
- Observed strong and weak points (per activity or overall impression): online classroom management, student motivation during online teaching, classroom interaction patterns, rapport on the online platform, use of aids, materials, online tools, realization of learning outcomes, achievement of aims and objectives, your role as a teacher. What are your general impressions and conclusions? What are the takeaways from this teaching and learning experience?
- **EPOSTL reflection—to be further developed in your final paper as well**
- Explore the areas of *Methodology*, *Conducting a Lesson* and *Lesson Planning* with the focus on online teaching and learning in the crisis situation, and identify at least 5 descriptors as presented in those sections by choosing the ones you believe require the greatest attention and discussion in the formation of your teaching competences and professional development in the given context.

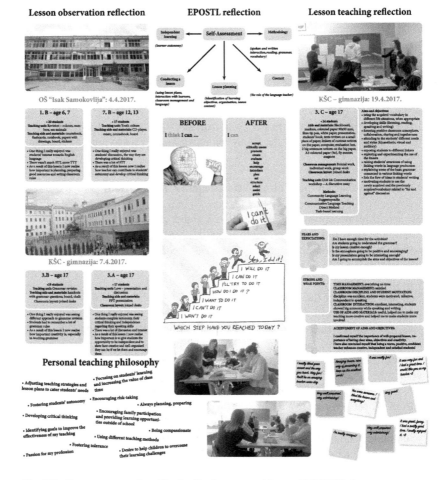

Fig. 6.2 Poster presentation: Final reflection on teaching and EPOSTL document

EPOSTL will encourage you to reflect on your didactic knowledge and skills necessary to teach EFL, help you assess your own didactic competences, and enable you to monitor your progress and to record your experiences of teaching during the course of your teacher education.
- **Personal teaching philosophy**

- This segment in the reflection should include your pedagogical conception of teaching and learning, a short description of how you teach and a justification for why you teach in a particular way. You can base your preferences on some theoretical principles that have been explored as part of the course or use some specific practice teaching examples to support your view.

As illustrated in the students' reflections, the use of the EPOSTL tool in language teaching pedagogy courses at the Department of English of the University in Sarajevo is seen as a very positive measure in teaching beginner teachers of English at the Teacher Education Program. While many descriptors were recognized for their universal potential to support teachers to become more reflective in their approach to teaching and learning languages, some aspects of the EPOSTL were also analyzed in the context-specific challenges that tailor the needs of a particular classroom, particular school, and particular country.

3 Case Study in English Language Learning: Linking Language Teaching Methodology and Theoretical Linguistics

In this section, we will introduce a case study from another class taught at the Department of English—Semantics and Pragmatics. The class is elective for the language teaching methodology program students and the original idea was to introduce the basic notions in semantics and pragmatics to future teachers, i.e., to students who choose English language teaching as a future profession. They are the same students who attend the Teaching Practice 1, Teaching Practice 2, and Interculturalism in English Language Didactics classes, where EPOSTL is introduced.

However, the experience showed that the students found little to no satisfaction or interest in being exposed to the linguistic content without any connection to the line of study they had chosen. This need has been expressed already by a number of authors (Schulze, 2015; Hatipoğlu, 2017, etc.).

In that respect, we found a solution in connecting the theoretical section of the class, prescribed by the curriculum with the in-class role-playing activities. The idea is rather familiar in the teacher training experience. For example, Nelson et al. (2016) stress that "academic role-play in a teacher education course with a service-learning component can improve course interaction between instructors and students and also between students and students, therefore strengthening the active-learning dynamic in a university classroom." Also, a very important argument in favor of our practice is that "role-playing is also used to teach critical thinking and prepare students to cope with stressful, unfamiliar, complex, or controversial situations by exposing them to real problems" (Crow & Nelson, n.d.).

We were led by the idea that the role-playing activities should be organized so as to depict imaginary situations with the themes concerning the average, expected issues teachers have with students sometimes. Those may entail the typical issues which may arise among students in class, when the teacher's intervention is necessary—for example, arguing over serious matters of identity (race, gender, etc.), or some typical situations arising from misunderstandings or arguments over matters such as different tastes in music, sports, film, etc. Of course, we are of the opinion that such themes are important for very different contexts worldwide, but we also bring them closer to the context of Bosnia-Herzegovina, a country which is still burdened by the unresolved narratives of the recent past—specifically, the war. In that respect, we would like to highlight some studies published on the topic: (1) Bosnian Post-War Transgenerational Trauma and Its Impact on Post-War Born Children, a paper by Amina Hadžiomerović (2018), (2) *Uspomene 677: the Transgenerational Trauma of Victims and Perpetrators (Part IV)*, a film by Bruce Clezy (2011), and (3) Application of an Ecological Framework to Clinical Practice with Adolescents: Transgenerational Transmission of War-related Trauma in Bosnia and Herzegovina, a paper by Mirsad Serdarević and Senija Tahirović (2020), etc.

Although today's students were born in the postwar period, they live through transgenerational trauma, and the recurring themes in our society in general are those that concern the issues of ethnic and religious affiliation and the past war. Hence, those are the specific societal circumstances where many social realities and relics of the past are part of the daily lives of the citizens of Bosnia-Herzegovina (BiH), regardless of age, ethnicity, class, etc.

This decision has proven quite logical, especially given the fact that those activities are part of the EPOSTL self-assessment section, primarily 1. *context* (c. the role of the language teacher), 5. *conducting a lesson* (d. classroom management; e. classroom language), and 7. *methodology* (a. speaking/spoken interaction, e. grammar, g. culture). Not only are students given an opportunity to integrate the skills they acquire during the Teaching Practice 1 and 2 courses, but they are also able to discuss possible issues related to the classroom management in a relaxed environment (the role-playing situation).

Although the curriculum for Semantics and Pragmatics contains several theories, the role-playing task currently concerns the politeness theory, which is extensively presented to the students of the teacher training program for two main reasons: (1) It is connected to the way in which teachers react to class misunderstandings and arguments, and (2) Interculturalism is important in order to present different possibilities of a reaction to situations across cultures (for example, Japan, Bosnia, the United States). Although interculturalism is taught, as we said earlier in the paper, as a separate subject in the teacher training program, and the links are established between the two subjects, we will focus here on the role-playing activity within the politeness theory framework for the purpose of achieving the real-life classroom atmosphere in an academic environment (that would more closely link the activity with the subjects Teaching Practice 1 and 2). We would like to emphasize here the study by Elaine Riordan entitled TESOL Student Teacher Discourse: *A Corpus-Based Analysis of Online and Face-to-Face Interactions* (2018) who dedicated a significant section of the book to politeness theory in the framework of relationship-building within the framework of S-T communication.

The introductory classes contain an overview of politeness theory as presented by Stephen Levinson and Penelope Brown, with a special emphasis on the notion of *face* (positive and negative) (Brown, 2000). The notion was first introduced in the 1960s by Erving Goffman (2013) and then further developed by Penelope Brown and Stephen Levinson (1987).

A replacement of the previous two-week instruction on *politeness theory*, whereby a professor would introduce the main characteristics and development and textual analyses in lectures and seminars, was now made with an interactive role-play where the principles of politeness theory are practiced *in situ* through different imaginary situations the future teachers could encounter in the EFL classroom.

Some of the imaginary in-class situations concerned the following topics:

a) A student is mocking another student for not providing a correct answer to the question.
b) A student is mocking another student for not being born in the place where he/she attends school.
c) A student is mocking another student for wearing second-hand clothes.

d) A student is mocking another student for not following the same religion as most of the class. Other students respond by laughing.
e) A student is telling a racially offensive joke (although the student is not aware of the true meaning of the joke).
f) A student is intentionally telling a joke in order to offend a teacher who wears traditional clothes.
g) A group of students fails to obey the teacher in performing a task.
h) A group of students engage in a fight in the middle of the class.
i) Students refuse to help their colleague who tripped and fell at the very beginning of the class, when they were all walking to their seats.
j) Last time, all students skipped class. This is the first time they meet their English language teacher after the incident.

Some of these imaginary issues may occur worldwide, but some have been observed rather frequently as social issues in BiH, meaning that there have been such incidents reported in class.

Students were tasked with the following three politeness-related tasks:

1. Choose the best in-situ reaction to the situation occurring.
2. What is the politeness strategy you would apply in the given situation? Why?
3. How would you avoid using an exaggerated *face-saving act*?

What makes this exercise challenging sometimes is that students are never pre-tasked, and that is in accordance with the reality of the classroom—such situations appear unexpectedly. Still, this is a joint exercise in *politeness theory* where the general idea is to encourage all students to reflect upon the proposed strategies and also predict difficulties that may arise if a selected politeness strategy is chosen as a response: when to use positive and when to use negative politeness strategies in in-class conflict resolution; how to discuss the face saving act strategies with the students after the escalation settles (how to talk to the students about the incident); encouraging apologies as mitigating devices in class between students in an attempt to settle misunderstandings.

Students reflect on the role-playing activity at the very end of the class. They have emphasized in most cases that the approach benefits them because they are able to understand the sometimes-confusing notions of the Brown & Levinson politeness model, and they are able to further practice the situations that may occur once they start teaching.

To the lecturer, such an approach to teaching *politeness theory* to future EFL teachers facilitates the efforts that had previously been made in explaining rather abstract linguistic notions that used to be presented and tested in a written form, containing linguistic tasks. Such an approach was rather irrelevant for their future profession and was too abstract since they did not choose linguistics as their major. More specifically, this enables students to (1) understand the main notions of Brown and Levinson's politeness theory; (2) recognize and use the linguistic devices stemming from the theory in role-playing problem-solving tasks, e.g. mitigating devices, negative and positive face, face threatening, and face saving acts, etc.; (3) reflect on the entire learning process as well as talk about ways in which they would perhaps be able to apply the knowledge of politeness theory in their own teaching practice in cases when they faced some unpredictable circumstances involving behavior of their own students.

However, there is space (and necessity) for improvement of the activity as well. This said, we primarily mean that the reflections should be handed in as a separate writing task, rather than just an oral post-activity assignment. Also, different kinds of tasks and topics related to the linguistic theories in the Semantics and Pragmatics elective course should be introduced. For example, Grice's Cooperative Principle, Speech Acts, and Humor. That would also enable diversification of tasks, not only in the sense of adding more EFL in-class situations, but also applying those linguistic theories so that the teaching experience itself is enriched.

4 Conclusion

The reflective tools, strategies, and activities illustrated in this paper reveal that reflective pedagogies have high potential of initiating and supporting self-reflection on language learning and language teacher competences across the language teacher education curriculum. They also assist student teachers with designing, developing, and structuring their reflection papers, reflection posters, or role-play scenarios, which support them in a more critical, more diverse, more nuanced, more dynamic, and more multi-perspective view of the language learning process as well as of their teaching practice.

As this paper illustrated, the language syllabus should be based on the comprehension and the assessment of the needs in the classroom that is reflective of a broader social, economic, and political reality, and oriented towards actual, current, and real-life tasks, constructed around meaningfully selected topics, notions, scenarios, and language functions. The reflective tools provide a good basis for monitoring the progress of linguistic and pedagogical competencies in teacher development, and they support teachers in their motivation and commitment to the teaching profession. The reflective nature of language learning and teacher development activities enable students to contextualize the process of learning and to critically reflect on important social and political issues that are still deeply embedded in the Bosnian society.

With this paper we wanted to illustrate and better understand how language classrooms can continue to be the spaces of possibility for reflection, freedom, and activism. In the words of Bell Hooks (2022), we are "urging all of us to open our minds and hearts so that we can know beyond the boundaries of what is acceptable, so that we can think and rethink, so that we can create new visions (…)." We sincerely hope that our reflections will add to the "collective call for the renewal in the teaching practices" (Hooks, 2022). We hope that new visions in language education will also entail the changes in the educational paradigm where language learners are seen as "social agents" (CEFR, 2020), who can "open their minds and hearts to know beyond those boundaries of what is acceptable," in order to act in the socially complex realities of today's world and in order to exert agency in the language learning process.

References

Brown, H. D. (2000). *Principles of language learning and teaching*. Longman.
Brown, P., & Levinson, S. C. (1987). *Politeness: Some universals in language use*. Cambridge University Press.
Common European framework of reference for languages: Learning, teaching, assessment: Companion volume (2020). Council of Europe.
Council of Europe. (2018). *Reference framework of competences for democratic culture. Volume II. Descriptors of competences for democratic culture*. Council of Europe Publishing.
Crandall, J. A. J. (2000). Language teacher education. *Annual Review of Applied Linguistics, 20*, 34–55. https://doi.org/10.1017/s0267190500200032
Crow, M. L., & Nelson, L. P. (n.d.). *The effects of using academic role-playing in a teacher education*. Available at: https://ijrp.subcultures.nl/wp-content/uploads/2015/01/IJRP5_CrowNelson.pdf
Cunningham, F. M. (2001). Reflecting teaching practice in adult ESL settings. *ERIC Digest*, 1–7.
Fat'hi, J., & Behzadpour, F. (2011). Beyond method: The rise of reflective teaching. *International Journal of English Linguistics, 1*(2). https://doi.org/10.5539/ijel.v1n2p241
Goffman, E. (2013). *Encounters: Two studies in the sociology of interaction*. Martino Fine Books.
Hadžiomerović, A. (2018). *Bosnian post-war transgenerational trauma and its impact on post-war born children*. International University of Sarajevo.

Hatipoğlu, Ç. (2017). Linguistics courses in pre-service foreign language teacher training programs and knowledge about language. *ELT Research Journal*. Retrieved January 10, 2023, from https://dergipark.org.tr/en/pub/eltrj/issue/28779/307997

Hooks, B. (2022). *Teaching to transgress: Education as the practice of freedom*. DEV Publishers & Distributors.

Huang, L.-S. (2021). *Improving learner reflection for TESOL: Pedagogical strategies to support reflective learning*. Routledge.

Jay, J. K., & Johnson, K. L. (2002). Capturing complexity: A typology of reflective practice for teacher education. *Teaching and Teacher Education, 18*(1).

Komšić, I., et al. (2010). *Spomenica 60. godišnice Filozofskog fakulteta u Sarajevu*. Filozofski fakultet.

Korthagen, F., & Nuijten, E. (2022). *The power of reflection in teacher education and professional development strategies for in-depth teacher learning*. Taylor & Francis Group.

Kumaravadivelu, B. (1994). The postmethod condition: (E)merging strategies for second/foreign language teaching. *TESOL Quarterly, 28*(1), 27. https://doi.org/10.2307/3587197

Kumaravadivelu, B. (2001). Toward a postmethod pedagogy. *TESOL Quarterly, 35*(4), 537. https://doi.org/10.2307/3588427

Kumaravadivelu, B. (2003). A postmethod perspective on English language teaching. *World Englishes, 22*(4), 539–550. https://doi.org/10.1111/j.1467-971x.2003.00317.x

Lam, R. (2018). *Portfolio assessment for the teaching and learning of writing*. Springer.

Liu, K. (2020). *Critical reflection for transformative learning: Understanding eportfolios in teacher education*. Springer.

Nelson, R. F., Winfield-Thomas, E., & Lew, M. M. (2016). Academic service learning and cultural competence in teacher education. In *Service learning as pedagogy in early childhood education* (pp. 47–57). https://doi.org/10.1007/978-3-319-42430-9_4

Newby, D. (Ed.). (2012). *Insights into the European Portfolio for Student Teachers of Languages (EPOSTL)*. Cambridge Scholars Publishing.

Newby, D., Allan, R., Fenner, A. B., Jones, B., Komorowska, H., & Soghikyan, K. (2007). *EPOSTL- European Portfolio for Student Teachers of Languages. A reflection tool for language teacher education*. European Center for Modern Languages. Council of Europe.

Orlova, N. (2011). Challenges of integrating the EPOSTL into pre-service teacher training. In D. Newby, A.-B. Fenner, & B. Jones (Eds.), *Using the European Portfolio for Student Teachers of Languages*. European Center for Modern Languages. Council of Europe Publishing.

Pine, G. J. (2009). *Teacher action research: Building knowledge democracies*. Sage.

Riordan, E. (2018). *TESOL student teacher discourse: A corpus-based analysis of online and face-to-face interactions*. Routledge.

Ryan, M. E. (2015). *Teaching reflective learning in higher education: A systematic approach using pedagogic patterns*. Springer.

Schulze, R. (2015). The significance of 'The social' in contemporary linguistics. *The Exercise of Power in Communication*, 17–42. https://doi.org/10.1057/9781137478382_2

Serdarević, M., & Tahirović, S. (2020). Application of an ecological framework to clinical practice with adolescents: Transgenerational transmission of war-related trauma in Bosnia and Herzegovina. *Epiphany, 13*(2), 9. https://doi.org/10.21533/epiphany.v13i2.351

Tabachnik, R., & Zeichner, K. (2002). Reflections on reflective teaching. In A. Pollard (Ed.), *Readings for reflective teaching* (pp. 13–16). Continuum.

Trim, J. L. (2007). *Modern languages in the Council of Europe 1954-1997: International co-operation in support of lifelong language learning for effective communication ...* Language policy division, Council of Europe.

Uspomene 677: the Transgenerational Trauma of Victims and Perpetrators (Part IV). (2011). [film]. Mirko Pincelli. dir. Pinch Media.

Widdowson, H. G. (1990). *Aspects of language teaching.* Oxford University Press.

Larisa Kasumagić-Kafedžić is Associate Professor at the Faculty of Philosophy, University of Sarajevo, at the Department of English Language and Literature. Her teaching, writing and research interests focus on intercultural, critical and peace pedagogies in teacher education and language and culture didactics. She is currently a visiting professor at Cornell University, USA, in residence during the 2022–2023 academic year as a Fulbright Visiting Scholar Fellow, where she is lecturing and conducting research on "Teachers as Agents of Change: Education for Peace and Social Responsibility". Contact: larisa.kasumagic@ff.unsa.ba; lk92@cornell.edu.

Selma Đuliman obtained her PhD in linguistics. She is an Associate Professor at the Faculty of Philosophy, University of Sarajevo, where she teaches semantics, pragmatics, translation theory and contemporary English language. Her main research interest is humor in linguistics. Her passion is translation, primarily non-fiction. She is an ardent proponent of interdisciplinary and multidisciplinary approaches to higher education teaching and research. Contact: selma.djuliman@gmail.com; selma.djuliman@ff.unsa.ba.

ELF-Aware Teacher Development: The Case of the ENRICH Continuous Professional Development Course

Yasemin Bayyurt, Lucilla Lopriore, and Stefania Kordia

1   Introduction

In the past 25 years, the function of English as a Lingua Franca (ELF), that is, English as a means of communication among speakers from various linguacultural backgrounds, has been at the heart of a growing discussion among linguists, researchers, teacher educators, and teachers. Significant insights have thus been generated, including, above all, that effective ELF interactions do not depend so much on strict adherence to norms of English as a Native Language (ENL) but rather on the use, for instance, of meaning negotiation strategies, accommodation strategies, and translanguaging. In this regard, there seems to be a broad consensus in the field that in order to help learners develop competencies that are required in ELF communication, we need to reconsider traditional practices in teaching English as a Foreign Language (EFL), where there is typically an overreliance on ENL norms. This overreliance is especially true when it comes to multilingual settings, where

---

Y. Bayyurt (✉)
Foreign Language Education, Boğaziçi University, Istanbul, Turkey
e-mail: bayyurty@bogazici.edu.tr

L. Lopriore
Foreign Languages, Literatures and Cultures, Roma Tre University, Rome, Italy
e-mail: lucilla.lopriore@uniroma3.it

S. Kordia
School of Humanities, Hellenic Open University, Patras, Greece
e-mail: stefania.kordia@ac.eap.gr

the role of ELF nowadays is hardly recognized even though it is extensively used even among learners themselves. On this basis, the notion of "ELF awareness" (e.g., Sifakis, 2019) has been recently expounded, focusing on how teachers can be encouraged to question, revise, and enrich their teaching so as to incorporate ELF in their classrooms. This process inherently involves, on the one hand, engagement in critical reflection on one's views and practices in relation to ELF and, on the other, action research, to determine what changes are necessary to be brought about and how (e.g., in terms of the tasks one needs to employ).

In this chapter, we present the Continuous Professional Development (CPD) Course developed in the framework of the EU-funded Project entitled "English as a Lingua Franca Practices for Inclusive Multilingual Classrooms – ENRICH," which, as its title suggests, aimed at empowering English language teachers to raise their ELF awareness and integrate ELF in their multilingual EFL classrooms. In order to achieve this aim, the ENRICH Project partners coming from five increasingly more multilingual countries, namely Greece, Italy, Turkey, Norway, and Portugal, first conducted an extensive needs analysis study focusing on the needs and requirements of teachers and learners in these countries as regards English language teaching (ELT) and ELF. Based on the findings, the CPD Course was afterwards developed, drawing as well on the partners' experience in similar smaller-scale ELF-aware teacher education programs carried out in the past (i.e., ELF-TEd, by Bayyurt & Sifakis, 2015a, 2015b; ELF-GATE, by Kordia, 2016; New English/es Landscapes, by Lopriore et al., 2022). The ENRICH CPD Course was implemented from February 2020 to June 2020, with the participation of 254 teachers from various parts of the world.

To provide a comprehensive picture of how ELF awareness was fostered through the ENRICH CPD Course, at first, we briefly present the theoretical background of ENRICH as regards the constructs of ELF and ELF awareness, as well as the key components of the previous ELF-aware teacher education programs. Then, the discussion turns to the needs analysis study carried out in the framework of the project, highlighting the most significant findings that emerged from it. The content and the methodology of the ENRICH CPD Course are afterwards discussed, with reference to the central role of critical reflection and action research. To provide a short glimpse into the participants' progress throughout the Course, indicative reflective data are finally discussed, illustrating as well useful insights pertaining to their action research in their classrooms so as to fulfill their learners' needs as ELF users.

1.1 English as a Lingua Franca

In order to understand the theoretical premises of ELF-awareness, as a well-established theoretical construct (Sifakis, 2019), it is important to revisit the definition of ELF in a historical perspective. In its earlier phases, ELF was defined as a "shared common language" (Firth, 1996; Seidlhofer, 2005, 2011) among people from different linguacultural backgrounds, that is, mainly non-native speakers, who resort to it not only for communication purposes but also for reasons pertaining to professional success and social inclusion. Research on sociolinguistic aspects of that type of communication has, in fact, been exceptionally rich, indicating the significance, for instance, of establishing mutual intelligibility over 'correctness' in relation to ENL norms, using a range of meaning negotiation strategies (e.g., repetition) and accommodating to the ways one's interlocutor employs English, based, among other things, on elements of one's first language and culture (for an overview of ELF research findings, see, e.g., Jenkins et al., 2018). As the world is becoming more and more multilingual and mobile, a need for redefining the use of English within this newly emerging multilingual context has materialized. Hence, Jenkins's (2015) definition of the new conceptualization of ELF as English as a Multilingua Franca (EMF) was timely in representing the true nature of ELF communication. She explained EMF as "… multilingual communication in which English is available as a contact language of choice, but is not necessarily chosen" (p. 73) encompassing the process of an individual's efforts to use all language resources or linguistic repertoires for successful communication overlapping, at times, with the definition of "translanguaging" (García, 2019).

In light of the above, the far-reaching implications of ELF for ELT in contexts where it is the primary means of international communication have become increasingly evident. As is often argued, we should consider teaching English not as a language with a fixed set of rules that *de facto* belongs to its native users, but as a dynamic and flexible means of communication which native and non-native users alike may claim ownership of (Cogo, 2018; Seidlhofer, 2018). In turn, this requires a shift away from traditional native-speaker models of language teaching, where emphasis is predominantly placed on native speakers (e.g., on ENL grammatical structures and ENL culture), towards a more global and inclusive approach that acknowledges the diverse needs and goals of English language learners as current or future ELF users (Rose et al., 2021). This is precisely what the process of ELF awareness is about.

1.2 ELF-Awareness in ELT

Recognizing the urgent need to respond to the pedagogical implications of ELF, ELF awareness (Sifakis & Bayyurt, 2018; Sifakis, 2019) refers to the process whereby teachers (but also other ELT stakeholders, such as curriculum designers) develop an understanding of the changing times in English language use and of the ways in which the gap between the way English is taught in the EFL classroom and the way it is employed in the real world can be bridged. As Sifakis and Bayyurt (2018, p. 459) highlight, this process essentially involves examining the findings of ELF research to find out how English is currently used, even by learners themselves and, on this basis, engaging (a) in critical reflection on one's experience, views, and practices as a language teacher to determine the extent to which they relate to ELF, and (b) in action research in one's classroom, through the "design, implementation and evaluation of instructional activities that reflect and localize one's interpretation of the ELF construct" (Sifakis & Bayyurt, 2018, p. 459).

Reflection, in this sense, goes beyond simply thinking about how to solve a practical problem (e.g., how to teach negotiation strategies). It entails looking deeply into oneself to re-structure one's definition of English language and communication and, thereby, re-define one's role as an English language teacher, through both reflection 'on action' and 'in action,' in Schön's (1987) terms. ELF awareness, therefore, is an inherently transformative process, in that it requires identifying and challenging deeply held beliefs about the 'superiority' of the native speaker as a language user and as a target model for language learners (Cogo et al., 2021; Sifakis & Bayyurt, 2018; Sifakis & Kordia, 2019, 2020).

In this regard, to clarify what teachers' reflection may concentrate on, Sifakis (2019) argued that ELF awareness has three distinct yet interconnected components: (1) *Awareness of language and language use*: awareness of the syntactic, morphological, phonological, pragmatic, lexical, and sociocultural components of English that are present in interactions with bilingual and multilingual English users both within and outside of the classroom; (2) *Awareness of instructional practice*: comprehension of teachers' own pedagogical practices, theories, and deeply held beliefs, for instance, about instruction and feedback, and about the cognitive and motivational needs of the language learners; and (3) *Awareness of learning*: acknowledgment of the learners' substantial use of English in their in-person and online encounters with local and international participants from diverse linguistic and cultural backgrounds.

What the above components imply is that English language teachers become more critical towards the nature of English and the essence of English language teaching as they develop their understanding of ELF and the need for integrating it in ELT. To this end, becoming a truly reflective practitioner necessarily includes acquiring a more comprehensive understanding of the characteristics of one's local context (Anderson, 2020). This understanding, of course, includes a critical evaluation of ELT materials and textbooks, as well as of instructional methods and techniques, in relation to the ways in which they approach, for instance, the ownership of English, the image of the native and the non-native speaker, meaning negotiation and accommodation strategies, and multilingualism and translanguaging. Such topics need to be highlighted in an ELF-aware teacher education program, in order to enable teachers to formulate their own theory of 'good practice' in their classrooms (Cogo et al., 2021; Dewey, 2012; Sifakis, 2019).

1.3 ELF-Aware Teacher Education Projects

To date, there have been three major projects on ELF-aware teacher education besides the ENRICH Project that will be described briefly in this section, however, more extensively throughout the other sections of the chapter. These major projects are the ELF-TEd Project (2012–2017); the ELF-GATE project (2014–2015); and the *New Englishes Landscapes: Revisiting English Language Teaching & Learning* Course (2018). In this section, we will be focusing on the ELF-TEd and the ELF-GATE projects as they are two pioneering projects before the ENRICH Project. The New Englishes Landscapes project was based on the ENRICH materials and implementation, and hence, will not be discussed in this section.

The ELF-TEd project began in October 2012 and completed all of its phases in December 2017. It took place in two major phases. In the first phase, the project aimed at raising in-service English language teachers' awareness towards ELF and ELF related issues (Bayyurt and Sifakis, 2015a, 2015b; Sifakis and Bayyurt, 2015, 2018). In the second phase, the teachers were expected to reflect back on their understanding of the ELF and the ELF-awareness constructs and implement their understanding through the materials they prepare for their actual classrooms. The original ELFTEd project was designed to train in-service English language teachers working in K-12 and higher education institutions. Out of many who showed interest in the course, 32 teachers (26 from Turkey, 3 from Greece, 1 from the Philippines, 2 from Australia) registered for the online course and accepted the invitation to attend the first meeting of the project in September 2012. However, only 12 teachers (11 from Turkey and 1 from Greece) attended the course regularly and completed the course. A project website was developed, and teachers were asked to participate in the portal where they needed to register and reach the training materials for the course. During the lifetime of the project, the participant teachers were expected to reflect on their understanding of English as a Lingua Franca (ELF) through the reading materials and tasks we provided on the project portal, develop teaching materials based on their understanding of the ELF construct, and share their opinions and experience in forum discussions on the project portal. The findings of the ELFTEd project inspired future projects based on the lessons learnt from the application of both "good practices of ELF in ELT" aspects of the project.

The ELF-GATE project (2015–2016) was developed by Stefania Kordia as part of her PhD thesis. The focus of the program was to develop an understanding of the potential benefits and challenges of the ELF-awareness in ELT from a transformative teacher education perspective. Fifty Greek in-service teachers were enrolled in the program on a voluntary basis. Again, the aim was to raise teachers' awareness towards issues related to ELF and ELF-awareness in ELT from a transformative teacher education perspective. The data were collected through reflective journals the participants kept throughout the program, which lasted four months; lesson plans and action research projects that teachers developed; and individual interviews with the participant teachers after the project was over. The teachers were expected to reflect on their ELF-aware practices during the project lifetime through the materials they prepared as well as forum discussions they participated in on the basis of the activities designed for the purposes of the course. According to Kordia (2016), this critical reflection enabled teachers to carry out research about how to integrate ELF into their teacher practices in their local context. This reflective practice enabled most of the participants of the ELF-Gate project to develop a deeper understanding of the constructs of ELF and ELF-awareness and how to integrate those constructs into their teaching practice from a critical point of view.

The ENRICH project and the ENRICH Italy project were developed within the framework of the European Union Erasmus+ project and used the materials and activities developed within the context of the ENRICH CPD. In the next section, we will discuss the key aspects of the ENRICH CPD development, needs analysis, and implementation in detail.

2 The ENRICH Project: The Needs Analysis Phase

2.1 Planning a Professional Development Course: Investigating English Language Teaching and Learning Needs

Learning to teach multilingual classes with students from migrant backgrounds is emerging as one of the major necessities felt by teachers, but not yet regarded as a priority by European educational authorities (European Commission, 2017), even though this knowledge is often stated by principals and teachers as one of the most important emerging teachers' training needs, and despite several attempts to foster integration in schools (European Commission, 2014).

Taking this principle as a starting point, the priority of the ENRICH project was to focus on the development of English language teachers' (ELTs) competencies based on extensive needs analysis carried out in different multilingual contexts of the project partners. The aim was to enhance English language teachers' understanding of the current role of ELF and of its integration in multilingual English Language Teaching (ELT) classrooms. However, this enhancement and integration required a change in traditional teacher education and demanded a new training construct for ELT (Lopriore, 2016). Although there were already existing completed projects on ELF-aware teacher education, ELF-related issues in ELT were still in their early stages as far as ELF-aware materials or teaching courseware (Galloway, 2018; Lopriore & Vettorel, 2015; Lopriore, 2019), as were large-scale teacher education projects across Europe and beyond (Bayyurt & Dewey, 2020; Dewey & Patsko, 2018; Sifakis & Bayyurt, 2015, 2018).

The ENRICH Project's priorities required us to study those educational contexts where English is taught, and to observe how English is taught; the main target groups were not only ELTs in countries where English is officially taught, but also a growing multilingual population that makes English a *de facto* lingua franca.

Since the main aim of the ENRICH project was to examine educational contexts where English was taught as a "foreign"/"second" language across Europe and beyond, a careful investigation of current ELT classroom practices in the partner countries, teachers' and learners' needs, and awareness and understanding of new forms of communication and learning through English seemed to be the main priority of the ENRICH project. This initial examination was a crucial step for the design and implementation of a Continuous Professional Development (CPD). The ENRICH team thus devised a research methodology inclusive of the design of a needs analysis (NA) aimed at gathering information about teachers' current practices and beliefs about ELT, particularly in multilingual classrooms, as well as of learners' opinions on their English language learning experience.

Specific attention had to be paid to the type of approach chosen to face the challenge of conducting a transnational study across five countries with different school systems, language policies, foreign language curricula, and teacher education models. It was important to ensure that identical collection and analysis procedures were conducted across all contexts; in view of this, the three-year Project duration required the design of a longitudinal model that would consider the drawbacks and the assets of this type of project (Enever & Lopriore, 2014; Ortega & Iberry-Shea,

2005; Neale, 2019), as described in the following paragraph on the needs analysis (NA) research design.

2.2 The Needs Analysis Research Design

NA has had a long-standing tradition in language teaching, originally meant to identify learners' language needs for designing specific language courses. More recently it has widened its scope and has become a relevant tool in fields such as English for Academic Purposes (EAP), as well as in research studies investigating teachers' and learners' practices, attitudes, and beliefs in language learning and teaching (Long, 2005).

It is within this tradition that the ENRICH NA survey was devised and carried out; its aims were to:

- investigate current English language teaching and learning practices, routines, attitudes, and beliefs in the five partner countries—with similar but different education systems
- carry out an analysis of both teachers' and learners' current teaching and learning needs in diverse ELT educational contexts.

A convenience sampling of the survey population, composed of teachers and students, was established with 600 ELTs (120 per country), 500 adolescents (100 per country), and 100 young learners (20 per country).

The NA survey research was devised and carried out through multiple choice (MC) questionnaires and focus groups involving teachers of English as well as their learners—across different school levels—within the five countries (Greece, Italy, Norway, Portugal, and Turkey) included in the project. The information collected was meant to be used to inform and develop the CPD components as well as to consider country variables. Information was collected through a questionnaire in English about ELTs' current practices as well as their personal beliefs and attitudes regarding ELT and new instantiations of English.

Similar information was also needed from the English language learners, namely their individual language learning habits and preferences, as well as their belonging to groups of migrants or refugees. The learners' group was subdivided into two groups: young learners (11–13 years) and adolescents (14–17 years) to meet their diverse needs and conditions. Questionnaires in the learners' local language were used with the adolescents, while focus groups were chosen as most appropriate for young learners.

2.2.1 Teachers' Questionnaire

The purpose of the teachers' questionnaire was to record teachers' training needs and beliefs regarding the following:

- the current role of linguistic diversity, social inclusion, and ELF.
- issues regarding multilingual classes, including learners from migrant backgrounds.
- the competencies needed to meet learners' current and future language needs.
- the integration of ELF in classroom practices.
- the use of innovative language teaching practices and cultural content.

The questionnaire—in English—was structured into 43 items, subdivided into sections with questions (Qs) alternated with statements (Ss) to elicit teachers' reflective response regarding the following:

- Biodata and professional & language background (Qs) & current teaching levels (Qs);
- Statements regarding teachers'

  - awareness of social context, school integration, language policies, and integration of migrant learners (Ss);
  - use and views of professional materials and coursebooks; teaching of language, culture, and standard and non-standard norms;
  - use of the Internet and of audiovisual materials;
  - views of native and non-native ELTs;
  - awareness of current status of English; and
  - areas of perceived training needs (Ss).

The questionnaire was delivered online via each partner country's professional associations and local educational authorities.

2.2.2 The Adolescents' Questionnaire

The questionnaire—in the learners' language of instruction—was specifically designed for language learners of their age group (14–17), including learners from migrant backgrounds. It was delivered locally via professional associations, local educational authorities, and school principals identified in each of the partner countries. This questionnaire aimed at investigating the following:

- what learners want to learn in the English classroom and how;
- the way they used English as well as ICTs in the classroom to communicate with their teacher and classmates and outside the classroom for real-life communicative purposes; and
- the way they expected they could use English to communicate in the future.

The questionnaire was structured into five sections in a total of 46 questions. Except for the first section, mainly composed of questions, all other sections included statements to which learners had to express their level of agreement or disagreement.

2.2.3 The Young Learners' Focus Groups

The young learners' focus groups FG (11–13 years of age) took place as face-to-face meetings in local schools in a conversation mode that would allow them to respond personally while interacting with their classmates. The FGs were led through a protocol, and each session lasted 20 min. A grid to observe the interaction between the interviewer and the children was used. The interactions were taken note of, and later reported to be centrally collected and analyzed. The main aims of the focus groups were the following:

- to elicit young learners' personal views of and responses to English;
- to gather information about learners' perceptions of English as a subject matter;
- to elicit learners' favorite app/website or game that would involve the use of English; and
- to find out whether the learners had ever been exposed to diverse Englishes or only to British English.

The interviewer elicited an open discussion on different topics by using stimulus questions and asked young learners to think back to their experiences as learners and users of English, based on a set of questions about their relationship with English, its varieties, and their favorite websites and apps. The main stimulus questions were the following:

1. What is the first image/sound that comes to your mind when you think of English?
2. Is English your favorite subject? If no, which one is it?
3. What is your favorite website/app or game?
4. During your English lessons have you ever been exposed to forms of English other than British, American, or Australian?

This open discussion triggered learners' personal responses and enhanced learners' reflections on their language learning experiences.

3 The NA Findings

The response rate to the questionnaires and focus groups exceeded expectations in all five countries, providing the necessary information to guide the research team's decisions on the development of the CPD Course. The use of innovative needs analysis procedures and the resulting findings have been reported in the chapter written by Lopriore published in the Handbook of English as a Lingua Franca, edited by Cavalheiro et al. (2021).

3.1 Teachers' Responses

The questionnaire received responses from 620 teachers, of which 532 were female and 88 were male. The majority of the teachers were non-native speakers of English. The number of participants per country was over 100, which was fairly representative of the five countries. Specifically, there were 151 teachers from Greece, 107 from Italy, 110 from Norway, 133 from Portugal, and 119 from Turkey who responded to the questionnaire.

The responses were beyond expectations, both for the number of responses and for the awareness of the relevance of exposing their learners to authentic uses of English in their teaching practice and of multilingual learners' needs. Most teachers provide their learners with opportunities to interact in English and use learning tasks that involve the use of the Internet, interactive applications, and social media. Over 55% expose their learners to uses of English like those they may be exposed to outside the classroom, while almost 90% teach Standard English pronunciation, usually referred to British English (BE) or American English (AE) and indicated in the country curriculum. Almost 80% of teachers develop their own teaching materials to address their multilingual learners' needs. Answers to the questions on attitudes show an overall understanding and awareness on the part of the teachers of the relevance of their role and function as non-native speakers, even if they do not yet integrate examples of non-native speakers in their lessons. Some contradictions emerge in their answers revealing at times native-speakerist assumptions, but also that they are transitioning from never challenged assumptions about traditional ELT practices, approaches, and models, as well as a preference for standard British or American English, all of which are gradually being affected by reality, to an awareness of the new multilingual language landscapes and of the new function and role of English.

3.2 Adolescents' Responses

The questionnaire was answered by a total of 505 students, with 140 respondents in Greece, 137 in Italy, 54 in Norway, 100 in Portugal, and 74 in Turkey. It is worth noting that learners' perceptions of effective learning approaches may differ from those of their teachers. Based on their responses, students appear to have a better awareness than their teachers of what they find most effective for their learning. For instance, the results indicate that while coursebooks are often considered useful for learning (38%), students tend to appreciate teachers who use authentic materials more often (37%). It is important to note that these findings do not necessarily contradict each other. Rather, they offer insight into how learners perceive their language learning experiences both in and outside the classroom. Moreover, when asked to provide examples of what they find most effective for their own learning, teachers' responses may provide further valuable information. For example, when teachers were asked whether their learners used English outside the classroom; 10% responded 'often,' and 45% 'sometimes.' Learners, on the contrary, stated that they learn English using it outside the classroom, namely 28% by using YouTube, 26% social media, 17% playing online games, and 55% watching movies in English. Asking both teachers and learners about their teaching and learning reveals how useful in research studies listening to both voices is.

3.3 Young Learners' Responses

The focus groups design proved very successful, as their organization provided initial questions meant to stimulate learners' interventions, triggered several responses and spontaneous conversation among the FG participants. Approximately 100 learners, 20 from each of the five countries, 48% male and 52% female, responded. Young learners' responses revealed specific aspects related to learners' awareness of ELT, their experiences, and their knowledge of the role of English and about multilingualism. The freedom of the focus group format allowed learners' responses to be quite varied and provided a good insight into learners' perceptions of their language learning experience. When asked if they use English outside school, almost all of them declare that they use it in various ways: "Sometimes I use some English expressions or words to make funny jokes with my friends or my parents. English gives the idea," thus showing their awareness of the potential of using another language and their self-confidence in using the language.

4 From the NA to the Professional Development Course Design

The overall NA research design had been highly structured to meet the challenges of a transnational survey, and to ensure the reliability and validity of the design, as well as the reliability of the construct, production, and administration of the tools used. The subsequent data analysis required careful consideration in order to design a course consistent with the emerging needs of both teachers and learners, specifically in multilingual contexts, and with the original aims of the project.

The analysis of the responses to the questionnaires and in the focus groups provided an overall picture that allowed us to compare internal country responses as related to the teachers, the adolescents, and the young learners. What emerged from the NA confirmed the initial hypotheses and aims of the ENRICH Project and informed the development of the CPD. The NA highlighted the following:

Teachers' overall awareness of

- the new communicative needs of multilingual classes,
- the need for authenticity of input and tasks, and
- the relevance of ICT use and of social media for language learning.

Learners' awareness of
- their learning processes,
- their self-concept as learners and as users of English, and
- the relevance of out-of-school experience on their language learning.

The ENRICH team took into consideration the NA findings to devise and plan the ENRICH CPD Course modules and activities to respond to the emerging needs of teachers and learners in multilingual contexts. The NA had also provided quite a few unexpected findings, regarding, for example, the number of similarities across the five countries, the degree of awareness teachers of English already have of the changes occurring in English, and of the necessity to provide learners with real life exposure to and the use of authentic English, but teachers need to be encouraged and sustained in their reflection in action aiming at enhancing reflective teaching.

The NA confirmed the original hypotheses of the ENRICH Project and highlighted the implications for a model of teacher education that needs to reshape teaching and learning practices through reflection and awareness, where teachers are, for example, presented with new instantiations of English, as in English as a Lingua Franca. This approach should be embedded throughout the course components, while learners' language experiences outside the classroom, or through social media, are valued in classroom life.

4.1 The ENRICH CPD Course

As noted in the earlier parts of this chapter, the development of the ENRICH CPD Course was undertaken as part of the ENRICH Project. The primary objective of the project was to establish a high-quality online educational infrastructure that would enable English teachers from across the globe to integrate ELF in their teaching contexts guided by the ELF awareness construct. To achieve this goal, the project drew upon the expertise and experience of researchers and teacher educators from Greece, Italy, Norway, Portugal, and Turkey, under the coordination of the Hellenic Open University (Greece). The ENRICH CPD Course, which lasted a total of 300 h, was designed to promote ELF awareness in multilingual and multicultural contexts. The course emphasized the development of critical thinking skills and focused on the main instances of ELF in current English usage, while encouraging reflective practices on ELF in EFL classrooms. The course structure was based on reflective practice and collaboration, and it was supported by a mentoring system.

The ENRICH course was conducted from February to July 2020 and was attended by more than 249 participants from the five countries involved, as well as from other geographic regions. The course was structured around three main areas: LEARNING, TEACHING, and USING ENGLISH (see Fig. 7.1).

As can be seen in Fig. 7.1, course participants were involved in the following:

- Exploring ELF, observing English as used in multilingual contexts;
- Learning about Linguistic Diversity and appreciating its value for language education; and
- Developing ELF awareness, the key that enhanced participants' involvement.

In addition, the course materials were composed of original videos, extra self-study, and self-reflection materials that enabled parties to respond to each other's questions through a reflective dialogue in the course Forums. At the end of the course, the participants were asked to prepare a Final Assignment that was peer reviewed by other course participants. In the next section we will present the research design and data collection.

7 ELF-Aware Teacher Development: The Case of the ENRICH Continuous... 131

Fig. 7.1 Course topics that are covered in the ENRICH CPD

4.1.1 Research Aims

Having discussed the theoretical background of the ENRICH CPD Course with respect to the integration of ELF in ELT, as well as the main characteristics of the Course, in what follows we offer a short glimpse into the transformative journey that participants coming from Greece, Italy, and Turkey went through towards fostering their ELF awareness. Even though, after expressing their wish to participate in the Course, participants from other countries (such as Pakistan and Brazil) had also joined these groups, we focus specifically on Greeks, Italians, and Turkish participants for one main reason. This is because the ELT contexts in these Mediterranean countries share a lot of similarities with each other, meaning that the participants, more or less, had a common starting point when entering the course. Such similarities include, for instance, the increasingly multilingual and multicultural character of ELT classrooms (e.g., Cavalheiro et al., 2021), the exceptionally high status that English enjoys in the educational system of each country, and the predominantly native-speaker-oriented mentality of ELT practices, which is evident in all domains surrounding ELT, from language curricula and syllabi to language testing and assessment frameworks (e.g., Bayyurt et al., 2019; Sifakis et al., 2018). It would be useful, therefore, to see how, amidst this context, the participants made sense of ELF and its role in their classroom.

In this sense, the study is exploratory in nature and adopts a phenomenologically oriented approach; it seeks to make sense of the participants' reflective insights about using, teaching, and learning English in relation to ELF and, thereby, to identify how their views may have potentially changed throughout the course. That said, this study constitutes part of a larger research project on the participants' overall professional development, including, for example, the ways in which they have actually integrated ELF in their classrooms at the end of the course and months afterwards. On this basis, the study intends to address the following research question: *How did the participants' views about the role of ELF in using, teaching, and learning English evolve while participating in the course?*

4.1.2 The Participants' Profile

The ENRICH CPD course was advertised locally in each partner country via social media platforms unofficially, and e-mails to universities, ministries of education, and schools officially. As mentioned earlier in the chapter, the ENRICH CPD Course was implemented from February 2020 to June 2020, with 249 participants in total from various countries around the world, who had the chance to select which sections of the course they would engage with, based on their own educational needs and priorities. Ninety-six of them chose to complete all of the sections. Among them, there were fifty-five participants from the countries we are focusing on in this paper; twenty-three of them came from Greece, seventeen from Italy, and fifteen from Turkey (Table 7.1).

More specifically, the group with the Greek, Italians, and Turkish participants consisted mainly of women (90%) who taught in a range of educational settings, such as state or private primary and secondary schools, universities, colleges, and other specialized institutions, for instance, with refugee learners. Although there were a few participants who were relatively young, most of them were between thirty-six and fifty-five years of age and had significant experience in teaching English; forty out of fifty-five participants, in fact, had been teaching for more than eleven years and half of them, that is, twenty participants, had been teaching for over twenty-one years. They were also very well-educated; all of them had a bachelor's degree in teaching English while more than half of them also held a postgraduate diploma, or even a doctorate. Finally, before the ENRICH CPD Course, the vast majority of them had not participated in a seminar or other educational program or event focusing on the role of ELF. As they reported, fourteen participants had indeed heard about ELF, mainly through short-term workshops, seminars, or conference presentations, and felt the need to learn more about it, which is what urged them to enroll in ENRICH in the first place.

Table 7.1 Participants' demographic information

	Category	N	%
Nationality	Greece	23	41.8
	Italy	17	30.9
	Turkey	15	27.3
	Total	55	100.0
Gender	Female	49	89.1
	Male	6	10.9
	Total	55	100.0
Teaching context	Primary education	15	27.3
	Secondary education	29	52.7
	Tertiary education	3	5.5
	Other	8	14.5
	Total	55	100.0
Age	25 or under 25	1	1.8
	26–35	16	29.1
	36–45	15	27.3
	46–55	19	34.5
	56 or more	4	7.3
	Total	55	100.0
Years of teaching Experience	1 or less	1	1.8
	2–5	5	9.1
	6–10	9	16.4
	11–20	20	36.4
	21 or more	20	36.4
	Total	55	100.0
Qualifications	BA or equivalent	21	38.2
	MA or equivalent	30	54.5
	PhD or equivalent	4	7.3
	Total	55	100.0
Participation in ELF-related Seminar, presentation or similar	Yes	14	25.5
	No	41	74.5
	Total	55	100.0

4.2 Data Collection and Analysis

Due to the exploratory nature of the research goals, qualitative data have been employed in order to explore the participants' transformative journey throughout the ENRICH CPD Course. These data have been gathered, first from the responses that the participants progressively provided in the forums of the sections 'Defining ELF,' 'Key issues in using ELF,' 'The ELF discourse,' and 'The content of ELF-aware teaching,' where they were asked to reflect on their experience and share their perspectives about the issue that each section focused on each time. Second, useful data have been drawn from a sample ELF-aware lesson plan that a participant designed for her learners at the end of the course. Qualitative content analysis was carried out through the MAXQDA software. As is usually the case, the process involved coding the data to eventually build general themes which would represent the overall meaning of the data (e.g., Cresswell, 2014). Due to space constraints, in this paper we focus on the following five themes which have emerged from this process: (a) *The image of the native and the non-native user of English*; (b) *The use of ELF in everyday life*; (c) *The meaning of ELF*; (d) *The aims of teaching and learning*; and (e) *The integration of ELF in one's classroom*.

4.3 The Participants' Transformative Journey

Despite their differences in nationality, age, teaching context, and educational background, the Greek, Italian, and Turkish participants seem to have followed a relatively common route in their ELF-aware transformative journey, while, at the same time, drawing on their own knowledge and experience with regard to using, teaching, and learning English. In this respect, their reflections at the beginning of the course essentially confirm the findings of the Needs Analysis study based on which the course had been developed; they illustrate, on the one hand, that the participants had an overall understanding of the global role of English and the changes that the language has been undergoing as a result of this, and, on the other, that they held a range of native-speakerist assumptions about English and their own role as teachers of it.

This rather ambivalent attitude is particularly evident in their introductory reflections concerning the *image of the native and the non-native user of English*. While describing how they perceived the terms 'native' and 'non-native' speaker and, respectively, the meaning of 'standard English,' 'correct English,' and 'good English,' most of the participants highlighted that Standard English, that is, the language that has traditionally been associated with native speaker discourse, is indeed synonymous to 'correct English,' which is what provides the norms for non-native speakers to abide by. 'Good English,' on the contrary, for them, refers mainly to establishing effective communication, that is, in ensuring that no confusion or misinterpretation may arise while exchanging messages with your interlocutors. In the indicative dialogue below, Giulia focused on the long-held belief that speaking as a native speaker *de facto* makes you an 'ideal' user of English, while, Marina, drawing probably on her experience in using ELF and her educational background, added that the differences between a native and a non-native speaker are rather blurred nowadays and, what is more, the forms deviating from native-speaker norms may not always cause communication problems:

> *Standard English* [is] *the official language which is grammatically correct, which has lexical richness, which perfectly distinguishes the use of the written and spoken form.* [It is] *the language spoken by users who have studied the language or lived in English-speaking countries and who speak it correctly, in formal and non-formal contexts. (Giulia, IT)*

> *The question here is who do we define as a native speaker? […]? What is wrong and what is right […]? Correct English* [means] *correct in terms of grammar, spelling, structure etc. compared with the native speakers' English* [but] *non-standard English* [includes] *variations which may or may not affect comprehension […]. Good English for me is the English which is fluent and comprehensive, with or without mistakes, native or non-native. (Marina, GR)*

Even when the participants showed a relative awareness of the significance of successful communication, "with or without mistakes," as Marina argued, their reflections on the role of the native speaker in teaching and learning clearly indicated how deeply entrenched in their way of thinking and acting native-speakerist assumptions had been. Viewing the native speaker as the only legitimate 'owner' of the language and, therefore, relating 'good' ELT practices with teaching 'correct English,' the vast majority of the participants described the image of the non-native English-speaking teacher as a professional who may indeed be consciously aware of the structures of the language but may never be as 'perfect' as a native one. For Burcu, Alice, and Kelly, native teachers are the only ones who have access to 'real English,' while non-native teachers, including themselves, are "permanent learners" (Hülmbauer, 2007, p. 6) of a language which, no matter how hard they try, could never be 'theirs' to use, let alone to teach:

> *When it comes to teaching, non-native speakers usually have a strong background and conscious knowledge of the language, as well as awareness about how the language works. What they sometimes miss is their lack of experience from 'real' language use [...]. What actually preoccupies a large number of* [them] *is their struggle with their own language deficiencies. (Kelly, GR)*

> *A native speaker is the speaker who speaks his* [sic] *own language which belongs to his country and his origin [...]. For a non-native speaker of English, it is more difficult to teach. As a teacher,* [you] *should do* [your] *best.* [You] *should improve. (Burcu, TR)*

> In this sense, the roles of a native and a non-native speaker are extremely different, in terms of teaching. A non-native teacher can be a good teacher, but there is always something lacking in his/her performances. (Alice, IT)

As the participants engaged more systematically with the characteristics of ELF discourse through the sections which described, for instance, how flexible and variable communication can be in various situations among non-native speakers, it became increasingly evident for them what *the use of ELF in everyday life* involved not only for them, as users of the language, but also for their students. While exchanging views with the rest of the participants about how they employed ELF in their personal and professional life, for instance, while traveling or participating in international conferences, Emre and Eleni, below, drew their colleagues' attention to the way their learners as well used ELF for their own communicative purposes, such as talking with friends and playing interactive games online. In doing so, they made a highly crucial observation: as their learners were creatively exploiting English and, thereby, 'changing' it to tailor it to their needs, what they were actually doing is making it their own and, in this sense, deviating from Standard English in a manner that made sense to them was exactly what made them feel self-confident and competent as users of English:

> *My students [...] often provide a variety of examples featuring especially morphosyntactic variations [...], which result from their flexible use of English. They are intelligible* [to them], *making students feel self-confident* [and] *competent enough to pursue communication. (Emre, TR)*

> [See] *the word 'unpaictable' and 'unpaictability'; to a native speaker it means nothing but to the Greek learner of English it refers to a person being awesome and their awesomeness* [by] *combining a Greek idiomatic/slang word with English [...];* [It] *is a way for the learners to make the language their own, to render it more to their own liking and, also, to make it more 'personal' to them. (Eleni, GR)*

In this regard, raising one's understanding of what 'real English' involves in lingua franca contexts was absolutely necessary in order for them to start embracing their and their learners' non-nativeness as a valuable asset rather than as a deficiency. This shift in perspective involved gradually reconsidering their strong attachment to the native speaker ideal and developing their own interpretation of the *meaning of ELF*, that is, what ELF represented to them both as users and teachers of the language. This is precisely the point when they started realizing that there might be a serious discrepancy between the way English functions in the real world and the way it is typically taught in their classrooms. As Isabella and Katerina argued, ELF, for non-native users, like themselves and their learners, meant connecting to each other through a shared language, which allows the interlocutors to use any resources they have available to express themselves, including, of course, their mother tongue and any other language they may feel close to. Then, for them, as non-native teachers, ELF involved gaining a sense of freedom from native-speaker constraints; most importantly, it meant overcoming feelings of inferiority and improving one's sense of self-efficacy:

> *To me ELF means [...] being closer to* [other] *speakers, regardless their native language, an opportunity to communicate negotiating meanings in a different way, relying not only on the language but also on other elements, such as [...] other languages or non-verbal communication [...]. Maybe ELF is the 'real' English. (Isabella, IT)*

> *The global aspect of ELF* [helps] *us, non-native English teachers, feel more free and less guilty when our use of the English language differs from that of a native speaker* [and] *no longer* [be] *ashamed of our accent, of not sounding like a native speaker. (Katerina, GR)*

Having explored the various characteristics and aspects of ELF communication and gained a fresh perspective of themselves and their learners, the participants progressively started reflecting on *the aims of teaching and learning* in their teaching situation. Their experience in teaching English for so many years, as well as their educational background, proved more than important in this respect. In their dialogue below, Kelly and Rosa focus on the significance of using authentic materials, such as videos, in raising their learners' awareness of how they could creatively negotiate the meaning in their ELF interactions, which, in turn, would enhance their communicative skills and improve their motivation and self-confidence. On this basis, Isra adds another crucial dimension: enriching ELT through an ELF-aware perspective essentially implies helping the learners identify and, to the extent that this is indeed possible, change their own native-speakerist assumptions. This involves facilitating their own transformative journey towards ELF-awareness while engaging them in a creative and reflective dialogue among themselves, much like the dialogue that their teacher had in the framework of the ENRICH CPD Course:

> *Making students feel free to communicate their own ideas and satisfy their need for creativity […] is of prime importance […]. Students need to be taught how to paraphrase, negotiate meaning* [and] *manage a conversation while using at the same time paralinguistic and extra-linguistic elements to complement verbal communication. (Kelly, GR)*

> *I can only see advantages in enriching the learning environment by taking an ELF-aware perspective. I think it could really boost the learners' motivation […]. Once educators are aware of this perspective, it's not too hard to find authentic ELF-oriented materials. (Rosa, IT)*

> *I think the best part of ELF-aware teaching is* [making] *learners feel more self-confident, autonomous and eager to use the language […].* [This] *may help […] in terms of enhancing creative thinking and changing* [their own] *convictions, old beliefs and assumptions toward the English language. (Isra, TR)*

Translating one's reflective insights into actual teaching practice, especially as far as ELF- awareness is concerned, is, however, not a straightforward task (Sifakis et al., 2018). After reflecting on various ELT related issues through the rest of the sections (e.g., '2.3 Methods, approaches and beyond'), the participants had the opportunity to work more systematically on *the integration of ELF in one's classroom*, in the safe environment of the ENRICH CPD Course. For the purposes of their Final Assignment, as mentioned earlier, they designed and taught an ELF-aware lesson plan for their own learners. Drawing on her highly fruitful reflective dialogue with her colleagues, including, for instance, the ideas that Kelly, Rosa, and Isra above had shared, Sofia, from Greece, decided to create a lesson aiming at developing her 11-year-old learners' listening and speaking skills, while, at the same time, increasing their motivation and self-confidence as non-native users of ELF (for more information on this lesson plan, see Sifakis and Kordia, in Cavalheiro et al., 2021).

Sofia's lesson was entitled 'Holidays in Greece,' which, as she noted, was one of her learners' favorite topics. To engage, therefore, her learners in a reflective dialogue with each other, at the beginning of her lesson, she employed a range of open-ended reflective questions to urge her students to share their own views and experiences in ELF communication. Taking into account her observations throughout the course about the ways in which they employed ELF in their personal lives, for instance, while traveling, her questions included the following:

What language do tourists use to communicate with Greek people while visiting Greece? Have you ever met people from different countries? What language did you use to speak to them?

Activating their background knowledge and experience as users of ELF was, in this regard, necessary in order for her to help them raise their awareness of how ELF works. To that end, she used, as a starting point, an authentic video she had found online, where several tourists in Athens discussed what they liked most about their holidays. In order to elicit her learners' perspectives about the speakers' usage of English and, thereby, their assumptions regarding, for example, the image of the native speaker and the nature of 'good English,' she employed a new set of reflective questions, including the following:

Are the people in the video native or non-native speakers? Where are they from? Did you understand them? Why or why not? Do they speak English 'well'? Why or why not?

On that basis, her lesson proceeded with a role-playing speaking activity, where the learners, in pairs, assumed the role of a Greek person and a tourist who had to communicate concerning their flights. As Sofia highlighted, her learners' responses were more than positive; despite their young age, they had indeed a lot to contribute to their reflective dialogue in class, showing her that enriching her teaching practice in the future with more ELF-aware activities, which could be progressively more demanding and influential, was essential in order for them to develop as confident and self-aware users of English. For Sofia, the most valuable lesson of her experience in the course was realizing that helping the learners feel free to use English in a way that makes sense to them, liberated from the pressure to be always 'correct' and 'proper,' is what matters the most; this was precisely what the vision of ENRICH has been and, the participants' journey throughout the Course indicated that this, in fact, could be realized:

The most important thing that I learned [...] is that there are ways we can use in class to make our students speak English more and more freely and at the same time make them more conscious of the fact that emphasis should be on understanding each other and not on pronouncing correctly or avoiding mistakes.

5 Conclusion

In this chapter, we presented the development and implementation of a Continuous Professional Development Course in the context of an EU-funded Project entitled "ENRICH - English as a Lingua Franca Practices for Inclusive Multilingual Classrooms." As we indicated in the earlier sections, the aim of the ENRICH project was to raise English language teachers' awareness and competence towards issues emerging in their multilingual and multicultural English language teaching contexts. We reported the stages of the development of the CPD in collaboration with the partners of the project from 5 different countries: Greece, Italy, Turkey, Norway, and Portugal. An extensive needs analysis was conducted before the development of the modules of the ENRICH CPD. The main focus of the ENRICH CPD was on ELF and its use among speakers from different linguacultural backgrounds. The aim of the course was to develop modules based on the needs analysis carried out in partner countries and to help teachers of English integrate that role of English in their classrooms through reflection on ELF, their local context, and their own role, as teachers through reflection on topics and activities raising their awareness towards ELF and ELF-related issues in ELT—i.e., ELF awareness. As Sifakis et al. (2022, p. 262) indicate:

> … teacher development is often associated with **critical reflection** leading to teacher autonomy … In this sense, an in-service teacher development course may engage teachers in **documenting, analysing** and **reflecting** on their own as well as their colleagues' **teaching practices, beliefs** and **attitudes**, in relation to the **needs** of their learners, the **requirements** of their teaching context and **new knowledge acquired** about the subject they teach.

As explained in the previous sections, critical reflection was achieved through tasks, assignments, and a final project that was assigned to the teachers as well as discussion forums among the teachers who participated to this study as well as the mentoring sessions which were carried out by getting together with the teachers both face-to-face (before pandemic) and online (during the pandemic). There were also online forums which gave teachers an opportunity to reflect on their own experience as well as other teachers' experiences with ELF-aware teaching. To illustrate this point further, it is important to see what teachers really thought about reflective practice during the ENRICH project:

> **Reading reviews** and **contact sessions** were the most useful part for me. **Things got clear** when **I read others' comments…** (Turkish Participant Teacher 1)

> **Joining discussions** in the **forum** are really beneficial for me because **it helps me understand** and **compare** the **teaching** and **learning context in different countries** (Turkish Participant Teacher 2)

In this chapter, we reported the findings of the needs assessment and its connection to CPD development by giving examples from teachers' reports on their journeys in becoming ELF-aware throughout the ENRICH project lifetime. The needs analysis informed the development of the CPD modules again documented in the sections above and the results of the implementation of the CPD course revealed that teachers' found the information presented throughout the project useful in their development as an ELF-aware teacher and the ENRICH project enabled them to see what their students could do with English in their classrooms when they were given a real chance to use English with an authentic purpose to use it. Hence, in our increasingly multilingual world, when given a real purpose to use language without any prejudices against the identities of teachers and students, both teachers and students will be able to use English more effectively. Further investigation is needed in order to develop a deeper understanding of the construct of ELF-awareness in relation to both ENRICH and other projects related to ENRICH.

Acknowledgments We extend our sincere thanks to the European Union Erasmus Plus Programme for supporting the "ENRICH: English as a Lingua Franca practices for inclusive multilingual classrooms Project" (2018-1EL01-KA201-047894).

References

Anderson, J. (2020). Reflection. *ELT Journal, 74*(4), 480–483.
Bayyurt, Y., & Dewey, M. (2020). Locating ELF in ELT. *ELT Journal, 74*(4), 369–376.
Bayyurt, Y., Kurt, Y., Öztekin, E., Guerra, L., Cavalheiro, L., & Pereira, R. (2019). English language teachers' awareness of English as a lingua franca in multilingual and multicultural contexts. *Eurasian Journal of Applied Linguistics, 5*(2), 185–202.
Bayyurt, Y., & Sifakis, N. (2015a). Developing an ELF-aware pedagogy: Insights from a self-education programme. In P. Vettorel (Ed.), *New frontiers in teaching and learning English* (pp. 55–76). Cambridge Scholars Publishing.
Bayyurt, Y., & Sifakis, N. (2015b). ELF-aware in-service teacher education: A transformative perspective. In H. Bowles & A. Cogo (Eds.), *International perspectives on teaching English as a lingua franca* (pp. 117–135). Palgrave Macmillan.
Cavalheiro, L., Guerra, L., & Pereira, R. (Eds.). (2021). *The handbook to English as a Lingua Franca practices for inclusive multilingual classrooms*. Humus.
Cogo, A. (2018). ELF and multilingualism. In J. Jenkins, W. Baker, & M. Dewey (Eds.), *The Routledge handbook of English as a lingua franca* (pp. 357–368). Routledge.

Cogo, A., Fang, F., Kordia, S., Sifakis, N., & Siqueira, S. (2021). Developing ELF research for critical language education. *AILA Review, 34*(2), 187–211.

Cresswell, J. W. (2014). *Research design. Qualitative, quantitative and mixed methods approaches*. SAGE Publications.

Dewey, M. (2012). Towards a post-normative approach: Learning the pedagogy of ELF. *Journal of English as a Lingua Franca, 1*(1), 141–170.

Dewey, M., & Patsko, L. (2018). ELF-aware teaching, learning and teacher development. In J. Jenkins, W. Baker, & M. Dewey (Eds.), *Handbook of English as a Lingua Franca* (pp. 441–455). Routledge.

Enever, J., & Lopriore, L. (2014). Language learning across borders and across time: A critical appraisal of a transnational, longitudinal model for research investigation. *System, 45*, 187–197.

European Commission. (2014). *Tackling Early Leaving from Education and Training in Europe: Strategies, policies and measures*. Publications Office of the European Union.

European Commission. (2017). *Rethinking Language Education in Schools*. Publications Office of the European Union.

Firth, A. (1996). The discursive accomplishment of normality: On 'lingua franca' English and conversation analysis. *Journal of Pragmatics, 26*(2), 237–259. https://doi.org/10.1016/0378-2166(96)00014-8

Galloway, N. (2018). ELF and ELT teaching materials. In J. Jenkins, W. Baker, & M. Dewey (Eds.), *The Routledge handbook of English as a Lingua Franca* (pp. 468–480). Routledge.

García, O. (2019). Translanguaging: A coda to the code? *Classroom Discourse, 10*(3–4), 369–373.

Hülmbauer, C. (2007). 'You moved, aren't?'—The relationship between lexicogrammatical correctness and communicative effectiveness in English as a Lingua Franca. *Vienna English Working PaperS, 16*(2), 3–35.

Jenkins, J. (2015). Repositioning English and multilingualism in English as a lingua franca. *Englishes in Practice, 2*(3), 49–85.

Jenkins, J., Baker, W., & Dewey, M. (Eds.). (2018). *The Routledge handbook of English as a lingua franca*. Routledge.

Kordia, S. (2016). Reflective practices in transformative ELF-aware teacher education: Insights from the ELF-GATE project. Paper presented at the ELF9 International Conference, Lleida, Catalonia.

Kordia, S. (2019). ELF-aware teaching in practice: A teacher's perspective. In N. Sifakis & N. Tsantila (Eds.), *English as a Lingua Franca for EFL contexts* (pp. 53–71). Multilingual Matters.

Long, M. (2005). *Second language needs analysis*. Cambridge University Press.

Lopriore, L. (2016). ELF in teacher education. A way and ways. In L. Lopriore & E. Grazzi (Eds.), *Intercultural communication. New perspectives from ELF* (pp. 167–187). Roma Tre Press.

Lopriore, L. (Ed.). (2019). NEW ENGLISH/ES and ELF: Investigating teachers' attitudes and ELT in the Italian context. *RILA-Rassegna Italiana di Linguistica Applicata, Special Issue, 1*, 21–74.

Lopriore, L., & Vettorel, P. (2015). Promoting awareness of Englishes and ELF in the English language classroom. In H. Bowles & A. Cogo (Eds.), *International perspectives on Teaching English as a lingua franca* (pp. 13–34). Palgrave Macmillan.

Lopriore, L., Canelli, A., Fiasco, V., & Sperti, S. (2022). Unveiling Teachers' Personal Responses to Innovation. *Boğaziçi University Journal of Education, 39*(1), 219–242. https://doi.org/10.52597/buje.1227207

Neale, B. (2019). *What is qualitative longitudinal research?* Bloomsbury.

Ortega, L., & Iberry-Shea, G. (2005). Longitudinal research in second language acquisition: Recent trends and future directions. *Annual Review of Applied Linguistics, 25*, 26–45.

Rose, H., McKinley, J., & Galloway, N. (2021). Global englishes and language teaching: A review of pedagogical research. *Language Teaching, 54*(2), 157–189.

Schön, D. (1987). *Educating the reflective practitioner: Towards a new design for teaching and learning in the professions.* Jossey-Bass.

Seidlhofer, B. (2005). English as a lingua franca. *ELT Journal, 59*(4), 339–341. https://doi.org/10.1093/elt/cci064

Seidlhofer, B. (2011). *Understanding English as a lingua franca.* Oxford University Press.

Seidlhofer, B. (2018). Standard English and the dynamics of ELF variation. In J. Jenkins, W. Baker, & M. Dewey (Eds.), *The Routledge handbook of English as a lingua franca* (pp. 85–100). Routledge.

Sifakis, N., & Bayyurt, Y. (2018). ELF-aware teaching, learning and teacher development. In J. Jenkins, W. Baker, & M. Dewey (Eds.), *Handbook of English as a Lingua Franca* (pp. 456–467). Routledge.

Sifakis, N., Bayyurt, Y., Cavalheiro, L., Fountana, M., Lopriore, L., Tsagari, D., & Kordia, S. (2022). Developing English language teachers' and learners' ELF awareness: The background, design and impact of the ENRICH project's continuous professional development programme. *Journal of English as a Lingua Franca, 11*(2), 255–279.

Sifakis, N., & Kordia, S. (2019). Promoting transformative learning through English as a lingua franca: An empirical study. In T. Fleming, A. Kokkos, & F. Finnegan (Eds.), *European perspectives on transformation theory* (pp. 177–192). Palgrave McMillan.

Sifakis, N., & Kordia, S. (2020). Mezirow meets Kegan: Conceptual links and insights for English as a lingua franca teacher education. In A. Kokkos (Ed.), *Expanding transformation theory: Affinities between Jack Mezirow and emancipatory educationalists* (pp. 106–122). Routledge.

Sifakis, N., Lopriore, L., Dewey, M., Bayyurt, Y., Vettorel, P., Cavalheiro, L., Siqueira, D. S. P., & Kordia, S. (2018). ELF-awareness in ELT: Bringing together theory and practice. *Journal of English as a Lingua Franca (JELF), 7*(1), 155–209.

Sifakis, N. C. (2019). ELF awareness in English language teaching: Principles and processes. *Applied Linguistics, 40*(2), 288–306.

Sifakis, N. C., & Bayyurt, Y. (2015). Insights from ELF and WE in teacher training in Greece and Turkey. *World Englishes, 34*(3), 471–484.

Yasemin Bayyurt (Ph.D.) is professor of Applied Linguistics at Boğaziçi University, Istanbul, Türkiye. Her current research on English and English language teaching/learning focuses on disciplinary literacies and CLIL in K12 and higher education, ELF-awareness in English language teaching/learning; EMI in higher education. Her publications include articles in various high impact journals (e.g., Language Culture and Curriculum, Journal of Multilingual Multicultural Development, Journal of English for Academic Purposes, RELC), edited books and book chapters published by international publishers. Her edited/co-edited volumes include "Current Perspectives on Pedagogy for English as a Lingua Franca" (2015) by De Gruyter, "Bloomsbury World Englishes Volume 3: Pedagogies" (2021) by Bloomsbury, and "English as a Lingua Franca in the Language Classroom: Applying Theory to ELT Practice" (2024) by Routledge. Contact: bayyurty@bogazici.edu.tr.

Lucilla Lopriore holds a MA in TEFL from Reading University, UK, and completed her PhD in Italian L2 at Siena, Italy. Besides her activities as a schoolteacher (1976–2000), she qualified as Teacher educator in 1988 (UK) and in 1989 (U.S.A.) and has worked in teacher education programs in Italy and abroad. In 2001 she moved to university, teaching English Linguistics, from 2006 at Roma Tre University, where she retired as full professor in 2021. Among research projects she was part of ELLiE, ENRICH and eCOST. Her current research focuses on teacher education, disciplinary literacies, early language learning, ELF, and plurilingual literacies. A course-book writer, she has published mostly in the field of applied linguistics. Contact: lucilla.lopriore@uniroma3.it; lucilla.lopriore@gmail.com.

Stefania Kordia holds a PhD from the School of Humanities, Hellenic Open University, Greece, focusing on the transformative potential of teacher education that aims at empowering teachers to overcome native-speakerism and integrate English as a lingua franca in their teaching practices. She has participated in various research projects, including EU-funded ones, and she has published several research papers appearing in international refereed journals, edited collections and conference proceedings. Her research interests include the pedagogy of English as a lingua franca, teacher education, transformative learning and critical reflection. Contact: stefania.kordia@ac.eap.gr.

8 Affection as a Professional Knowledge in German as a Foreign Language Teachers' Initial Education in Rio de Janeiro

Mergenfel A. Vaz Ferreira and Anelise F. P. Gondar

1 Introduction

German language has been offered as a school subject in Brazil ever since German immigrants settled in parts of the states of Rio Grande do Sul, Santa Catarina and, to some extent, Paraná in the nineteenth century (Uphoff, 2011). Still, the command of the German language on Brazilian soil can be characterized by heterogeneity: in different parts of the country and in different periods of Brazilian history, explorers, merchants, businesspeople, farmers, and families settled, traded, and attempted to adapt to a new country and home while trying to preserve their (linguistic) ties to their *Vaterland*.

It was still in the nineteenth century that German began to be offered as a foreign language at one of the oldest and most prestigious public institutions in Brazil: *Colégio Pedro II*. Throughout the twentieth century, the offer of German language at schools in Brazil witnessed periods of expansion and periods of retraction, according to the different political and educational scenarios in the country throughout the

M. A. Vaz Ferreira (✉)
Faculdade de Letras, Setor de Alemão, Federal University of Rio de Janeiro, Rio de Janeiro, Brazil

A. F. P. Gondar
Department of Modern Foreign Languages, Federal Fluminense University, Niterói, Brazil
e-mail: anelisegondar@id.uff.br

© The Author(s), under exclusive license to Springer-Verlag GmbH, DE, part of Springer Nature 2024
P. Voerkel et al. (eds.), *Tools, Techniques and Strategies for Reflective Second & Foreign Language Teacher Education*,
https://doi.org/10.1007/978-3-662-68741-3_8

years. The creation of undergraduate courses (double degree in Portuguese-German) in all states of the federation and of *Goethe Institutes* (in the capital cities of Porto Alegre, Rio de Janeiro, São Paulo, Salvador, Curitiba, and Brasília), both of them in the past 60 years, expanded the access to German language in institutional spaces and contributed to the consolidation of the GFL profession.

Currently, teachers' initial education in German as a FL takes place in 17 higher education institutions spread throughout the Brazilian territory and has dedicated itself, for the most part, to teachers' training (the so-called 'licenciaturas') and to bachelor's degrees (the so-called 'bacharelados') (Voerkel, 2017).

In the State of Rio de Janeiro, which has a low presence of communities of German descent, the development of German language undergraduate courses has taken place over the last fifty years. In Rio de Janeiro, there are three public universities offering the Portuguese-German double major—two federal universities and one state university. The three universities have been historically involved in teachers' training (Voerkel, 2017) and their activities, some of them in cooperation with one another. This has contributed to the democratization of the wider community's access to learning German as a FL as well as in helping to constitute a professional profile for the German FL teacher, who's ready to work for free/commercial courses and in private schools.

Not only has there been a gradual advance in the dissemination of German courses, but there has also been an advancement of research on subjects related to teaching German as a FL. According to Araújo and Uphoff (2019), research in the field of German in Applied Linguistics has been advancing since the 1990s in key areas that are equally relevant to teaching practice: textbook usage in university-level FL education, curricula and language policies, in general concerning the promotion of the German language in Brazil, as well as the performance of other players (the Goethe Institutes and other cultural agencies, such as the local German consulates) in fostering the German language. Many studies are also devoted to sharing experiences gathered within the so-called 'teaching initiation programs' (*programas de iniciação científica*) and extension courses (*cursos de extensão*) (Idem: 279).

In previous research pieces we attempted to understand classrooms as multi-level learning spaces, in which students with different competencies in FL seek to improve their knowledge in a cooperative learning setting (Gondar & Ferreira, 2021), and also to investigate new perspectives on teacher professionalization (Gondar & Ferreira, 2020). This chapter, thus, aims to discuss the importance of affectivity in a teacher's initial education and in the professionalization process of future teachers in the context of undergraduate courses in Rio de Janeiro.

Many authors (Ribeiro & Jutras, 2022; Ribeiro, 2010; Carstensen et al., 2019, among others) have emphasized the need for undergraduate courses on teacher training to take knowledge and skills based on affectivity into consideration. These authors advocate that affectivity and emotions should be tackled in many subjects of undergraduate courses. The renowned Brazilian educator Paulo Freire (2002) considers affectivity to be an essential pedagogical pillar of the teaching experience, which would inform the pedagogical knowledge that is key to teachers' development: that of knowing how to do things 'o saber-fazer' (know-how) and that of knowing how to be a teacher 'o saber-ser' (Freire, 2002). In one of his masterpieces, 'Pedagogy of the Autonomy,' Freire (2002, pp. 39–41) calls for the teacher's reflexive posture as being a key element of his/her own and the pupils' autonomy. For him, teaching practices stemming from epistemological curiosity foster the connection between theory and practice, leading to the betterment of one's own pedagogical practice. For Paulo Freire (2002, pp. 138–143), affectivity is also a pillar of the teaching experience. This theoretical background leads us to the following research question: What is the relevance of the affective dimension in German as a FL teacher training? The chapter is structured as follows: First, we offer a brief and non-exhaustive presentation of the main features of GFL teacher training in Rio de Janeiro, then we move on to the discussion about so-called essential teaching knowledge and skills as explicated by specialists in the field of Education widely discussed in our teaching practice courses such as Tardif (2002), Perrenoud (2002), Saviani (2016), and Freire (2002). We argue in favor of the need to discuss affectivity in teacher training based on the idea that they make up an essential feature of GFL teachers' professional identity while they are still in their undergraduate courses. To underpin this argument, we turn to a survey conducted in 2019 with undergraduate students from both the Federal University of Rio de Janeiro (UFRJ) and the State University of Rio de Janeiro (UERJ). While aiming at understanding features related to professional identity building, we noticed that the respondents spontaneously mentioned several aspects related to what we interpret as 'socio-affective knowledge.' By returning to those responses in light of the above-mentioned authors, we came to the conclusion that they not only consider those socio-affective aspects they themselves mentioned as paramount to their education as GFL teachers, but they also understand those skills to be important in their own practice.

2 German Language Teacher Training in Rio de Janeiro - Brazil

The presence of the German language in Brazil dates back, in general, to the first territorial explorations in colonial Brazil as well as the presence of scholars and explorers in the imperial period (Montez, 2007; Sallas, 2010). However, the presence of the German language in Brazil is also largely due to immigration of German citizens from various regions of Germany to Brazil, an immigration that dates back 200 years, as well as more recent immigration in the twentieth century, motivated by the horrors of World War II (Kestler, 2005).

German language education can be thus historically found in two settings: One of them being that of official schools such as the federal primary and secondary school *Colégio Pedro II* in Rio de Janeiro in which German was one of the foreign languages taught to the Brazilian elite as to complement their humanistic education (Couto, 2012). The other one is that of community primary and secondary schools that were created in the nineteenth century in the southern states of Rio Grande do Sul, Santa Catarina, and Paraná to serve the local immigrant communities (Stanke & Bolacio, 2015).

In the State of Rio de Janeiro, which registers a smaller presence of German immigrants, German has historically not been part of primary and secondary school curricula. In the city of Rio de Janeiro, German as a FL is offered in three institutions of private education—namely, the *Escola Alemã Corcovado* (EAC), the *Escola Cruzeiro*, with two branches (*Centro* and *Jacarepaguá*), and the *Escola Suíço-Brasileira*—with German also being offered in bi-cultural schools, such as the *Lycée Moliére*. Also at the elementary school level, German is taught in three public elementary schools and one high school in the state of Rio (Godiva, 2020). In addition, German as a FL has been taught at the *Goethe Institut Rio de Janeiro* for nearly 60 years and the two major private language institutes, Baukurs (since 1978) and Instituto Cultural Germânico—ICG (since 1995). Together, therefore, we have an educational landscape that covers both primary and higher education as well as complementary education (through commercial courses) providing a relevant job market for future German teachers.

The double major undergraduate courses in Portuguese-German in Rio de Janeiro were created in the second half of the twentieth century in the state's capital, in Rio de Janeiro, following the same experience as in other parts of Brazil (Heise, 1994; Voerkel, 2021). Currently, teacher training in German as a FL takes place in the *Letras* institutes of the following universities: the Federal University of Rio de Janeiro (UFRJ), the Fluminense Federal University (UFF), and the State

University of Rio de Janeiro (UERJ). The course curricula of these three universities, with the exception of some subjects being taught only in some of them (such as 'Cultura Alemã', which is solely offered at UERJ), offer courses in German language and literature, Germanic philology, and courses in pedagogical practice. With the consolidation of the undergraduate courses throughout the 1980s and 1990s, these universities began to offer internship opportunities in their language courses aimed at the external community—this was the case at UFRJ, with the creation of the CLAC project (*Curso de Línguas Abertos às Comunidades*), also at UFF, with the PROLEM program (*Programa de Línguas Estrangeiras Modernas*) and finally at UERJ as well, with the LICOM project (*Línguas para a Comunidade*) (Stanke & Bolacio, 2015).

Faculty members from the three universities have been working in close cooperation for years in many research areas, be it regarding the choice of textbook to be adopted in the undergraduate courses in all three universities, joint activities and workshops within the scope of APA-Rio (Association of German Teachers of Rio de Janeiro) as well as efforts with the Secretary of State for Education to offer German as a FL in public state schools (Stanke & Bolacio, 2015).

The joint effort of the three universities' faculties in Rio de Janeiro in enhancing the pedagogical education of future teachers double majoring in Portuguese-German is widely presented and discussed among scholars of the field of German studies in Brazil (Meirelles, 2020; Gondar & Ferreira, 2020).

For the past five years, the authors of this chapter have been conducting research on the knowledge and skills that would be considered essential to the professionalization of future German teachers. If we assume that pedagogical and experiential knowledge development play a special part in defining the education of German language teachers, what would be the importance of affectivity and reflexivity in educational practice, and what place could this dimension effectively occupy in teacher training? This is the core question that leads us, in the next section of this chapter, to a brief overview of the literature on reflexive knowledge and affective practices based on Tardif (2002), Perrenoud (2000, 2002), Saviani (2016), and Freire (2002).

They highlight the importance of experiential knowledge, aimed at overcoming the challenges of countless orders in the complex routine of the classroom. This type of knowledge can cast a new light on the syllabi of undergraduate courses as it does also help students to understand that their experiential knowledge emerges from their accumulated experience in years of formal and informal learning and the dimension of affectivity they experienced as both learners and (soon to be) teachers. We argue that 'affective' knowledge can be linked to the perception of a teaching practice that is meaningful both to teachers as well as to students. Thus, the next section will set the theoretical foundation for the arguments that we put forward in this research: We will present theorizations on the 'essential knowledge/ skills of teachers, and further on we will discuss affectivity in the teaching-learning relationship in the context of German FL teachers' education based on the student's own point of view.

3 Theorizing: A Teacher's Essential Knowledge

Theorists of the Education field have written extensively on the topic of the so-called 'teacher knowledge' and its relevance to the advancement of what we call the development of teacher professionalization and teachers' identity.

Tardif (2002), a theorist dedicated to research on 'teaching knowledge,' draws on a sociological perspective to discuss the experience of work in the lives of individuals. When speaking of knowledge mobilized by teachers in their daily work practice, Tardif (2002) understands "knowledge" in "a broad sense, which encompasses the knowledge, competence, skills (or aptitudes), and attitudes of teachers, what was often called 'knowing,' both 'knowing how to do' and 'knowing how to be'" (Tardif, 2002, p. 60).

Tardif (2002) stresses three important dimensions that need to be taken into consideration while approaching teachers' professional knowledge: 'identity,' 'time,' and 'space.' The identity dimension involves a negotiation between what individuals make of themselves and how individuals are perceived by others, pointing out that jobs performed by people throughout their lives necessarily mark their identities, that is, in the author's words: "his identity carries the marks of his own activity, and a good part of his existence is characterized by his professional performance" (Tardif, 2002, p. 56). 'Time' is also an important factor since professional decisions involve experiences of individuals as students throughout their lives, skills learned during their undergraduate studies, and the competence acquired during their daily work as teachers.

The 'spatial' dimension of skills development is related to the institutional and informal learning environments in which teaching takes place—it has to do with places and spaces in which the teachers and students share their thoughts and attitudes. Tardif (2002) understands that the dimensions of space and time create situational experiences and that those are relevant for the creation of professional knowledge. The importance of space for practice in initial teacher education should be emphasized, given that many of the tasks required of the profession, and situations that teachers go through professionally, require knowledge, techniques, aptitudes, and attitudes that are often only gained from their experience in similar situations.

Still, according to Tardif (2002), teacher knowledge is complex and encompasses a great diversity of objects, issues, and problems, all directly or indirectly related to teaching practice. Thus, the teacher's professional knowledge, according to the researcher, plural and heterogeneous, involves various cognitive, methodological, and social factors, stemming from different sources. While collecting narratives of many teachers over the years, Tardif lists aspects such as knowledge of the subject and knowledge related to the planning and organization of classes, knowledge about materials and textbooks, and attitudes such as liking teaching, being able to motivate learners, and having creativity and imagination, all of which highlights the role of experience in building professional competence.

In his research and theories about the teaching profession and initial and continuing teacher education, Perrenoud (2000, 2002) opts for the concept of competencies to refer to teachers' aptitudes to

> face a multitude of analogous situations, mobilizing in a correct, fast, pertinent and creative way, multiple cognitive resources: knowledge, skills, micro-competencies, information, values, attitudes, perception schemes, evaluation and reasoning. (Perrenoud, 2002, p. 19).

For the author, a large part of these competencies would be developed along the teachers' daily practices, so they can be understood as "experiential knowledge" (Perrenoud, 2002, p. 19). However, he advocates the importance of developing a group of competencies during teachers' initial education. A problem identified by Perrenoud is that most initial teacher education courses do not base their programs on an empirical analysis regarding the skills and competencies needed in the daily lives of teachers. Instead, a good part of undergraduate course curricula focuses on (and are limited to) issues concerning the mastery of the content to be taught as well as pedagogy and didactic principles.

Still, with regard to the constitutive knowledge mobilized in teaching practice, Dermeval Saviani (2007, 2012, 2013, 2016) brings important contributions to this discussion. While recognizing the multifactorial, complex, and diverse nature of knowledge involved in educational practice, he defined certain common characteristics related to analytical procedures based not only on curriculum studies but also on formative processes in different spaces shared with colleagues and teachers in initial training. Those features led to the following knowledge categories (Saviani, 2016, pp. 65–66):

- attitudinal knowledge, which would be linked to behavioral and socio-emotional aspects, such as discipline, coherence, dialogue with learners, etc.
- critical-contextual knowledge, related to the socio-historical conditions of the context in which the teachers are inserted, and, therefore, a type of knowledge that contributes to tackling present and future needs of learners.
- specific knowledge, which would be linked to knowledge of the subjects and contents to be taught.
- pedagogical knowledge, mentioned by Saviani (2016, p. 66) as the knowledge linked to educational sciences and educational theories, that is, knowledge that relates directly to the teacher's work activities, such as planning and organizing classes, themes, contents and teaching materials, knowledge about teaching approaches and methodologies, among others.
- didactic-curricular knowledge, which would be linked to the knowledge that teachers should have about education guidelines in different spheres (federal, state, and municipal), also according to each level of education, in addition to the pedagogical projects of each school or institution (Saviani, 2016, pp. 65–66).

Among the essential knowledge for teachers highlighted by the authors mentioned so far, reflection seems to permeate different fields such as the "attitudinal knowledge," by Saviani (2016), the "identity" and "time" dimensions, postulated by Tardif (2002), considering in the "time" dimension the practical knowledge built from experience. This is a view that is similar to the position of Perrenoud (2002), when he points out experiential knowledge emerging from aspects such as attitudes, perception, and reasoning schemes. He sees them as competencies to be developed by the teacher. However, reflection as an attitude or fundamental knowledge for professional teaching appears more prominently in authors such as Donald Schön (1992) and Paulo Freire (1987).

Donald Schön mentions (1992, 2000) the importance of experience through the construct which he calls "knowledge in action." When considering the teacher's daily practice and its complex nature, often marked by unexpected or conflicting situations, the author highlights the "reflection in action" component as a valuable instrument in teaching practice, which needs to be systematically developed.

Freire goes further by adding "reflection" to the teacher's essential toolbox. He organically connects both the 'reflection' and the 'action' dimensions (1987). For him, the binomial 'action' and 'reflection' make up what he calls "praxis", which is the driving force for the transformation of the teacher's professional practice. Thought and reflection would thus be at the heart of the teacher's action. The reflective ability can be seen, therefore, as an important tool to be developed by teachers so that their knowledge can be better understood, mobilized, and transformed by them. This brief literature review on essential knowledge categories and competencies in teaching practices points to several common elements, perhaps the main one being the recognition of the complexity involved in daily teaching and the diversity of aspects teachers need to deal with: curricula, pedagogical projects, teaching materials, planning and methodologies, as well as critical-reflective tools that allow them to remake and rethink paths for the development of new understandings and new ways of knowing-how and knowing-how to be.

It is equally important to note the mismatch, in general terms, pointed out by the authors, between initial teacher training curricula and the needs commonly experienced in the day-to-day of the profession in schools and classrooms. In light of the above, there seem to be gaps and inconsistencies in training curricula as far as the teaching-learning of attitudinal or socio-emotional knowledge is concerned.

In the next section, therefore, we will dive more specifically into attitudinal or socio-emotional knowledge (Ribeiro & Jutras, 2022) and present Paulo Freire's always-sharp perception of the affective and reflexive dimensions of teaching-learning. It is with this magnifying glass that we will present and discuss the data generated in a survey we carried out with Portuguese-German undergraduates from two universities in Rio de Janeiro. The results reinforce the aspects that are dealt with here.

3.1 Affectivity as Teaching Knowledge

The importance of the affective dimension among several other aspects involved in teaching practice, more specifically in language teaching and learning, such as didactic and pedagogical aspects and the knowledge related to the contents to be taught, has been gaining more and more interest from researchers. In this sense, different authors highlight affect as essential for the building up of an educational relationship that enables and promotes the exchange of knowledge and the development of learners' knowledge. For Ribeiro and Jutras (2022, p. 39), this dimension would be linked not only to teachers' and students' attitudes and the relationships they establish among themselves, but also to the relationships they establish with subjects and their contents, as well as how they relate to the experiences of success and frustration in the teaching-learning process. In this way, it can be seen as the propeller of all processes connected to teaching and learning activities. In Moll's words (1999, p. 180): "the affective relationship enables the relationship with knowledge." Thus, it is evident that affectivity should occupy a constitutive space in teachers' initial formation.

In the attempt to inquire what place this dimension effectively occupies in teacher education, we first resort to Ribeiro and Jutras' (2022) study. In an analysis of different undergraduate curricula, they discovered that the affective component did not find a balanced place in comparison to other components, such as teaching content and issues of didactics and pedagogy (Ribeiro & Jutras, 2022, p. 40). However, the authors observe that affective aspects are still mentioned in official guidelines and documents for teacher training in Brazil. In the document *Referência para a formação de professores* (Brasil, 1999, p. 25), the importance of developing "cognitive, affective, physical, ethical, aesthetic, social insertion, and interpersonal relationship" skills in learners is highlighted. According to the same document, the affective relationships established in the teacher-learner dialogue play a fundamental role in creating the necessary ground for learning and for the social integration of students (Brasil, 1999, p. 27). Moreover, the affective dimension appears in different parts of the document. For example, it mentions "ethics" in the teaching-learning process, related to mutual respect, dialogue, solidarity, recognition, and respect for diversity, while also stating that "the adoption of a welcoming attitude towards students and their families, mutual respect and commitment to justice, dialogue, solidarity, and non-violence" (Brasil, 1999, p. 69).

Freire (1987, 1997, 2002) offers an indispensable contribution to the debate regarding social-affective-emotional knowledge and competencies in teacher practice. In Pedagogy of Autonomy (Freire, 2002), the author weaves several reflections on teaching practices, based on the assumption that teaching and learning are processes that irrevocably overlap and are imbricated in each other: One learns while teaching and teaches while learning.

For Freire, respect for the learner's autonomy is directly linked to the promotion of critical and ethical pedagogy and to respect for the other's dignity. It is in this sense that Freire stresses that an ethical pedagogical practice that respects the dignity and autonomy of learners must necessarily involve not only methodological rigor, and solid didactics and pedagogy, but above all, the awareness that all knowledge implies an equally important affective dimension. In the preface of his book, the educator Edina Oliveira tackles the necessary knowledge for educational practice and refers specifically to the knowledge that involves ethical rigorousness, which was also so dear to Paulo Freire:

> Like all other knowledge, this knowledge demands permanent action from the educator. It is in the loving coexistence with their students and in the curious and open posture that they assume and, at the same time, provokes them to assume themselves as social-historical-cultural subjects of the act of knowing, that the teacher can speak of respect for the dignity and autonomy of the learner. [...] The technical-scientific competence and the rigor that the teacher must not give up in the development of his

or her work are not incompatible with the loving care necessary for educational relationships (Oliveira, 2002, p. 7).

The teaching-learning practice demands the active participation of the subject in a "total, directive, political, ideological, gnoseological, pedagogical, aesthetic, and ethical experience in which beauty goes hand in hand with decency and seriousness" (Freire, 2002, p. 14). Among the qualities of the ethical and respectful practice of pedagogy, we highlight those related to the social and emotional aspects of the teaching practice and that, in a way, are in close dialogue with many of the qualities pointed out by future teachers, our undergraduate students who answered the questionnaire mentioned in this chapter.

One of the first qualities mentioned by Freire is humbleness, described as the teacher's virtue in recognizing that nobody knows everything, and nobody is a tabula rasa, that is, teachers need to show respect and listen to their learners. The author adds to the quality of humbleness the quality of loving-kindness, which has not only to do with the way students should be treated but, above all, should be constitutive to the very act of teaching-learning. In this sense, he considers that teaching means "being open to wishing others well," which is an act of courage stemming from both the students as well as the very educational practice (Freire, 2002, p. 72). Courage as a social-affective knowledge is related to the creation of an empowering learning environment that can gradually lead students to overcome negative emotions related to foreign language learning (Marx, 2020, p. 132). Another quality he mentions is tolerance, pointed out as the virtue that teaches us to live with what is different.

Humbleness, loving-kindness, courage, and tolerance are elements that are closely related to the affective characteristics of teacher know-how, as mentioned by the students, and shown in the following section.

4 What Undergraduate Students of German as a Foreign Language Say About Affectivity

In 2019 we conducted a survey aimed at investigating the professionalization processes of soon-to-be teachers of German as a foreign language enrolled in double major courses in Portuguese-German at two public universities in Rio de Janeiro. In general terms, the survey sought to collect information about the possibilities and challenges involved in the process of professionalization of teachers of German as an additional language, focusing on aspects that could affect the development of the professional self-image of these students (Gondar & Ferreira, 2020, 2021).

In this sense, the questionnaire addressed the following themes as possibly determining factors in the construction of the professional self-definition of German teachers in initial training:

(1) Their personal motivations for choosing the course,
(2) the subjects or academic activities during their initial training that contributed the most to the construction of their professionalization,
(3) their perception of the main characteristics or competencies they consider important for German teacher practice, and
(4) their main professional expectations as German teachers.

The questionnaire consisted of seven questions and was answered by students who had studied didactics and teaching practice or who had participated in projects focused on practical activities with German teaching. In all, 27 students of two undergraduate courses in Rio de Janeiro participated in the research. In previous articles (Gondar & Ferreira, 2020, 2021) we had focused on two topics: The professional self-definition of these teachers in training and the role of subjective theories on their professionalization process. The question of knowledge and characteristics pointed out by the students as fundamental to the profession of teaching German as an additional language had been mentioned a few times by the informants in the survey, but until now it had not been analyzed.

In general terms, the knowledge or competencies listed by the respondents of the questionnaire can be organized into three categories:

- one related to knowledge on contents and objects to be taught by German teachers in their daily practice, which was described by the respondents as knowledge of the German language and culture;
- didactic-pedagogical knowledge, which constitutes a sound command of different methodologies and ways of teaching to be able to reach as many students as possible and meet their needs;
- and last, knowledge such as "patience," "respect," "empathy," "care,"and "love," among others, which we identified as belonging to the socio-emotional sphere.

Our attention was drawn to the fact that knowledge related to didactics was mentioned by 19 of the 27 respondents. A few students justified their choice for these aspects, highlighting the difficulty that, in general, learning German represents for Brazilian learners. That difficulty would make knowledge about didactic choices essential, according to their point of view. However, although this aspect linked to the difficulty of learning the language can be associated with the need for further development of cognitive knowledge about the linguistic and cultural content of the German language, we were surprised that knowledge relating to an emotional dimension came second in the respondents' mentions: 16 out of 27 answers.

In this way, knowledge, or characteristics such as "like what you do," "dedication," "patience," "know how to listen to students and co-workers," "empathy," and "sensitivity" were very recurrent answers in the questionnaire.

More than 50% of the interviewees, therefore, made spontaneous references to affective elements with a normative character, that is, a social-affective knowledge that is important to 'teaching knowledge.' The spontaneous references to socio-affective elements are important indications of two phenomena: (1) the concrete identification of these knowledge types in their training, demonstrating that in some way those have contributed to student learning up to that point, and (2) that these socio-affective features need to be part of the teaching practice of trained professionals.

5 Final Considerations

The present chapter aimed at theoretically discussing socio-affective knowledge as teaching knowledge based on the actuality of the theme, both in specialized literature and in the perception of Portuguese-German undergraduates. Assuming that affectivity is a relevant aspect of educational practice, we sought to try to identify what place this dimension effectively occupies in teacher training.

To this end, we briefly presented teacher education in the state of Rio de Janeiro, arguing that, although the region does not concentrate on the largest German immigrant colonies in Brazil, it still stands out as a region of relevant training and professional practice. We also discussed authors who have addressed the essential knowledge to the teaching profession, with emphasis on attitudinal knowledge and practical knowledge coming from experience. The Freirean understanding of pedagogic reflection helped us to address various conceptions of knowledge. In order to deepen the discussion and to introduce the central argument of this article, we conducted a brief and non-exhaustive literature review in the area of Education that deals with teacher knowledge. This chapter's central argument is that social-affective knowledge has an undeniable relevance in the initial educational experience of German language teachers. This supposition is confirmed by the occurrence of affective aspects voiced in the survey about professional identity conducted by the authors and applied to sixth, seventh, and eighth-semester students from two public universities in the state of Rio de Janeiro.

We conclude that the empirical elements offered by the undergraduates of the two public universities that participated in the research largely corroborate the argument that affective knowledge is constitutive to the formation of professional competence.

We have seen that, for the students, issues such as 'patience,' 'empathy,' 'love,' and 'sensitivity' were important throughout their initial training and are also paramount to 'teaching knowledge' that will guide their future professional practice.

In this chapter, we aimed thus at showing that theoretical arguments, as well as empirical evidence, reaffirm the need to value affective competencies as an essential component of the development of know-how within the daily practice of teachers of German as a Foreign Language.

References

Araújo, F. R., & Uphoff, D. (2019). Historiografia de estudos brasileiros sobre o ensino-aprendizagem de alemão como língua estrangeira. In D. Uphoff, L. Leipnitz, P. C. C. Arantes, & R. C. Pereira (Eds.), *Alemão em contexto universitário: ensino, pesquisa e extensão* (pp. 79–102). Humanitas.

Brasil. (1999). *Secretaria de Educação Fundamental. Referenciais para formação de Professores*. MEC

Carstensen, B., Köller, M., & Klusmann, U. (2019). Förderung sozial-emotionaler Kompetenz von angehenden Lehrkräften. Konzeption und Evaluation eines Trainingsprogramms. *Zeitschrift für Entwicklungspsychologie und Pädagogische Psychologie, 51*(1), 1–15.

Couto, L. C. (2012). Sobrevoo pela História do Ensino de Alemão-LE no Brasil. *Revista HELB*. Available at: http://www.helb.org.br/index.php/revista-helb/ano-6-no-6-12012/199-sobrevoo-pela-historia-do-ensino-de-alemao-le-no-brasil. Last access: 04.03.2023.

Freire, P. (1987). *Pedagogia do oprimido* (17th ed.). Paz e Terra.

Freire, P. (1997). *Professora sim, tia não: Cartas a quem ousa ensinar*. Olho d'Água.

Freire, P. (2002). *Pedagogia da autonomia: saberes necessários à prática educativa* (18th ed.). Paz e Terra.

Godiva, S. (2020). Ações glotopolíticas para o ensino de alemão na rede pública do Rio de Janeiro. In D. Daher, C. Maria, T. Pereira, & M. Savedra (Eds.), *O ensino plurilíngue na escola pública: Desafios em tempos de globalização*. Editorarte.

Gondar, A., & Ferreira, M. A. V. (2020). Herausforderungen der Professionsbildung angehender DaF-Lehrerinnen und -Lehrer in Rio de Janeiro: Bestandsaufnahme auf der Grundlage subjektiver Theorien und Aussichten für die Forschung. *InfoDaF, 47*, 1–16.

Gondar, A. F. P., & Ferreira, M. V. (2021). Formação docente e autodefinição profissional de formandos em ensino de alemão como língua adicional no Rio de Janeiro. *DELTA: Documentação E Estudos Em Linguística Teórica E Aplicada, 36*(2), 1–25.

Heise, E. (1994). Língua e Literatura Alemã. *Estudos Avançados, 8*(22), 463–466. Available at: http://www.scielo.br/pdf/ea/v8n22/65.pdf

Kestler, I. (2005). A Literatura em Língua Alemã e o período do Exílio (1933-1945): a produção literária, a experiência do exílio e a presença de exilados de fala alemã no Brasil. *Itinerários, Araraquara, 23*, 115–135.

Marx, N. (2020). Positive Psychologie und die Fremdsprachendidaktiken. In E. Burwitz-Melzer, C. Riemer, & L. Schmelter (Eds.), *Affektiv-emotionale Dimensionen beim Lehren und Lernen von Fremd- und Zweitsprachen. Arbeitspapiere der 40. Frühjahrskonferenz zur Erforschung des Fremdsprachenunterrichts* (pp. 132–144). Narr.

Meirelles, C. (2020). DACH-Prinzip e pluricentrismo na formação de professores de alemão no estado do Rio de Janeiro. Dissertação (Mestrado em Estudos de Linguagem) - Instituto de Letras. Universidade Federal Fluminense.

Moll, J. (1999). La dimension affective dans la formation des adultes. In G. Chappaz (Ed.), *La dimension affective dans l'apprentissage et la formation* (pp. 103–130). SFPUNAPEC.

Montez, L. (2007). O Brasil para os europeus. Três narrativas de viajantes germânicos no Rio de Janeiro entre os séculos XVIII e XIX. In L. M. C. Gazzaneo (org.), *Espacialização, Patrimônio e Sociedade* (pp. 107–123). Editora da UFRJ.

Oliveira, E. (2002). Prefácio. In P. Freire (Ed.), *Pedagogia da autonomia: saberes necessários à prática educativa* (18th ed.). Paz e Terra.

Perrenoud, P. (2000). *10 novas competências para ensinar*. Artmed.

Perrenoud, P. (2002). A formação dos professores no séc. XXI. In P. Perrenoud, M. G. Thurler, L. de Macedo, N. J. Machado, & C. D. Alessandrini (Eds.), *As competências para ensinar no século XXI: a formação dos professores e o desafio da avaliação* (pp. 11–27). Artmed Editora.

Ribeiro, M. L. (2010). A afetividade na relação educativa. *Estudos de Psicologia. Campinas, 27*(3), 403–412.

Ribeiro, M. L., & Jutras, F. (2022). Representações sociais de professores sobre afetividade. *Estudos De Psicologia, 23*(1).

Sallas, A. L. F. (2010). Narrativas e imagens dos viajantes alemães no Brasil do século XIX: a construção do imaginário sobre os povos indígenas, a história e a nação. *Hist. cienc. saude-Manguinhos, 17*(2), 415–435.

Saviani, D. (2007). *Educação: do senso comum à consciência filosófica* (17th ed.). Autores Associados.

Saviani, D. (2012). *Escola e Democracia* (42nd ed.). Autores Associados.

Saviani, D. (2013). *Pedagogia Histórico-Crítica: primeiras aproximações* (11th ed.). Autores Associados.

Saviani, D. (2016). Educação Escolar, Currículo e Sociedade: O Problema da Base Nacional Comum Curricular. *Movimento – Revista de Educação*, 54–84.

Schön, D. A. (1992). Formar professores como profissionais reflexivos. In A. Nóvoa (Ed.), *Os professores e sua formação*. Dom Quixote.

Schön, D. A. (2000). *Educando o Profissional Reflexivo: um novo design para o ensino e a aprendizagem*. Trad. Roberto Cataldo Costa. Artmed.

Stanke, R. S., & Bolacio, E. S. A. (2015). O Ensino de Alemão no Ambiente Escolar e a Formação de Professores. In H. P. E. Galle & V. S. Pereira (Eds.), *Anais do 1° Congresso da Associação Brasileira de Estudos Germanísticos (ABEG) 09-11 de novembro 2015 – USP São Paulo*. ABEG. http://germanistik-brasil.org.br/wp-content/uploads/2016/05/Stanke-Bolacio1.pdf

Tardif, M. (2002). *Saberes docentes e formação profissional*. Vozes.

Uphoff, D. (2011). Uma pequena história do ensino de alemão no Brasil. In R. Bohunovsky (Ed.), *Ensinar alemão no Brasil: contextos e conteúdos* (1st ed., pp. 13–30). Ed. UPPR.

Voerkel, P. (2017). *Deutsch als Chance: Ausbildung, Qualifikation und Verbleib von Absolventen brasilianischer Deutschstudiengänge.* Friedrich-Schiller-Universität Jena.

Voerkel, P. (2021). Zu Entstehung und Entwicklung der Deutschstudiengänge in Brasilien. In P. Voerkel, H. D. Gruhn, & D. Uphoff (Eds.), *Germanistik in Lateinamerika. Entwicklungen und Tendenzen* (pp. 191–218). Universitätsverlag.

Mergenfel A. Vaz Ferreira has been an Associate Professor of German Language at the Federal University of Rio de Janeiro since 2011. Between September 2022 and July 2023, she was a Visiting Professor at the Friedrich Schiller Universität Jena with the German Academic Exchange Service (DAAD). She holds a master's and PhD in Language Studies from the Pontifical Catholic University of Rio de Janeiro and her main areas of interest are the processes of teaching and learning additional languages/cultures, focusing mainly on the education of teacher's additional languages and didactic approaches for additional languages from a critical and decolonial perspective. Contact: megvazferreira@letras.ufrj.br.

Anelise F.P. Gondar is an Assistant Professor of German Language at the Federal Fluminense University in Niterói, Rio de Janeiro. She studied Political Science and Education at the University of Heidelberg (2008) and completed the double degree 'Especialização em Ensino de Alemão' from the Universities of Kassel and UFBA (2012) and the German Teacher Training ("Grünes Diplom") from the Goethe Institut. She completed her Ph.D. in International Politics in 2018 at PUC-Rio on the topic of 'Women's Colonial Schools in Germany'. Her main areas of work include teacher training in German as a Foreign Language, language mediation and German colonialism. Contact: anelisegondar@id.uff.br.

Teachers as Researchers: Voices from Experts

Sonja Brunsmeier

1 Introduction

In his influential meta-study, Hattie (2012, p. 22) pointed out the importance of the teacher: they have "the most powerful influence in learning." Hence, the education of excellent teachers can be regarded as a major aspect for quality teaching. In Germany, the *Qualitätsoffensive LehrerInnenbildung*, which was launched by the Federal Ministry of Education and Research in 2015, as well as recently published research findings (e.g., Diehr, 2018; Livingston & Assunção Flores, 2017) as well as conferences (e.g., annual conferences organized by the Association for Teacher Education in Europe) indicate that the necessity to look at teacher education in order to ensure good quality in teacher education has been noticed. Nevertheless, the discussion about what the characteristics of "good" primary English as a foreign language (EFL) teacher are, as well as about which practices, concepts, and ideas are needed in high-quality teacher training prevail (e.g., Caspari & Grünewald, 2022). On the basis of comprehensive empirical evidence as well as the insights of the interview study, this chapter intends to look at the suitability and effectiveness of pre-service teacher instruction, existing concepts and models, and provide suggestions for developing these further.

S. Brunsmeier (✉)
University of Passau, Passau, Germany
e-mail: Sonja.Brunsmeier@uni-passau.de

© The Author(s), under exclusive license to Springer-Verlag GmbH, DE, part of Springer Nature 2024
P. Voerkel et al. (eds.), *Tools, Techniques and Strategies for Reflective Second & Foreign Language Teacher Education*,
https://doi.org/10.1007/978-3-662-68741-3_9

2 Relevance of Teacher Training

This chapter concentrates on pre-service teacher education at the university level in the subject of English in primary schools. As the *lingua franca*, English is of particular importance in today's globalized world, and the positive effects of starting to learn a foreign language (FL) early have been shown in several studies (e.g., BIG-Kreis, 2015; Edelenbos et al., 2006). The report "Languages in Education and Training" shows that children start learning a FL in Europe at the average age of 7.7 years (European Commission, 2014). According to the "Foreign Language Learning Statistics," 99–100% of all pupils opt for English as their first FL (Eurostat, 2016). In Germany, 15 out of the 16 federal states teach EFL as a mandatory subject in primary school.

2.1 The Importance of Subject-Specific Teacher Education

Several researchers have identified a research gap in FL education and an even larger gap in the area of EFL education (Wilden & Porsch, 2017). In the European context, neither of the two important European documents, the "European Portfolio of Language Teacher Education" (Kelly & Grenfell, 2004) or the "European Portfolio of Student Teachers of Languages" (Newby et al., 2007), address the specific requirements for primary EFL teachers. By taking a closer look at the situation between individual countries within Europe, differences with regard to standards and recommendations for teacher education can be noticed: In contrast to other European countries, Germany has already defined standards for quality in teacher education (KMK, 2019). The standards describe requirements for the actions of teachers. They refer to competencies and, thus, to abilities, skills, and attitudes that a teacher should have in order to (re)act professionally in daily school life. Professional action also includes the competence to cooperate with colleagues and with other professions and institutions. In concrete terms, competencies are formulated for teaching, educating, assessing, and innovating. These different competencies must be acquired during teacher training (KMK, 2019). Moreover, individual German associations suggest school and subject specific teacher competencies (Deutscher Anglistenverband und Deutsche Gesellschaft für Amerikastudien, 2009; BIG-Kreis, 2007). The exemplarily aforementioned country-specific documents support the idea that it is important to conceptualize teacher education in a subject specific manner.

2.2 The Importance of High-Quality University Education

In teacher education, professional development is understood as the development of "an individual's skills, knowledge, expertise and other characteristics as a teacher" (OECD, 2009, p. 49). The conveyance of knowledge is necessary since it forms the basis for reflection upon practical experience. However, knowledge does not automatically transfer into professional actions in the classroom (Legutke, 2008, p. 19). This fact explains why the theory-practice rationale is a much-discussed issue in the context of pre-service teacher education at universities. Different seminar concepts integrate theory and practice into university courses. In the following paragraphs, three seminar concepts are described in greater detail (e.g., Dausend, 2017): (A) microteaching, (B) self-experience, and (C) teaching videos. (A) Microteaching can be very effective in teacher education for the acquisition of teaching skills and the development of favorable attitudes towards teaching in a relatively short amount of time. (B) Self-experience puts the individual experiences of students in the center. This includes the experience and reflection on different teaching situations in relation to theory. (C) Watching and working with videotaped primary EFL lessons in university lectures, seminars, and tutorials increases subject specific knowledge and can serve as a reflective tool. All three outlined seminar concepts emphasize that teacher development

> is not viewed as translating knowledge and theories into practice but rather as constructing new knowledge and theory through participating in specific social contexts and engaging in particular types of activities and processes. This (…) is the source of teachers' practices and understandings (Burns & Richards, 2009, p. 4).

In this respect, classroom action research plays an important role because this approach views teachers as agents (Burns, 2009, p. 116). It provides teachers with the opportunity to explore their own teaching and learning contexts and directly change and improve aspects in their particular situations. This means that introducing and supporting pre-service teachers at the university level in conducting action research projects (e.g., during their internships at schools) allows them to implement their knowledge and expertise from their studies immediately (Rossa, 2017, p. 199). Hence, "one benefit of action research is that teachers become able to connect theoretical and practical aspects of their education in a meaningful way" (Benitt, 2017, p. 134). In this way, 'in-service as well as pre-service teachers can learn from action research in various ways and on different levels' (Benitt ibid.: p. 129). Seminar concepts that are subject-specific (e.g., primary EFL teachers) and research oriented (e.g., allowing pre-service teachers to conduct their own research) are needed in professional pre-service teacher education.

2.3 The Importance of Instructors in Teacher Education

The constitutional principle of academic freedom includes the freedom of teaching. This principle entails the right for university instructors to determine the content of and methodological approaches within their classes. As previous research (e.g., Oleson & Hora, 2014) has shown, several factors—ranging from beliefs, professional knowledge, and expertise across knowledge of the subject matter to individual characteristics, institutional culture, and local organizational factors—are interdependent and influence how instructors plan and teach their classes at the university. Hence, it is of interest to understand how instructors conceptualize their classes for pre-service teacher education and why they do so.

3 Research Questions

The results published in this chapter are part of a larger research project which aims to develop, implement, and evaluate subject-specific teaching concepts for the education of pre-service primary EFL teachers. The overall aim of the research project is to provide a model for teaching approaches in teacher education in order to ensure a high-quality education of pre-service teachers.

The focus of this chapter lies on the instructors and their everyday pre-service teacher practices as well as their ideas on the education of pre-service teachers. With the help of problem-centered interviews, daily practices, opinions, and visions on the education of pre-service teachers in the subject of English in a German university context are explored. These perspectives provide valuable insights into the education of primary EFL teacher in one particular context and aim to answer the following two research questions:

R1: What characterizes a "good" primary EFL teacher?
R2: What practices, concepts, and ideas are suitable for primary EFL pre-service teacher education?

The results of this case study portray characteristics that an ideal primary EFL teacher should possess and deduce implications for seminar concepts in primary

EFL pre-service teacher education, which will guarantee high quality in teacher education.

4 Materials and Methods

At this current stage of knowledge, an explorative and qualitative study provides insights into everyday teaching practices in pre-service teacher education and supports the finding of solutions for the conceptualization of seminar concepts for this particular target group. For this purpose, one particular context (i.e., a German university that is specialized on teacher education) is investigated (= case study).

Within this case study, semi-structured expert interviews (Richards, 2009, p. 185) were conducted as a preliminary study. Problem-centered interviews were chosen because they allow focus on the participants (i.e., stakeholders at the German university specializing in teacher education) and how they experience and interact with a phenomenon (i.e., teaching pre-service teachers) at a given point in time and in a particular context (i.e., German university specializing in teacher education). This chapter presents the results of the preliminary interview study.

4.1 Context and Participants

The interviews were conducted at one of the six Universities of Education in Germany. The six Universities of Education (*Pädagogische Hochschulen*) are all located in the state of Baden-Württemberg. They concentrate on educational science issues both in research and teaching. The university trains educators for primary schools, general secondary schools (*Hauptschule*), middle-ranking secondary schools (*Realschule*), and special schools. Practical experiences (such as a 6-month-school internship) are part and parcel of teacher education. These Universities of Education offer doctoral and post-doctoral degrees and are, therefore, on a par with full universities.

The interviewed cohort comprised the university's president, vice presidents, the study's dean, the institute's director, and the head of the English department, as well as several professors and lecturers from the English department. Since the university specializes in teacher education, all of the 13 interviewees can be considered experts. Their context specific insights, their professional knowledge, and their everyday experience reveal how they go about their everyday teaching practices and would go about the education of well-qualified pre-service teachers (i.e., their visions regarding pre-service teacher education). The semi-structured expert interviews were conducted between November, 2018 and April, 2019. Since the experts and the interviewer share the same scientific background and knowledge about the relevant system, a high level of motivation on the part of the experts to participate in the interview was noticeable. Additionally, "the professionalism of people familiar with being in the public eye; silent awareness of the scientific and/ or political relevance of their field of activity (…); the desire to help 'make a difference', professional curiosity about the topic and field of research; an interest in sharing one's thoughts and ideas with an external expert" (Bogner et al., 2009, p. 2) led to smooth and thought-provoking conversations.

4.2 Instruments

The semi-structured expert interviews were based on two different interview guides: one for participants from the management level (university's president, vice presidents, the study's dean, the institute's director) and one for interviewees from the English department (head of the English department, professors, and lecturers). Both interview guides contained more or less similar key topics that were addressed in the conversations and helped to structure the talks. The interview guide for participants from the management level focused more on political and structural issues of teacher education, while the interview guide for the English department additionally asked for subject specific aspects in educating future language teachers. The questions were formulated in a way that the respondent had enough freedom to answer with whatever was important to them, giving them the feeling that they 'participated in a conversation with a purpose' (Richards, 2009, p. 196)—in this case on the issue of educating well-qualified pre-service teachers at a university that is specialized on teacher education.

4.3 Data Analysis

The different stakeholders from the university were asked to share their opinions, experiences, and visions with regard to primary EFL pre-service teacher education. Hence, the semi-structured interviews captured the diverse perspectives of the experts in the field of teacher education. To elucidate these perspectives, the audio recordings were first transcribed, anonymized, and then analyzed using Qualitative Content Analysis (Mayring, 2014). The Qualitative Content Analysis is a systematic qualitative-oriented text analysis procedure that is bound to the concrete material. This method allows researchers to reconstruct the subjective views and

Table 9.1 Overview of categories

Category	Subcategory
Teacher competencies	General competencies
	Subject-specific competencies
Pre-service teacher education	Structure
	Teaching practices
	Role of research

opinions of the experts. Five deductive categories were derived from the interview guidelines and formulated prior to the analysis (see Table 9.1).During the process of coding, the answers of the experts were clustered according to the topics they addressed. This way inductive categories were derived from the material itself and added to the category system. To ensure reliability of the results, a second person also coded the data (Mayring & Fenzl, 2019, pp. 636–637).

5 Results

The results from the diverse perspectives and experiences of the experts allow us to deduce (1) characteristics that an ideal primary EFL teacher should possess, as well as (2) practices, concepts and ideas for pre-service teacher education (see Fig. 9.1). The two areas will be supported with statements from the experts.

(1) *Characteristics of a "good" teacher*

According to the experts, a "good" teacher should generally possess the following:

- content knowledge (*Fachwissen*),
- pedagogical content knowledge (*Fachdidaktisches Wissen*),
- learner orientation, and
- reflective competence.

Furthermore, a "good" primary EFL teacher needs

- to know specifics of different age groups, and
- to speak English fluently.

These characteristics will be further explained in the following section and supported with quotations from the interviews.

The experts consider *content knowledge (Fachwissen)* as a fundamental basis in pre-service teacher education (04_E_Z.8). Additionally, the experts emphasize the importance of pedagogical content knowledge (*Fachdidaktik*) (12_A_Z.2).

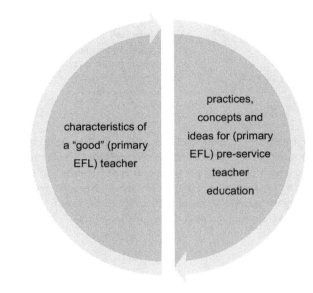

Fig. 9.1 Overview of results

Therefore, it is considered of vital importance to teach content knowledge in direct relation to the concrete classroom (06_A_Z.2). Furthermore, "primary teacher education means to take the future classroom that the pre-service teachers will be working in, as a concrete starting point from which more abstract concepts and contents can be taught, understood, and reflected" (07_A_Z.50). Moreover, the experts discuss the interconnectedness of different areas:

> Profession-oriented primary teacher education involves the profound conveyance of content knowledge, pedagogical content knowledge, educational science and integration of reflective training phases (school internships) – keeping in mind that our future primary teachers have to take care of individual differences in their classrooms – ranging from children with special educational needs to highly gifted children (12_A_Z.12).

According to this statement, they weigh and value the various fields of primary EFL pre-service teacher education differently: "The three fields language competence, content knowledge, and pedagogical content knowledge form the basis in foreign language teacher education. But in my eyes the area of pedagogical content knowledge is most important in primary teacher education" (01_E_Z.10). Since "teachers teach children and not subjects" (03_A_Z.4), the aspect of *learner-orientation* is of vital importance. By bringing in content and pedagogical content knowledge in relation to the context (i.e., the classroom setting, individual learners), teachers can design and teach topics, tasks, and the language in an engaging way (03_A_Z.31 and 07_A_Z.2), while respecting and valuing individual differences in a classroom (04_E_Z.2). Therefore, teachers need *reflective competence*. Self-reflection is seen as a prerequisite for any teacher: "This means that he (…) constantly monitors and adjusts his teaching to the setting" (12_A_Z.2) and "is able to go back and forth between theory and practice and vice versa" (04_E_Z.8).

Additionally, a "good" primary EFL teacher needs to know about *age-group specifics*. This background entails knowledge about how children learn language and which methodology is suitable to do so (04_E_Z.2). The majority of experts agree that primary EFL teachers need *to speak English fluently* (11_E_Z.4). Furthermore, they "need to adjust their language to the language level of the children" (07_A_Z.2).

(2) **Practices, concepts, and ideas for primary EFL pre-service teacher education**

According to the interviewed experts at the university, subject-specific teacher education should

- allow for the further development of FL competence,
- convey pedagogical content knowledge,
- integrate knowledge from different fields (i.e., from subject-specific to general pedagogical knowledge), and
- offer teaching practice (i.e., school internships).

Research-led teaching concepts

- support a reflective attitude,
- involve students, and
- lead to a gain in knowledge.

The above-mentioned features of pre-service teacher education will be further explained in the following paragraphs and supported by the voices of the experts.

"I think it's important, obviously, that we train them to a high enough level in their language knowledge. We train them to practice their language to raise it to a high enough level so they have knowledge, enough knowledge in their language" (02_E_Z.12-14). This quote reveals that instructors at the university see students' *further development of FL competence* as a central part of EFL teacher education. Another instructor explains that the integration of language practice in EFL teacher education is a particular strength of universities of education (i.e., German universities that are specialized in teacher education):

> By looking at the history of English, language practice has been treated as an orphan. In contrast to the universities that I have studied and worked at, the integration of language practice is a unique feature offered by universities of education. I do personally consider language practice as a key feature in foreign language teacher education – especially for primary EFL students (01_E_Z.16).

In EFL teacher education, students need to know how they can use their own language competence to develop the language competence of the children in their future classrooms. I.e., future teachers need *pedagogical content knowledge*:

> And also that we teach them how children learn and how children specifically learn languages, so that they can use that knowledge to develop appropriate activities to do with the children in the classroom and that the activities are appropriate for the children's age so they know something about child development and child psychology and that kind of thing I think is important (02_E_Z.4).

It becomes obvious that content, knowledge, and language should go hand in hand in teacher education: "As an instructor of teaching methods I consider it as important to discuss content knowledge in light of teaching and learning aspects. Actually, these cannot be separated" (06_A_Z.10). It is exactly this *interplay of knowledge from different fields (i.e., from subject-specific to general pedagogical knowledge)* that is seen as a particular strength of the universities of education (09_A&E_Z. 18):

> I think that teacher education needs to look at various fields. University courses need to be filled with information from, for example, pedagogical content knowledge and educational and psychological science. Lessons in school can only be planned when we also have our children in mind. (..) We need holistic approaches to help our student teachers to answer the question: What makes my teaching successful? (07_A_Z.4).

This approach allows teachers "to link theory and practice in an accessible and professional way" (10_E_Z.36). Especially, the *teaching practice within the study programme* is considered as a valuable experience to link theory and practice: "Teaching is a skill that needs practice. This is why I think that our 6-month internship is a really good idea. After our students have spent 6 months in school, they come back as a different person. When they then continue their studies, they are able to see and discuss things differently" (11_E_Z.48). Nevertheless, the experts also point out room for development with regard to how the mandatory 6-month internship could and should be integrated in the study agenda: "The interplay of theory and practice during the internships needs more profound guidance. That is, we should think about how the reflection of teaching practice can become professional and which roles the schools and we play in that particular process" (12_A_Z.4).

The experts discuss several advantages and challenges of research-based teaching concepts in pre-service teacher education. First and foremost, the majority of the participants said that "research-based teaching and learning means to *develop a reflective and critical attitude*" (01_E_Z.76). Beyond this idea, the experts hope that the pre-service teachers will also profit from this attitude later in their teaching: "It means thinking of ways to teach English in schools and thinking of different ways to teach it, trying them out and then analyzing how it went, and what happened, and what you have to change for next time" (02_E_Z.90). By *engaging the students in research* via, for example, little research projects in the context of the Bachelor and/or Master thesis (03_A_Z.14), formulating individual research questions and thinking about (methodological) ways to find an answer to these (06_A_Z.50) and/or reading published research findings (10_E_Z.23), they can learn about research's importance and discover its relevance for teaching practice also leading *"to a gain in knowledge"* (08_E_Z.74).

6 Discussion, Conclusion, and Implications

The voices of the experts underline the important role of a teacher and his responsibilities in the teaching and learning processes. Since previous research (e.g., Borg et al., 2014; Crandall & Christison, 2016, p. 7) has shown that changes in beliefs of teachers are most likely brought about during the pre-service phase, the necessity of which is underlined by identifying factors that allow for development of well-qualified primary EFL teachers at the university level. By sharing insights from their daily practices, the experts shed light on important characteristics of a "good" primary EFL teacher as well as key principles in pre-service primary EFL teacher education at their university. In the following section, results from the interviews are discussed and contrasted and/or aligned to previous research results. Beyond this, conclusions and implications for the organization and structure of academic settings are given (these are indicated by a small square ☐).

(A) Teachers matter because …

their competence influences the quality of teaching (Hattie, 2012). The necessity of high standards in teacher education programs is expressed by all the interviewees.

Therefore, the experts first of all think about competencies that a primary EFL teacher should possess and then continue to discuss which role subject-specific teaching concepts could play in teacher education at universities. Thereby, it is especially the question of how to link the development of subject-specific knowledge with practical experience—and vice versa—that continues to prevail the discussion on how to best structure and conduct the academic phase of teacher education (Legutke et al., 2022, p. 3).

☐ More research in and on primary EFL pre-service teacher education is needed (Legutke & Schart, 2016; Wilden & Porsch, 2017). On the basis of comprehensive empirical evidence, the suitability and effectiveness of pre-service teacher instruction can then be evaluated, existing concepts and models can be further developed, and specific standards for teacher education formulated.

(B) A "good" primary EFL teacher needs to ...

have general competencies as well as subject-specific competencies. This answer is in line with other researchers (e.g., Hoinkes & Weigand, 2016; Nunan, 2016). Irrespective of the subject, the experts name general competencies that primary EFL teachers need to have: they should know about teaching and learning processes (content knowledge), be experts on their contexts (i.e. the pupils in their classroom), have a methodological repertoire (pedagogical content knowledge), be motivated and enthusiastic about their job (teacher personality), and constantly reflect on what they do and—if necessary—change their teaching accordingly (reflective competence) (Kohonen, 2015). Moreover, a primary EFL teacher needs subject-specific competencies (Bondi & Poppi, 2007; Kirchhoff, 2016). One needs to have good language competence and know how to adapt it to the particular group of learners. Additionally, one must have linguistics, cultural and literary knowledge, and know about age-group specifics (e.g., how young children learn FLs). But what makes a "good" EFL teacher continues to be critically discussed and still needs further research. As Gerlach (2022) points out "additional conceptual and empirical approaches are necessary in order to better understand the complex construct of the 'foreign language teacher'" (p. 29).

☐ The question that arises is how pre-service teachers can be equipped with general competencies as well as subject-specific competencies during the course of their studies. Students at university need to receive content knowledge in general classes (e.g., psychology and educational science) as well as subject-specific content knowledge in their chosen subjects (e.g., English, Math, etc.). This content knowledge should then be taught, analyzed, and reflected on in relation to pedagogical content knowledge and the concrete classroom context. This way, the students' understanding and application of theory to practice (and vice versa) is supported. If university subjects like psychology, etc. work closely together with subjects like English, etc., cross-connections (e.g., developmental prerequisites and their influence in learning) can be made, and students can be encouraged to link information that they have learned.

(C) Universities' teacher education has the responsibility to ...

educate highly qualified teachers. The experts discussed how teaching and learning does and/or could take place in pre-service teacher training programs at university: They consider the idea of integrating knowledge from different fields (i.e., from subject-specific to general pedagogical knowledge) and encouraging students to always see theory and practice (and vice versa), in relation to each other, as important. Dausend (2017, p. 117ff.) exemplarily outlines three approaches for seminar concepts: microteaching, self-experience and teaching videos (see above "Introduction"). These approaches can be used in class to integrate theory and practice in university courses. In all three, students must be engaged actively in different types of activities and can, thereby, obtain new knowledge and theory through participation. Furthermore, some of the experts suggest that the 6-month mandatory internship could play a key role in experiencing theory in practice (and vice versa). The experts point out that internships need to be closely supervised, in cooperation with university and school staff, because

> field experiences lead both to desirable and undesired learning outcomes. This entails that amongst others practical skills as well as reflective practice are not automatically developed but need to be systematically and consciously developed (e.g. Farrell & Jacobs 2016). Additionally, the studies so far reveal shortcomings in the arrangement of field experiences (e.g., in terms of supervision quality and learning support) (Hascher, 2012, p. 110).

The experts also discuss what role research-led teaching and learning could play in pre-service teacher education at universities. By engaging the students in research, it is hoped that the pre-service teachers develop a critical attitude that develops their knowledge and teaching skills further. Burns and Richards (2009) suggests the approach of action research allows teachers to conduct research in their own classrooms.

☐ Several practice phases (i.e., school internships), which are supervised by the university in close cooperation with the schools, should become mandatory in teacher education. The internships allow students to see theory in practice and reflect on what they have learned in their universities' classes. Moreover, students can carry out their own (classroom) research and develop their teaching further.

7   Summary and Outlook

The current density of publications (e.g., Diehr, 2018), projects (e.g., Qualitätsoffensive LehrerInnenbildung/Federal Ministry of Education and Research Germany), and conferences (e.g., annual conferences organized by the Association for Teacher Education in Europe) about the role of a teacher reveal the necessity to look at quality factors in pre-service teacher education. The results of this interview study add the perspective of different stakeholders, who are actively involved in designing and teaching classes to pre-service teachers. The outcome of this study informs researchers in the field of teacher education, primary EFL teachers, university staff and students alike about teaching concepts in pre-service teacher education. From these insights, different groups of people can learn, discuss, and use the results for and in their respective contexts. For example, the outcomes of the interview study may support political decisions (e.g., definition of standards for quality in teacher education, curricula development for universities) and bring changes to schools (e.g., cooperation among teachers, innovative school lessons). Overall, the results of this interview study are meant to contribute to high quality pre-service teacher education.

References

Association for Teacher Education in Europe. *Annual Conferences*. https://atee.education/conferences/

Benitt, N. (2017). Primary EFL teachers as researchers. Benefits and challenges. In E. Wilden & R. Porsch (Eds.), *The professional development of primary EFL teachers. National and international research* (pp. 129–140). Waxmann.

BIG-Kreis (Ed.). (2007). *Fremdsprachenunterricht in der Grundschule. Standards für die Lehrerbildung*. Domino Verlag.

BIG-Kreis (Ed.). (2015). *Der Lernstand im Englischunterricht am Ende von Klasse 4. Ergebnisse der BIG-Studie*. Domino Verlag.

Bogner, A., Littig, B., & Menz, W. (2009). Introduction: Expert interviews – An introduction to a new methodological debate. In A. Bogner, B. Littig, & W. Menz (Eds.), *Interviewing experts* (pp. 1–16). Palgrave Macmillan.

Bondi, M., & Poppi, F. (2007). Devising a language certificate for primary school teachers of English. *PROFILE, 8*(2007), 145–164.

Borg, S., Birello, M., Civera, I., & Zanatta, T. (2014). The impact of teacher education on pre-service primary English language teachers. In *ELT Research Papers, 14 (03)*. British Council.

Burns, A. (2009). Action research. In J. Heigham & R. A. Crocker (Eds.), *Qualitative research in applied linguistics. A practical introduction* (pp. 112–134). Routledge.

Burns, A., & Richards, J. C. (Eds.). (2009). *The Cambridge guide to second language teacher education*. Cambridge University Press.

Caspari, D., & Grünewald, A. (Eds.). (2022). Themenheft "Fachdidaktisches Wissen in der Lehrkräftebildung". *ZFF, 33*/1.
Crandall, J. A., & Christison, M. A. (2016). An overview of research in English language teacher education and professional development. In J. A. Crandall & M. A. Christison (Eds.), *Teacher education and professional development in TESOL. Global perspectives* (pp. 3–34). Routledge.
Dausend, H. (2017). Theory and practice in primary English teacher education. In E. Wilden & R. Porsch (Eds.), *The professional development of primary EFL teachers. National and international research* (pp. 109–125). Waxmann.
Deutscher Anglistenverband und Deutsche Gesellschaft für Amerikastudien. (2009). *Positionspapier: Lehrerinnen- und Lehrerbildung im Studienfach Englisch. Endbericht der Studie EAC 89/04.* Europaeische Kommission.
Diehr, B. (Ed.). (2018). *Universitäre Englischlehrerbildung. Wege zu mehr Kohärenz im Studium und Korrespondenz mit der Praxis.* Peter Lang.
Edelenbos, P., Johnstore, R., & Kubanek, A. (2006). *The main pedagogical principles underlying the teaching of languages to very young learners Languages for the children of Europe.* Published Research, Good Practice & Main Principles. Final Report of the EAC 89/04.
European Commission. (2014). *Languages in Education and Training. Final Country Comparative Analysis.* Eurostat. 2016. *Foreign Language Learning Statistics.* https://ec.europa.eu/eurostat/statistics-explained/index.php/Foreign_language_learning_statistics#Primary_education
Farrell, T. S. C., & Jacobs, G. M. (2016). Practicing what we preach: Teacher reflection groups on coopertaive learning. *The Electronic Journal for English as a Second Language, 19*(4)., o.P.
Gerlach, D. (2022). Das Wissen der Fremdsprachenlehrpersonen – und Grundsätzliches zu seiner Beforschung. *Zeitschrift für Fremdsprachenforschung, 33*(1), 29–50.
Hascher, T. (2012). Lernfeld Praktikum – Evidenzbasierte Entwicklungen in der Lehrer/innenbildung. *Zeitschrift für Bildungsforschung, 2*(2), 109–129.
Hattie, J. (2012). *Visible learning for teachers: Maximizing impact on learning.* Routledge.
Hoinkes, U., & Weigand, P. (2016). Der Aufbau des fachspezifischen Professionswissens angehender Fremdsprachenlehrerinnen und -lehrer in der ersten Ausbildungsphase: Wege zur Entwicklung einer quantitativen Messung. In M. K. Legutke & M. Schart (Eds.), *Fremdsprachendidaktische Professionsforschung: Brennpunkt Lehrerbildung* (pp. 47–74). Narr.
Kelly, M., & Grenfell, M. (2004). *European profile of language teacher education.* University of Southhampton.
Kirchhoff, P. (2016). Was sollte eine gute Englischlehrkraft wissen? Über die Auswahl von Items im FALKO-E Test zum fachspezifischen Professionswissen. In M. K. Legutke & M. Schart (Eds.), *Fremdsprachendidaktische Professionsforschung: Brennpunkt Lehrerbildung* (pp. 75–98). Narr.
KMK – Ständige Konferenz der Kultusminister der Länder in der Bundesrepublik Deutschland. (2019). *Standards für die Lehrerbildung: Bildungswissenschaften.* KMK.
Kohonen, V. (2015). Reflective teacher professionalism in foreign language education: enhancing professional growth through ELP-oriented pedagogy. In H. P. Krings & B. Kuehn (Eds.), *Fremdsprachliche Lernprozesse: Erträge des 4. Bremer Symposions zum Fremdsprachenlehren und -lernen an Hochschulen (Fremdsprachen in Lehre und Forschung (FLF))* (pp. 11–29). AKS-Verlag.

Legutke, M., Saunders, C., & Schart, M. (2022). Zwischen den Disziplinen: Anmerkungen zur Fachspezifik des Professionswissens von Fremdsprachenlehrkräften. *Zeitschrift für Fremdsprachenforschung, 33*(1), 3–27.

Legutke, M. K. (2008). Zur Qualifikation von Sprach- und Kulturvermittlern für die fremdsprachliche Früherziehung. In M. K. Legutke & M. Schocker-von Ditfurth (Eds.), *E-Lingo. Didaktik des frühen Fremdsprachenlernens. Erfahrungen und Ergebnisse mit Blended Learning in einem Masterstudiengang* (pp. 9–22). Narr.

Legutke, M. K., & Schart, M. (Eds.). (2016). *Fremdsprachendidaktische Professionsforschung: Brennpunkt Lehrerbildung*. Narr.

Livingston, K., & Assunção Flores, M. (2017). Trends in teacher education: A review of papers published in the European journal of teacher education over 40 years. *European Journal of Teacher Education, 40*(5), 551–560.

Mayring, P. (2014). *Qualitative content analysis: theoretical foundation, basic procedures and software solution*. Klagenfurt. Retrieved June 20, 2020, from http://nbn-resolving.de/urn:nbn:de:0168-ssoar-395173

Mayring, P., & Fenzl, T. (2019). Qualitative Inhaltsanalyse. In *Handbuch Methoden der empirischen Sozialforschung* (pp. 633–648). Springer.

Newby, D., Allan, R., Fenner, A.-B., Jones, B., Komorowska, H., & Soghikyan, K. (2007). *European portfolio for student teachers of languages. A reflection tool for language teacher education*. European Centre for Modern Languages.

Nunan, D. (2016). Epilogue. In J. A. Crandall & M. A. Christison (Eds.), *Teacher education and professional development in TESOL. Global perspectives* (pp. 257–264). Routledge.

OECD. (2009). *Creating effective teaching and learning environments. First results from TALIS*.

Oleson, A., & Hora, M. T. (2014). Teaching the way they were taught? Revisiting the sources of teaching knowledge and the role of prior experience in shaping faculty teaching practices. *Higher Education, 68*(2014), 29–45.

Richards, K. (2009). Interviews. In J. Heigham & R. A. Crocker (Eds.), *Qualitative research in applied linguistics. A practical introduction* (pp. 182–199). Routledge.

Rossa, H. (2017). You teach what you believe in. BELT – Beliefs about Effective Language Teaching. In E. Wilden & R. Porsch (Eds.), *The professional development of primary EFL teachers. National and international research* (pp. 197–208). Waxmann.

Wilden, E., & Porsch, R. (Eds.). (2017). *The professional development of primary EFL teachers. National and international research*. Waxmann.

Sonja Brunsmeier is Professor of Didactics of English Language, Literature and Culture at the University of Passau (Germany). Her research interests include EFL education in primary and secondary schools and EFL teacher education at university level. She is a member of the editorial board of the academic journal Grundschule Englisch. Before joining the Department of English and American Studies at the University of Passau, she held positions as a professor at the University of Vechta, a junior professor at Ludwigsburg University of Education and a research assistant at University of Education Freiburg. She also has experience as a primary and secondary school teacher and headteacher. Contact: sonja.brunsmeier@uni-passau.de.

A Corpus-Based Analysis of Ideologies in Chilean SLTE Policies

10

Rodrigo Arellano

1 Introduction

This discursive study is located in Chile, a Latin American country with 19.828.563 inhabitants. This includes 12.8% self-declared as indigenous (2.185.792) and at least 8.2% foreigners (1.462.103), though this later number might be much higher due to massive migratory processes in recent years (National Institute of Statistics, 2017). This rich combination of cultures challenges the prominent role of Spanish as the de facto language of this nation, which is spoken by 95.9% of Chileans (Cervantes Institute, 2021). In addition, six autochthonous languages are still in use with different degrees of vitality; four of them are taught in schools (Arellano et al., 2020) together with the use of German, Italian, and other community languages. Furthermore, with only 2.5% of the population being certified to speak English in Chile (Romero, 2017), the role of English within Chilean society is understood as a foreign language positioned in the expanding circle of World Englishes (Kachru, 2017).

The current research project is an exploration of beliefs in EFL teacher training programs in Chile through the analysis of relevant policy discourses in order to provide for explicit reflection on the ways those beliefs both shape policy and affect classroom practices. This study aims to answer the following research question:

R. Arellano (✉)
Department of Languages, Literature and Communication, Universidad de la Frontera, Temuco, Chile
e-mail: rodrigo.arellano@ufrontera.cl

© The Author(s), under exclusive license to Springer-Verlag GmbH, DE, part of Springer Nature 2024
P. Voerkel et al. (eds.), *Tools, Techniques and Strategies for Reflective Second & Foreign Language Teacher Education*,
https://doi.org/10.1007/978-3-662-68741-3_10

What language-in-education ideologies are evident in policy discourses about EFL teacher training in Chile? To this end, a corpus-based methodology was used to detect the most salient ideological foci in a complex set of language-in-education policies. Then, this investigation used a mixed-methods approach, which combined KWIC with the examination of salient excerpts in context. Importantly, a discursive exploration such as this one can help educational stakeholders to reflect on the way language teacher education is enacted. In this way, a corpus-based semi-automatic analysis can shed light on the emphasis of policy documentation by systematizing the study of beliefs based on linguistic data to foster critical thinking and the improvement of instructional practices.

2   Literature Review

2.1   The Discursive Study of Policy Ideologies as Sets of Beliefs

Ideologies are mental constructs or sets of beliefs about the world that are created over time and stored in the speakers' minds under the influence of specific sociocultural and political contexts. The delimitations of the construct of ideology are unclear (Skott, 2015) as there are no disciplinary domains, literature, or unique research methods specifically associated with their study (Schieffelin et al., 1998). Importantly, ideologies operate in the intersection of society, discourse, and cognition, whose abstract nature makes their study a challenging endeavor. Indeed, van Dijk (2005) defined ideologies as the "foundation of the social representations shared by a social group" (p. 2), although ideologies can be debated and contested within the same communities (Wodak & Meyer, 2016). At first, the study of ideologies was originally conceived as a science of ideas, but quite soon these networks of beliefs started to be perceived negatively by the influence of politics. Within the context of the French Revolution, ideologies gained a negative connotation and were understood even pejoratively. This was based on the supposed distortion of ideas in society, although ideologies can represent positive values as well.

Importantly, when these ideologies are verbalized or transformed into textual data, they can be best studied as discourses and reflected upon in order to make improvements in both policies and practices. From this perspective, discourse analysis offers a useful set of methods because textual data is both "socially shaped and socially constitutive" (Fairclough, 1995, p. 131) and can help us comprehend the participants' views about the phenomena under investigation. To accomplish this, it is important to develop "thick descriptions" (Geertz, 1973, p. 7) to truly capture the individuals' intended meanings. In other words, a detailed account of the situational context of the participants (or policymakers) needs to be provided to understand their stories and narratives (Punch, 2009) to focus on the analysis of language in context.

Regarding pedagogy, it is clear that ideologies as belief systems influence the teachers' praxis (Colina, 2002), particularly as educators go into the classroom with a set of preconceptions about language learning and language content (Baldauf & Kaplan, 2005). Nevertheless, these mental constructs are not always rational as they are influenced by the teachers' experiences and emotional factors. Additionally, a cognitive perspective can be considered by observing teachers' practices in connection with understanding what they think, believe, and know (Borg, 2008). Remarkably, this struggle between emotional and rational components can lead to the teachers' justification of certain ideologies even when opposite evidence is presented to refute them. Therefore, people can accept truth as given or they can challenge others' views by exercising their sense of agency based on mental networks constructed through the speakers' personal experiences, which can be studied discursively.

Then, by recognizing that teaching is ideological, a rich source to explore the construction of these sets of beliefs is language policy. These policies are situated in a curricular space where language and education views are made explicit, and once identified and reflected upon can be accepted or contested by educational stakeholders. Undoubtedly, the analysis of these policies can inform researchers and policymakers about the way EFL teacher training is conceptualized and enacted. Especially considering the pervasive effect of policies in educational processes, but also their inherent gaps between design and implementation. Importantly, there is evidence that in many countries EFL training serves social, economic, and political agendas (Phillipson, 1992; Pennycook, 2021). In this line of thought, it is still believed that there is a direct correlation between EFL instruction and social development, despite the acknowledgment of many other factors to achieve a nation's prosperity (Lo Bianco, 2010). Somehow, this belief is anchored on ideas about neoliberalism, which is the topic of the next section of this chapter.

2.2 Second Language Teacher Education in a Neoliberal Market

The term second language teacher education (SLTE) was originally coined by Richards (1990) to "cover the preparation - training and education - of L2 teachers" (Wright, 2010, p. 260). It aimed to provide a space to study the learning processes of foreign language teacher trainees and the skills they will have to learn and use in classrooms. Traditionally, SLTE has comprised pre-service teachers and in-service teacher education, where training in language-related areas and educational disciplines is offered. The problem is that teacher training is not ideology-free and these "sets of beliefs" (Silverstein, 1979, p. 193) have a tremendous impact on the way teachers are prepared at universities, which is the area of inquiry of this discursive research.

Within the Chilean context, the tendency in SLTE programs is to emphasize language-related disciplines during years 1–3 with educational courses at the end of the program (Barahona, 2016). After this focus on English learning, a second commonality is that most SLTE training includes practicum experiences from year 2, where trainees visit schools to observe and teach. These visits are normally part of language teaching methodology courses and trainees are mentored by a university instructor and a practicing language teacher. There is normally a 1-year final practicum in years 4 or 5, in which trainees need to teach at least one group of students, while they write a research thesis or complete a project about a topic of interest. Finally, most EFL teacher training programs require trainees to undertake a Cambridge examination to demonstrate a C1 level.

Another relevant factor to address in these SLTE programs has been the implementation of more active methodologies based on changes in the current educational paradigms. Historically, a teacher-centered approach has been used (Schiro, 2013) in which the focus of EFL and SLTE training was based on accuracy and attainment of grammatical knowledge. Current models, however, are more aligned with student-centered practices (Ertmer & Newby, 2013) in which students attempt to interact using the language of instruction to practice their receptive and productive language skills. In this context, communicative approaches have emerged as the preferred option for policymakers to promote the use of constructivist pedagogical practices, at least in theory.

Notwithstanding, most of the foreign language models to design these SLTE programs have been imported to Chile despite the profound differences in terms of the political, socio-cultural, and educational realities of students and teachers. Currently, the tendency is the rejection of foreign one-size-fits-all policies, toward the elaboration of contextualized frameworks, including those for teacher training, as Kamhi-Stein et al. (2017) explain:

> They (policies) are not being readily transplanted and adopted from other countries. Instead, what the region is witnessing is the development of models that are initiated in the countries, then brought out into the open and examined through practice and contested by confronting them with existing perspectives (p. 2).

The educational policies in Chile have not been the exception to these contextualizing trends, and their analyses can shed light on the stakeholders' understanding of educational and linguistic beliefs to set the stage for reflection and improvement. Nevertheless, concerning SLTE practices, a neoliberal shift has been observed in the last decades, in which the access to university programs has been mostly determined by the capacity of the teacher candidate to pay the university fees. These practices, aligned with the privatization of universities, have created a vicious cycle that has lowered the quality of teaching degrees (Romero, 2017). Hence, the marketization of educational processes has had tangible effects on education and policy design at all levels. In this respect, the market regulates the offer and demand of teacher training programs, but with few regulations from the State or other ad hoc agencies.

This new type of access to higher education resulted in a sharp increase in the universities' enrolment, but with a "focus on income generation and profitability rather than teaching and research" (OECD, 2012, p. 31). What is more, there is evidence that many Chilean institutions mark the parents' preferences to educate their children with students and teachers from the same socioeconomic groups, leading to segregation practices and reproduction of social classes (Schneider et al., 2006). These practices are partly based on the assumption that prosperity and well-being are only measured in economic terms. This view also ignores the real socioeconomic status of most of the Chilean population, which earns $US509 a month, although Chile is classified as a high-income nation (World Bank, 2020). This discrepancy is explained by Pennycook and Makoni (2020):

> An emphasis on national GDP, for example, suggests that when it rises above a certain point, a country may move into the Global North (various South American countries, such as Chile, are sometimes now shown as part of the Global North), overlooking the deep internal inequalities within nations (p. 6).

Nonetheless, despite recent attempts to move away from neoliberal practices that have been labeled as successful in macroeconomic terms (Ahumada, 2019), there is still a pervasive effect of business-oriented practices in the Chilean educational system (Brunner & Alarcón, 2023). Then, it is against this backdrop that this discursive research is positioned to understand the ideological construction of language-in-education policies during SLTE processes in Chile.

3 Methodology

This study is based on the analysis of a set of language-in-education policies using discourse analysis techniques. By examining relevant policy documents, beliefs were unmasked to have a deeper understanding of the way policymakers understand SLTE processes at different levels of implementation. To do this, policy documentation was analyzed in three layers:

i. macro-level: SLTE national standards (16.257 words)
ii. meso-level: SLTE curricula and programs descriptions of 34 universities (23.998 words)
iii. micro-level: 35-course outlines of an SLTE program of a university in Southern Chile (25.200 words).

This set of policy documentation is mostly available for public access. Firstly, in the case of the macro-level policies, the standards (Ministry of Education of Chile, 2014) can be easily downloaded from the corresponding ministerial webpage. Secondly, regarding the meso-level policies—curricula and program descriptions—they can be accessed from the webpage of each university. Finally, the micro-level policies were obtained from the head of the SLTE program in a Chilean regional university.

A mixed-methods approach was used through a combination of quantitative and qualitative strategies to reduce the weaknesses and maximize the advantages of both approaches (Creswell, 2012; Newby, 2014). By using discursive strategies, the focus was positioned on the exploration of discourses and meanings constructed by individuals rather than on the search for a single truth (van Dijk, 2009; Wodak & Meyer, 2016). This examination was carried out using NVivo12 and AntConc software packages to store the data, organize it hierarchically, and reexamine relevant units of analysis.

From this perspective, two strategies were employed. Firstly, a poststructuralist inductive keyword analysis was used to analyze the linguistic data. To start, keywords analysis (Fairclough, 2000, 2003) is a way to approach texts which focus on concepts that are statistically more frequent in a given dataset, especially when they are compared to other texts of similar characteristics (Baker, 2010). In the case of this research, the repeated keywords were compared across policy levels regarding their frequency ranking as well as the collocations of each recurrent keyword included in these policies. In other words, the strategy of keywords-in-context was used in terms of lexical frequency, but also through the analysis of the co-texts of interest, which were grouped to thematize the data (Arellano, 2018). Secondly, key excerpts were analyzed using elements from critical discourse analysis, especially at the lexical level (Fairclough, 1995) to illustrate the language-in-education ideologies findings. This perspective includes the analysis of the language choices in the examined policies to understand how they portray their beliefs about EFL teacher training processes (Waring, 2018).

Accordingly, the analysis focuses on the chosen lexico-grammatical features used, particularly keywords-in-context as powerful indicators of ideological construction. Specifically, this study investigated the frequency of the ten most frequent content keywords, whose repeated lexical items appeared across datasets (*'learning,'* *'student,'* and *'English'*) to be reanalyzed using their collocations (Fairclough, 2000, 2003). Furthermore, the analysis also contemplated the count of the courses in the Chilean SLTE curricula to detect the ideological foci of the data. This results in an eclectic approach, in which discursive tools were utilized to analyze these datasets in Spanish, whose key findings were translated into English.

Finally, the textual data had to be prepared for its analysis in these software packages. For instance, some of this information was presented as images, so transcriptions were necessary to have all the data in the same format. This can be a time-consuming process, but it allows the correct reading of words by NVivo12 and AntConc.

4 Findings

4.1 The Context: Quantification of SLTE Curricula

To contextualize this study, the set of SLTE courses provided by these teaching programs were broadly classified into (i) specialization (ii) pedagogy and (iii) others (Table 10.1). This analysis was based on a quantification supported by NVivo12 using the 'query option,' which was complemented with manual analysis. This section presents the examination concerning the categorization of courses on the public information provided by Chilean universities about their SLTE degrees.

Table 10.1 General classification of courses in Chilean SLTE programs

Area	N° of courses	% of coverage
1. Specialization (English)	944	52.54%
2. Pedagogy	693	38.56%
3. Others	160	8.90%
Total	**1797**	**100%**

Broadly speaking, more than half of the offered courses in these SLTE programs correspond to the English specialization (52.54%), followed by pedagogy (38.56%) and other courses (8.90%) that complement the language-related and educational training of EFL teachers. Nevertheless, it is worth mentioning that, on the one hand, the contents of some areas may overlap and, on the other hand, some courses may have been designed with the purpose of supporting English proficiency attainment or methodological competencies. Then, if this analysis is broken down, it is possible to observe that two sets of courses concentrate the training in language-related areas. Firstly, *'English'* courses aim at the development of proficiency (36.04%), and secondly, *'language teaching methodology courses'* (15.95%) develop pedagogical proficiency, as seen in Table 10.2 below.

This focus on the specialization is complemented with pedagogy courses (Table 10.3), in which *'practicum'* experiences are the most frequent modules in the data (25.8%). This is followed by *'psychology'* training (11.4%) and courses aligned with investigative skills, such as *'capstone'* projects (8.66%) and *'research'* (8%). Finally, an array of other teaching components completes the training of EFL teacher candidates, as seen below.

To finish, a third category comprises other courses (Table 10.4). Firstly, *'general training'* includes modules related to the university context, and courses about communication, amongst others. Secondly, *'electives'* includes optional foreign languages, arts, sports, etc. Finally, *'theological'* courses are linked with Christian

Table 10.2 Specialization courses

Specialization courses	N° of courses	% of coverage
1. English	344	36.04%
2. Language teaching methodology	151	15.95%
3. Anglo-Saxon literature	79	8.5%
4. Phonetics and phonology	79	8.5%
5. Syntax	67	7.09%
6. Culture	49	5.19%
7. Second language acquisition	43	4.5%
8. General linguistics	41	4.3%
9. Specialized electives	23	2.4%
10. Morphology and lexicon	22	2.3%
11. Text and discourse	20	2.11%
12. Spanish	17	1.86%
13. Translation	8	0.8%
14. Semantics and pragmatics	1	0.1%
Total	**944**	**100%**

Table 10.3 Pedagogy courses

Pedagogy courses	N° of courses	% of coverage
1. Practicum	179	25.8%
2. Psychology	79	11.4%
3. Capstone	60	8.66%
4. Research	55	8%
5. Curriculum	51	7.3%
6. Educational management	45	6.48%
7. Educational studies	41	5.91%
8. Assessment	32	4.61%
9. ICTs	29	4.17%
10. Diversity	26	3.76%
11. Sociology	23	3.31%
12. Counselling	16	2.3%
13. Ethics	15	2.15%
14. Philosophy	13	1.9%
15. Identity	12	1.73%
16. Anthropology	5	0.72%
17. Maths	4	0.6%
18. History	4	0.6%
19. Educational policies	4	0.6%
Total	**693**	**100%**

Table 10.4 Other courses

Other courses	N° of courses	% of coverage
1. General training	84	52.4%
2. Electives	60	37.5%
3. Theological	16	10.1%
Total	**160**	**100%**

values, considering that 7 out of the 34 analyzed universities are founded or owned by the Catholic Church or other religious denominations.

There are marked differences when comparing the language, education, and general training curriculum within these Chilean SLTE programs. The language-related courses focus on English proficiency, where the students' linguistic background is not the emphasis. There is also a strong focus on language teaching methodology, where practicum components are highly valued, together with training in diverse academic areas, such as research and psychology, amongst others. Furthermore, elective courses deal with general training, where there are communicative courses in Spanish as well as theological preparation.

In addition, a monolingual ideology can be observed by the strong advocacy for English during instruction, the little training in Spanish and the absence of courses about indigenous or community languages. What is more, the extensive focus on practicum experiences is related to a social efficiency ideology, where trainees need to learn how to operate successfully as teachers in schools. Finally, there are also traces of scholarly academicism as trainees need to be acquainted with disciplinary areas, including research as an academic practice. This quantification of courses is helpful to provide a backdrop to understand the foci of instruction in Chilean SLTE as well as to triangulate the data when compared against frequency counts and collocations, which are presented in the next section.

4.2 Quantitative Analysis: Keywords-in-Context Across Datasets

This section summarizes the corpus-based analysis of different content KWIC across the different policy layers. The national standards provide a focus on '*learning*' (N = 229) and '*students*' (N = 165), positioning teacher training as a learner-centered process. However, at universities, the emphasis is placed on proficiency in which '*English*' is the most frequent KWIC in the program descriptions (N = 255) and course outlines (N = 638). In this case, universities treat the specialization or content as the core of the SLTE program, despite the emphasis of the Ministry of Education to enhance the importance of pedagogy. This institutional focus on proficiency can be confirmed by the keyword '*language*' (N = 82) at the meso-level and '*level*' (N = 221) and '*evaluation*' (N = 161) at the micro-level. Table 10.5 presents the 10 most repeated content keywords related to SLTE, their position within each corpus and their respective tokens.

However, a raw count of frequencies can be of little value if the linguistic context of the keywords under examination is not considered. Therefore, to delineate the study of KWIC about SLTE processes in Chile, the three repeated keywords across datasets (highlighted in Table 10.5) were analyzed regarding their most frequent collocations. This frequency count can be found in Table 10.6.

At the macro-level (national standards), the collocation analysis confirms the focus on pedagogy and learning, which is replaced by teaching and English as the core components of training at the meso-level (program descriptions). This is somehow replicated in the micro-level (course outlines) through a deeper focus on evaluation and the proficiency levels of EFL teacher candidates. These three keywords will guide the use of excerpts provided in the next section, which will exemplify the ideologies at play within Chilean SLTE processes.

Table 10.5 Frequency analysis of the three most repeated words across datasets

Standards (macro-level)	Tokens	Program descriptions (meso-level)	Tokens	Course outlines (micro-level)	Tokens
2. **Learning**	229	2. *English*	255	2. *English*	638
3. Standards	228	3. Professional	163	3. Subject	238
4. Students	165	4. Education	147	4. Level	221
6. *English*	165	5. **Learning**	125	5. Development	186
7. Development	92	6. Teaching	122	6. **Learning**	166
8. Knows	90	8. Career	96	7. Students	164
9. Teaching	88	9. Teacher	79	8. Evaluation	161
10. Education	82	10. Language	82	9. Communicative	140
11. Knowledge	67	11. Students	71	10. Abilities	126
12. Skills	66	12. Contexts	68	11. Knowledge	125

Table 10.6 Collocation analysis of repeated KWIC across datasets

KWIC	Macro-level (National standards)	Meso-level (Program descriptions)	Micro-level (Course outlines)
1. **Learning**	i. Process (N = 51) ii. Outcomes (N = 39) iii. Objectives (N = 23)	i. The English language (N = 103) ii. Professional(ism) (N = 88) iii. Academic degree/title (N = 70)	i. Teaching methodology (N = 21) ii. Teaching-learning process (N = 21) iii. Improvement of learning and standards (N = 20)
2. **Students**	i. Learning (N = 32) ii. Social aspects (N = 11) iii. Skills development (N = 11)	i. Their (students) (N = 30) ii. The (students)—generic (N = 25) iii. The (students)—female (N = 10)	i. The (students)—generic article (N = 48) ii. Their (students) (N = 46) iii. Have to (N = 20)
3. **English**	i. EFL teaching program (N = 65) ii. Disciplinary and pedagogy standards (N = 20) iii. Proficiency (N = 15)	i. Teacher of (N = 34) ii. Secondary education (N = 30) iii. Teaching (N = 10)	i. (English) language (N = 315) ii. In (English) (N = 152) iii. Level (N = 36)

4.3 Qualitative Analysis: Illustration of Ideologies Using Relevant Excerpts

This section presents the thematization of the data using KWIC as a guide. To present the thematic foci in this multi-layered policy dataset is that this analysis has been presented in two macro sections. First, the English and Pedagogy standards (section 'English and Pedagogy Standards') and second, the SLTE programs descriptions and one regional university (section 'SLTE Programs Descriptions and One Regional University') despite the possible overlap of ideological forces in both of them. In addition, the sets of beliefs identified in this second section share most ideological components at the meso-level (all the examined universities) and micro-level (a regional university outside the capital of Chile as a case study) so only the differences or tensions will be made salient.

4.3.1 English and Pedagogy Standards

At the national level, the data positions the learner (teacher candidate) as the protagonist of the teacher training process. In this line of thought, the Ministry of Education emphasizes the theoretical and practical trainees' capabilities as well as their development of linguistic and educational skills. The analysis of collocations confirms this 'learner-centered' approach in national policies in which showing *'proficiency'* (N = 15) is only one component of their university preparation. In this respect, the focus is put on the students' learning practices, in which the teacher is only a mediator for learning, as seen in Excerpts 1–2.

Excerpt 1. Learner-centered approach (I)

Standard 6 (pedagogy description)

(The teacher) knows how to apply evaluation methods to monitor the <u>students</u>' progress and knows how to use the results to provide feedback for learning.

Excerpt 2. Learner-centered approach (II)

Standard 2, criterion 1 (pedagogy)

(The teacher) knows how to design, implement and assess teaching-learning strategies to promote the <u>students</u>' personal and social development.

As seen above, the subject of the sentence (The teacher) was not mentioned explicitly as this is optional in Spanish and is only used for emphasis or clarification. In other words, this KWIC (in brackets) was not used to focus on the '*students' progress*' (Excerpt 1) and the '*students' personal and social development*' (Excerpt 2). Nevertheless, this learner-centered approach is supposed to be achieved through a strict monolingual policy. In this case, languages other than English are not allowed or endorsed in EFL classrooms in the specialization section of these national standards.

Excerpt 3. English-only policy

Standard 6, criterion 8 - Specialization

(The teacher) speaks in English, effectively, 100% of the time in the class.

Interestingly, it is assumed that learners and teachers speak the same (first) language in the pedagogy section of these guidelines. It is worth noticing that this section of the standards is the same for all teaching programs in Chile regardless of the discipline or area of study (Excerpt 4). Then, they are not linked to any language teaching degree, so the language of instruction is not mentioned. This perspective is based on the assumption that the use of Spanish as the de facto language is used by all teachers and students while ignoring the existing linguistic diversity of the classroom, especially among migrant children.

Excerpt 4. Use of Spanish

Standard 9 - Pedagogy

(The teacher) can communicate himself/herself in oral and written form, coherently and correctly within academic and professional contexts related to his/her field.

This implicit use of Spanish, the high frequency of the word '*English*,' as well as the absence of other languages, provides information about linguistic ideologies. Accordingly, all the occurrences for '*English*' are found in the specialization section of the standards and the university programs, but languages are not mentioned in the pedagogy components, suggesting the presence of double monolingual ideologies. In this case, English is the content as well as the medium of instruction in the language component of SLTE programs, but Spanish is exclusively used for the teacher trainees' pedagogical training. However, 'Spanish' seldom appears in the whole dataset (N = 4) as it is assumed all learners use it. This is so while aboriginal languages or other community languages are not mentioned, despite their inclusion and endorsement in recent policies. This position demonstrates the belief that Chile is perceived by policymakers as a homogeneous and monolingual culture.

4.3.2 SLTE Programs Descriptions and One Regional University

The learning of '*English*' is what matters the most at the meso- and micro-levels (N = 638) as opposed to the learner-centered approach endorsed by the national policies. Universities promote high levels of linguistic competence, in which teacher candidates should be able to demonstrate proficiency, as seen in Excerpts 5–6.

Excerpt 5. Proficiency (I)

(The teacher) demonstrates mastery of the communicative resources of the English language, in an academic register, allowing him/her to understand and produce various types of discourses, both oral and written at an advanced level. (University 16)

Excerpt 6. Proficiency (II)

(The teacher) demonstrates mastery of the comprehension and production of oral and written skills of the English language to implement meaningful learning experiences. (University 2)

At the institutional level, '*English*' is the most frequent lexical item in the SLTE program descriptions (N = 255) as well as in the selected university (N = 638). As seen above, English is the object of study to develop proficiency through language awareness to '*demonstrate mastery*' (Excerpts 5–6) of the L2. This is also clear at universities, where there is complementation between proficiency and the transmission of academic content, showing traits of a scholarly academic ideology.

Excerpt 7. Focus on content

(The teacher) analyzes and relates historic and cultural aspects of English-speaking countries to his/her own culture, literature and history. (University 16)

Excerpt 8. Technical and specialized language

Learning outcome: To defend ideas verbally, justifying a position through the utilization of a technical and specialized language according to the level of their study. (University 3)

However, university discourses evidence other non-linguistic ideologies as well. The most salient one is neoliberalism through the promotion of their programs as products to be sold in the educational market. This is evidenced by keywords such as '*career*' (N = 96) and '*professional*' (N = 163) within the top 10 most frequent words. These keywords portray a future projection of the student if the client (teacher candidate) decides to purchase the access to these specific teaching programs.

Excerpt 9. Quality assurance

From a solid training in linguistics, literature and English-speaking cultures, the teacher incorporates the knowledge and the competencies that are needed for the professional application of the teaching and learning of English as a foreign language to comply with the requirements of the new educational paradigms by contributing competently with the development and quality of English teaching (University 25).

Excerpt 10. Academic degree

This professional has an academic degree that certifies the approval of an advanced cycle dedicated to the profound, updated and critical study of the pedagogical disciplines. (University 12)

As seen in Excerpts 9–10, the policy discourses that promote this university training are aligned with marketization practices. In this way, only positive elements are mentioned when describing these SLTE programs, while weaknesses or flaws are never mentioned. On the one hand, the program descriptions overuse positive features of these teaching degrees, while emphasizing that teacher candidates will become competent '*professionals.*' However, on the other hand, the education they provide is not always consistent with the description provided by these programs, as seen below:

Excerpt 11. Spanish teaching

The EFL teacher from University (institution's name) plans, executes and evaluates teaching situations, which allows him/her to work in public and private educational institutions at different levels, as well as teaching Spanish as a foreign language in productive companies or bilingual services (University 14).

Excerpt 12. Working in other fields

You will be able to work in public and private institutions in kindergarten, primary and secondary education, professional institutes, technical schools, language academies, mines, tourism agencies and community centers, amongst others (University 5).

For instance, Excerpt 11 promotes this SLTE program with the promise that teacher candidates would be able to teach Spanish, based on the assumption that being a native speaker is enough to teach a given language. Nevertheless, the count of courses (see section 'The Context: Quantification of SLTE Curricula') shows there are only 17 courses of Spanish offered nationally within these teaching programs (1.86%) with no courses about Spanish teaching. This means that half of the existing 34 TESOL programs in Chile provide no training about the students' L1 or this is kept to the minimum. In addition, that number falls to only 8 courses (0.8%) in the whole country when it comes to training about translation, while no courses were found concerning indigenous languages, which provides additional evidence for the existence of a strict English-only policy. A similar fallacy was observed in Excerpt 12, as the teacher candidate would be able to work in *'mines, tourism agencies and community centers;'* however, no courses were identified in the examined policies to prepare EFL teacher candidates to work in these areas.

A relevant element, particularly in the regional university used as a case study, was the tension between student-centered and teacher-centered models. The descriptions of these SLTE programs as well as the course outlines of the specific institution under examination attempt to promote active methodologies. Additionally, these micro-policies aim to create links between the (language) academic content and learning strategies so that teacher candidates can use them with their students in the future, as illustrated in Excerpts 13–14.

Excerpt 13. Methodology (I)

Methodology: Practical work of recognition and reproduction of phones in the language laboratory: Exercises, creation and composition of rhymes, tongue twisters, songs, chants, preparation of audiovisual material for their learning).

(Course outline of 'Pronunciation workshop')

Excerpt 14. Methodology (II)

Methodology: Practical work

Examples: Games and creation of material for one's learning

(Course outline of 'Applied grammar I')

These course outlines enhance not only the learning of specialized linguistic content, but also use methodological choices to design teaching aids to learn pronunciation and grammar. Consequently, these teaching materials can be used in their practicum experiences so that these teacher candidates can learn how to teach these language components in the EFL classroom. However, this enhancement of active methodologies contradicts how teacher candidates are evaluated in these language-related courses, as shown in Excerpts 15–16.

Excerpt 15. Assessment (I)

The assessment system for this subject will be theoretical (50%) and practical (50%) components. The assessment types will be:

Assessment instrument	Learning outcomes	Weight
1. Reading quizzes and workshops	(1,2,3,4,5)	25%
2. Test 1	(1,2)	25%
3. Test 2	(3,4)	25%
4. Research project	(5)	25%

(Course outline of 'Second Language Acquisition')

Excerpt 16. Assessment (II)

The assessment system for this subject will be theoretical (50%) and practical (50%) components. The assessment types will be:

Assessment instrument	Learning outcomes	Weight
1. Test 1	(1,2)	25%
2. Test 2	(3,4)	25%
3. Reading workshops and quizzes	(1,2,3)	25%
4. Analysis of language samples	(4,5)	25%

(Course outline of 'Introduction to linguistics')

These two extracts show the assessment information in two courses in the area of linguistics. Despite the description of balanced *'theoretical (50%) and practical (50%) components'* (Excerpts 15–16), 3 out of the 4 evaluations correspond to tests or quizzes, which are assessment strategies that foster memorization practices. Only the final assessment in both courses is more aligned with research, in which teacher candidates would need to design a research project or analyze real language samples. However, although this assessment promotes active learning and higher thinking skills, it is placed as the final evaluation of the course at the end of the academic term. Another interesting example to illustrate this tension is the use of the word *'teacher'* or *'profesor/a'* in Spanish, in which the educator is placed as the protagonist of the sentence, either as the subject or in a salient noun phrase position. This analysis was conducted in the original language of the data using

AntConc and, therefore, the data is presented in Spanish to preserve the structures and meanings (Fig. 10.1).

These concordances illustrate the focus on *'teacher'* (*profesor/a*) within the sentence in which not only the optional subject in Spanish is made explicit at the beginning or end of sentences, but also gender-inclusive language is used. Indeed, the policy datasets use these discursive strategies throughout the three layers of policy analysis. Spanish is a language that uses some morphological markers for nouns, articles, and adjectives. Amongst others, '*or*' is frequent to talk about male entities/people, while '*a*' is used with female entities/people. Within these policies, the strategy of '*syntactic duplication*' has been used to include a word with both genders through the repetition of the morphemes '*(a).*' Interestingly, the male marker is always positioned as the first option in all the identified cases in the data, but the use of gender-inclusive language is not systematic in any of the policy datasets under examination.

Finally, in the university discourses, '*learning*' (N = 125) and '*teaching*' (N = 122) as well as '*teacher*' (N = 79) and '*student*' (N = 71) are practically identical in terms of frequency within the most repeated 10 content KWIC. These frequencies oppose the focus on learning provided in the macro-level policies in which '*teacher*' is not one of the most frequent words, while '*learning*' (N = 229) and '*students*' (N = 165) rank much higher than '*teaching*' (N = 88).

5 Discussion

In summary, regarding these national teaching standards, this analysis revealed the importance of learning through the development of the trainees' proficiency and pedagogical skills. This focus is achieved by the complementation of advanced linguistic capabilities to serve communicative purposes, which includes an empha-

El **profesor(a)** de Inglés formado(a) en la Universidad
El **profesor(a)** de Inglés ejerce su profesión
El **profesor** presenta problemas, dilemas, preguntas
El **profesor** presenta aspectos teóricos de diseño curricular
del papel de los y las **profesores(as)** en los procesos políticos-sociales

según paradigmas y características del ser **profesor(a)**. Este curso permite la
prácticas evaluativas desarrolladas por los **profesores** en el aula. La idea central es que
este curso permita al futuro **profesor(a)**, reflexionar sobre la importancia del
Reconocer el rol de **profesor** tutor y/u orientador en la formación
la comunidad escolar en que el **profesor** se desenvuelve. En las clases

Fig. 10.1 Teacher-student tension

sis on language teaching methodology components. There is an English-only policy that is not considering the students' first language or other languages of the community as teaching resources. This theme is practically invisible, but this 'silenced topic' is evidence of the priorities of policymakers. In fact, when contrasting the English and pedagogy standards, it is possible to observe that English and Spanish are strictly used in different domains of the trainees' spheres of activity. English as an L2 is the object of study as well as the medium of instruction in the specialization, while pedagogical courses are delivered in Spanish only, assuming this is the language spoken by all students. Hence, this language focus in coursework evidences a double monolingual ideology, where these two different languages are used in mutually exclusive contexts: English for language studies and Spanish for pedagogy instruction.

Overall, a range of ideological forces is evident in the university datasets as well. One of the most salient ones is neoliberalism, through the extensive display of marketing and discourses of advertising (Cook, 2001), where access to language and education are products that can be purchased in higher education institutions. Hence, access to the university is understood mostly as an economic practice through the idealistic promotion of these SLTE programs. These policies describe future EFL teachers as active agents who will become competent professional educators in the future with SLTE programs depicted as ideal. The focus also relies on proficiency and practicum-based experiences through monolingual practices that give little space to the use of other languages. In the case of the university under examination, there was a tension between teacher-centered and student-centered practices, in which discourses of academicism and gender-inclusive language were identified. Also, there is a discourse of expertise, where trainees are aimed to be very skillful in certain academic areas, while others simply support the presence of scholar academicism at various degrees. To finish, educational courses seek to train the candidates in the academic language teachers need to use once they enter the teaching profession.

This qualitative analysis served to thematize the data to deepen the understanding of the most salient ideologies in Chilean SLTE policies. Nonetheless, not only the most frequent words but also the way the message is constructed provides information about the policymakers' sets of beliefs. Because of these findings, more contextual scrutiny was needed to complement the frequency and collocation examination of the discursive data. In addition, what is not said or included is also relevant as it reinforces the foci of the policymakers. This absence of topics about indigenous languages or the minimal frequency of themes about Spanish, amongst others, highlights this importance.

6 Conclusions

This chapter has reported on the ideologies identified in a multi-layered SLTE policy set in the Chilean context. This analysis has revealed a set of salient sets of beliefs, which have been explained and exemplified through keywords-in-context, frequency counts, and collocations. At the national level, there is an emphasis on learning practices, while at the institutional level, universities depict trainees as professionals, who are mostly perceived as clients in the context of a neoliberal market. Universities do highlight proficiency in English as a focus, but they combine it with language awareness elements through a struggle between teacher and student-centered models depicted through the use of gender-inclusive language. The specific university under examination reflects these national and institutional policies, including the use of English and Spanish in different paths of the SLTE instruction.

The findings highlight the importance of pedagogy and learner-centered approaches to EFL teacher education, while universities focus largely on the development of proficiency and language-based disciplinary knowledge. However, the obsession to achieve a high command of the L2 can limit the training of prospective EFL teachers. Especially if English-only policies or (double) monolingual ideologies guide the pedagogical training, the language potential of bilingual/multilingual students can be hindered or lost. This is also a call for action for the training and inclusion of Spanish, local, and community languages and to become critical of the quality of some SLTE programs anchored in marketing strategies and neoliberal discourses.

Finally, the policy analysis reveals the potential for improving reflexivity regarding instructional practices. In this way, educational stakeholders must be critical of the ideologies evident in policy discourses. Therefore, by engaging in reflective practices, lecturers and trainees could show a sense of agency to challenge some pervasive ideologies such as neoliberalism or monolingualism, amongst others. This critical stance should be useful in order to train EFL teachers who could also unmask and reflect upon language-in-education beliefs within instructional practices as well as in policy documents within Chilean SLTE and beyond.

Acknowledgment This work was funded by the National Agency for Research and Development (ANID)/Scholarship Program/DOCTORADO BECAS CHILE/2017-72180169 and The Australian Government Research Training Program Scholarship.

References

Ahumada, J. M. (2019). *The political economy of peripheral growth: Chile in the global economy*. Springer International Publishing - Imprint: Palgrave Macmillan.

Arellano, R. (2018). A corpus linguistics application in the analysis of textbooks as national teaching instruments of English as a Second language in Chile. *Revista Actualidades Investigativas en Educación, 18*(1), 1–19.

Arellano, R., Reinao, P., Marianjel, A., & Curaqueo, G. (2020). Un estudio comparativo entre las metodologías usadas en la enseñanza del mapudungun como segunda lengua y el inglés como lengua extranjera. *Forma y Función, 33*(1), 87–114.

Baker, P. (2010). Corpus methods in linguistics. In L. Litosseliti (Ed.), *Research methods in linguistics* (pp. 93–113). Continuum.

Baldauf, R., & Kaplan, R. (2005). Language-in-education policy and planning. In E. Hinkel (Ed.), *Handbook of research in second language teaching and learning* (pp. 1013–1034). Lawrence Erlbaum.

Barahona, M. (2016). *English language teacher education in Chile*. Routledge.

Borg, S. (2008). *How to research teachers' beliefs and knowledge*. Unpublished paper presented at the 42nd Annual TESOL Convention.

Brunner, J. J., & Alarcón, M. (2023). Evolution of Chilean higher education from the governance equalizer perspective. *Research Square (preprint)*, 1–21.

Cervantes Institute. (2021). *El español, una lengua viva: Informe 2021*. Cervantes Institute.

Colina, S. (2002). Second language acquisition, language teaching and translation studies. *Translator, 8*(1), 1–24.

Cook, G. (2001). *The discourse of advertising* (2nd ed.). Routledge.

Creswell, J. (2012). *Educational research: Planning, conducting, and evaluating quantitative and qualitative research* (4th ed.). Pearson.

Ertmer, P., & Newby, T. (2013). Behaviorism, cognitivism, constructivism: Comparing critical features from an instructional design perspective. *Performance Improvement Quarterly, 26*(2), 43–71.

Fairclough, N. (1995). *Critical discourse analysis: The critical study of language*. Longman.

Fairclough, N. (2000). *New labour, new language?* Routledge.

Fairclough, N. (2003). *Analysing discourse: Textual analysis for social research*. Routledge.

Geertz, C. (1973). *The interpretation of cultures - Selected essays* (3rd ed.). Basic Books.

Kachru, B. B. (2017). *World Englishes and culture wars*. Cambridge University Press.

Kamhi-Stein, L., Díaz-Maggioli, G., & de Oliveira, L. (Eds.). (2017). *English language teaching in South America: Policy, preparation and practices*. Multilingual Matters.

Lo Bianco, J. (2010). Language policy and planning. In N. Hornberger & S. McKay (Eds.), *Sociolinguistics and language education* (pp. 143–176). Multilingual Matters.

Ministry of Education of Chile. (2014). *Estándares Orientadores para Carreras de Pedagogía en Inglés*. MINEDUC.

National Institute of Statistics. (2017). *Resultados definitivos Censo 2017*. Government of Chile.

Newby, P. (2014). *Research methods in education* (2nd ed.). Routledge.

OECD. (2012). *Quality assurance in higher education in Chile*. OECD Publishing.

Pennycook, A. (2021). *Critical applied linguistics: A re-critical introduction*. Routledge.

Pennycook, A., & Makoni, S. (2020). *Innovations and challenges in applied linguistics from the Global South*. Routledge.
Phillipson, R. (1992). *Linguistic imperialism*. Oxford University Press.
Punch, K. (2009). *Introduction to research methods in education*. SAGE.
Richards, J. (1990). The dilemma of teacher education in second language teaching. In J. Richards & D. Nunan (Eds.), *Second language teacher education* (pp. 3–15). Cambridge University Press.
Romero, G. (2017). *Novice teachers of English: Participation and approach to teaching in school communities of practice in Chile* (Unpublished doctoral thesis). University of Ottawa.
Schieffelin, B., Woolard, K., & Kroskrity, P. (1998). *Language ideologies*. Oxford University Press.
Schiro, M. (2013). *Curriculum theory: Conflicting visions and enduring concerns* (2nd ed.). SAGE Publications.
Schneider, M., Elacqua, G., & Buckley, J. (2006). School choice in Chile: Is it class or the classroom? *Journal of Policy Analysis and Management, 25*(3), 577–601.
Silverstein, M. (1979). Language structure and linguistic ideology. In P. Clyne, W. Hanks, & C. Hofbauer (Eds.), *The elements* (pp. 193–248). Chicago Linguistics Society.
Skott, J. (2015). The promises, problems, and prospects of research on teachers' beliefs. In H. Fives & M. Gill (Eds.), *International handbook of research on teachers' beliefs* (pp. 13–30). Routledge.
van Dijk, T. (2005). Politics, ideology and discourse. In R. Wodak (Ed.), *Elsevier encyclopedia of language and linguistics. Volume in politics and language* (pp. 728–740). Elsevier.
van Dijk, T. (2009). *Society and discourse: How social contexts influence text and talk*. Cambridge University Press.
Waring, H. (2018). *Discourse analysis: The questions discourse analysts ask and how they answer them*. Routledge.
Wodak, R., & Meyer, M. (2016). *Methods of critical discourse studies* (3rd ed.). SAGE.
World Bank. (2020). *Chile data*. Retrieved June 10, 2020, from https://data.worldbank.org/country/chile
Wright, T. (2010). Second language teacher education: Review of recent research on practice. *Language Teaching, 43*(3), 259–296.

Rodrigo Arellano is a foreign language teacher (English/Spanish), an applied linguist and a teacher trainer. He is an Assistant Professor at *Universidad de la Frontera* (Chile) and he holds a PhD in Applied Linguistics obtained at The University of New South Wales (Australia), where he works as a lecturer teaching linguistics and research courses. His fields of interest include Discourse Analysis, Second Language Acquisition and Second Language Teacher Education. Currently, he is working on projects researching multilingualism, the linguistic landscape of Spanish in Sydney, the ideologies behind teacher training practices and the learning and teaching of linguistics. Contact: rodrigo.arellano@ufrontera.cl.

11 Epilogue: Tools, Techniques, and Strategies for Reflective Second & Foreign Language Teacher Education

Paul Voerkel, Nancy Drescher, and Mergenfel A. Vaz Ferreira

Reflection as a means of professional growth and development is a multifaceted concept that takes on various forms and meanings, depending on the context in which it is applied. In the field of language teacher education, Farrell (2020) defined reflection as the systematic examination of principles and practices about teaching and learning, as well as related assumptions, beliefs, and values. For the professional action of educational staff, this means to be able to analyze, re-think, and change our own behavior while teaching. This action is fundamental to promoting more positive practices and experiences for all those involved in the teaching process, and it needs to be one of the foundations upon which teacher educators build their curricula.

P. Voerkel (✉)
Schmalkalden University of Applied Sciences, Schmalkalden, Germany

N. Drescher
Department of English, Minnesota State University, Mankato, MN, USA
e-mail: nancy.drescher@mnsu.edu

M. A. Vaz Ferreira
Faculdade de Letras, Setor de Alemão, Federal University of Rio de Janeiro, Rio de Janeiro, Brazil

© The Author(s), under exclusive license to Springer-Verlag GmbH, DE, part of Springer Nature 2024
P. Voerkel et al. (eds.), *Tools, Techniques and Strategies for Reflective Second & Foreign Language Teacher Education*,
https://doi.org/10.1007/978-3-662-68741-3_11

Throughout this final chapter, we will attempt to comment on the intricate ways in which reflection shapes teachers' perceptions, influences their decisions, and ultimately contributes to their personal and professional growth and self-awareness that have been developed throughout the book. Although it is, of course, an ambitious undertaking that cannot be fully realized in the context of such a brief treatise, the following will attempt to present reflection in more detail in three aspects based on the considerations from this anthology:

(1) Reflection is both an attitude and an instrument for education. It is dependent on some basic skills and individual traits, such as empathy, but can and should be practiced and developed in teacher education programs.
(2) Reflection is not an automatic process and must be practiced and encouraged. In this respect, Paulo Freire (1987) points out the importance of the link between reflection and action and confirms that both are a main force for transforming teachers' practices (Freire, 1987, p. 38). To this end, strategies, techniques, and instruments for promoting reflection play a major role.
(3) Reflection can be considered as a link between theory and practice. In this sense, it is an important instrument to foster objective understanding in teaching situations and represents the relevance of further research.

1 Reflection in Education

Reflection is a key concept for teacher training, both for pre-service and in-service teachers. Because of this pivotal role it plays, teacher reflection stands at the crossroads between several disciplines that deal with teacher training, mainly didactics and applied linguistics, but also linguistic subdisciplines, language policy, cultural studies, and pedagogy.

There is more awareness today about the key role of reflection in teacher training (especially in pre-service teacher training), but that doesn't mean it is productively developed as a tool within all university education programs, as there are some restraining elements. First of all, we need to mention the importance of teaching environments and curricula as a context within which the development of teacher training occurs. The context has a profound influence on the teaching of reflection (if it is done, how much it is done, and in which way it is done). At the same time, it is not easy to create the conditions in the daily training routine in which reflection can succeed, such as a direct reference to the field of action of the teachers, a systematic approach, collegial dialogue, and the voluntary nature of the process (e.g., Mohr & Schart, 2016, p. 295f.).

Additionally, an important role lies within the teacher instructors themselves as they particularly exercise influence on the students and shape their future professional behavior (e.g., Gerlach, 2020). It is, thus, important to examine and evaluate teachers' beliefs and attitudes (such as was done in the Brunsmeier chapter).

In general, reflection is an indispensable tool for teachers seeking to continuously improve their teaching practices, adapt to changing educational landscapes, and provide the best possible learning experiences for their students. It fosters self-awareness, encourages innovation, and promotes a culture of lifelong learning among educators, ultimately benefiting both teachers and the students they serve. But especially, it also helps to maintain a constant curiosity towards teaching and learning processes and to establish an attitude towards one's own practice and a direct relation to everyday life (e.g., Farrell, 2015).

2 How to Support Reflection

University level education programs have a crucial role to play in supporting the development of teacher reflection. One way to support this development is the use of specific instruments that guide students toward deeper reflection. This book has provided insights into a number of tools for examination such that we can choose which one fits when coming to implementation.

We find, for example, the development of several frameworks, rubrics, and grids to visualize and develop reflection within professional teacher training (such as what was done in the Rütti-Joy and the Drescher & Urzúa chapters) from a wide range of context around the world. We saw in the chapter by Urzúa and Drescher, after an extensive review of the literature surrounding reflection, a description of their investigation of reflective writing that aimed to uncover common discourse moves and steps in U.S. teacher candidates' reflective writing through the development and use of a specially tailored, user-friendly rubric that is intended for use in the growth and development of teachers. The chapter by Rütti-Joy, then, presented the rationale, design, and implementation of an intervention study with a focus on the application of an assessment rubric as a reflective tool in the Swiss L2 teacher education context. Yamaguchi, Yoneda, Osada, Adachi, and Kurihara in their chapter further answered the questions of what areas of teaching are perceived as differently important at different stages of teaching and what the pedagogical implications of teaching English are in the case of elementary schools in Japan.

The anthology moved to broader contexts of application within teacher development courses with a chapter by Voerkel, who pursued the question about the extent to which tools used by Action Research can be a useful instrument for German teacher education students in Brazil. It was shown that action research can be used profitably even at the undergraduate level, but that this requires close supervision and that an orientation based on concrete procedural steps towards reflection has proven its worth. The next chapter, by Kasumagić-Kafedžić and Đuliman, focused on a Bosnian context and examined the use of the EPOSTL tool in language teaching pedagogy courses and how students used this document to reflect on their own linguistic and didactic competencies as well as in planning and assessing their own professional development by keeping a record of their teaching experiences provided for them as in-class simulations, in-class observations, or in-class and school practice teaching. Bayyurt, Lopriore, and Kordia then presented an original Continuous Professional Development (CPD) Course for EFL teachers with an overt ELF-aware orientation within a network of teacher educators from Greece, Italy, Norway, Portugal, and Turkey. The establishment of mentoring partnerships and transnational teacher communities was highlighted in both phases, aiming at promoting critical reflection on one's views, attitudes, and practices, encouraging constructive dialogue, and providing, when appropriate, intellectual challenge and emotional support. In this chapter, they emphasized the challenges and opportunities encountered throughout the course development and implementation, as well as on the implications for teacher development.

The anthology then addressed the perspectives of teachers and experts in the field with a chapter by Ferreira and Gondar, who aimed to discuss the importance of affectivity in a teacher's initial education and in the professionalization process of future teachers in the context of undergraduate courses in Rio de Janeiro.

The book also examined the use of practical experiences especially in classrooms. There are models that showed that long term internships (starting from 6 month onwards) are especially helpful. In her chapter, Brunsmeier attempted to show how universities in a German context "translate" the policies into their everyday pre-service teacher instruction and why they opt for specific seminar concepts. And finally, there is a chapter by Arellano that aimed at reviewing a multi-layered set of SLTE policies in Chile to unmask their hidden ideologies, how language-in-education ideologies are evident in policy discourses about EFL teacher training in Chile.

By integrating these kinds of strategies into teacher education programs and examining them within a broader context, university teacher education programs around the world can and should help pre-service and in-service teachers develop the essential skills of reflection, equipping them to become more effective, adaptable, and self-aware educators in their future careers. Ultimately, this integration and development benefits not only individual teachers, but also the students they will go on to teach.

3   About the Relevance of Research

Research serves as the compass guiding our understanding of reflection within teacher education programs. It is the conduit through which we illuminate the intricacies of how reflection works, the essential components encompassed within reflective skills, and the pathways through which individuals, particularly educators, can acquire and hone these skills. Moreover, research sheds light on the transformative impact of teacher training on the practice of reflection and offers insights into the myriad ways in which institutions can provide crucial support in this journey of self-improvement.

The high relevance of reflection for teacher action is illustrated, among other things, by the fact that more and more publications directly or indirectly address and explore reflective processes in teaching and learning. For example, the 2/2023 issue of *Kontexte*, a journal for the professionalization of teachers of German as a foreign language, deals with the teacher training program DLL and repeatedly addresses the role of reflection for foreign language teacher education from different perspectives. This is not surprising insofar as "reflexive teaching as a goal of developing teaching competence" (Krumm, 2016, p. 312) has now gained an undisputed place on the educational policy agenda. For more than ten years, approaches to reflexive teacher education have been circulating in the German-speaking academic community (e.g., Abendroth-Timmer, 2011), the ultimate aim of which is to turn the educator's own experience into professional expertise through reflection.

Furthermore, as we navigate the complex landscape of academia and praxis, a commitment to precision in terminology and concepts is paramount. It enables us to communicate effectively, fostering a shared understanding that, in turn, propels the evolution of reflection and, ultimately, the enhancement of educational practices. Therefore, our collective pursuit of knowledge and refinement from wide ranging contexts in the domain of reflection remains not only relevant but imperative, ensuring that educators all around the world can continue to adapt, innovate, and thrive in the dynamic world of education.

References

Abendroth-Timmer, D. (2011). Reflexive Lehrerbildung: Konzepte und Perspektiven für den Einsatz von Unterrichtssimulation und Videographie in der fremdsprachendidaktischen Ausbildung. *Zeitschrift für Fremdsprachenforschung, 22*(1), 3–41.

Farrell, T. S. C. (2015). *Promoting teacher reflection in second language educaton: A framework for TESOL professionals*. Routledge.

Farrell, T. S. C. (2020). Professional development through reflective practice for English-medium instruction (EMI) teachers. *International Journal of Bilingual Education and Bilingualism, 23*(3), 277–286. https://doi.org/10.1080/13670050.2019.1612840

Freire, P. (1987). *Pedagogia do oprimido* (17th ed.). Paz e Terra.

Gerlach, D. (2020). *Zur Professionalität der Professionalisierenden. Was machen Lehrerbildner*innen im fremdsprachendidaktischen Vorbereitungsdienst?* Narr.

Krumm, H.-J. (2016). Kompetenzen der Sprachlernenden. In E. Burwitz-Melzer et al. (Eds.), *Handbuch Fremdsprachenunterricht* (6th ed., pp. 311–314). A. Francke.

Mohr, I., & Schart, M. (2016). Praxiserkundungsprojekte und ihre Wirksamkeit in der Lehrerfort- und Weiterbildung. In M. Legutke & M. Schart (Eds.), *Fremdsprachendidaktische Professionsforschung: Brennpunkt Lehrerbildung* (pp. 291–322). Narr.

Paul Voerkel is a passionate language teacher. He studied German as a Foreign Language, History, Hispanic Studies and Educational Sciences at the University of Leipzig (Germany) and received his PhD on teacher education in Brazil at Jena University (Germany). Since 2007, he has been active at various universities in Germany, Ecuador and Brazil, among others as an invited DAAD lecturer. At present, he works as a the head of the Department of Studies and International Relations at Schmalkalden University of Applied Sciences (Germany). His research interests include teacher education, methodology-didactics, cultural studies, and language policy. Contact: paul.voerkel@gmail.com.

Nancy Drescher is a full Professor in the Teaching English to Speakers of Other Languages at Minnesota State University, Mankato. She has a Ph.D. in Applied Linguistics from Northern Arizona University. Her teaching focuses on English language teaching, teacher education, sociolinguistics, and literacy. Her main research interests include teacher development, educational policies, and reflection. She has taught English at the K-12 level in the United States and overseas and currently works primarily at the university level. Contact: nancy.drescher@mnsu.edu.

Mergenfel A. Vaz Ferreira has been an Associate Professor of German Language at the Federal University of Rio de Janeiro since 2011. Between September 2022 and July 2023, she was a Visiting Professor at the Friedrich Schiller Universität Jena with a grant of the German Academic Exchange Service (DAAD). She holds a master's and PhD in Language Studies from the Pontifical Catholic University of Rio de Janeiro and her main areas of interest are the processes of teaching and learning additional languages/cultures, focusing mainly on the education of teacher's additional languages and didactic approaches for additional languages from a critical and decolonial perspective. Contact: megvazferreira@letras.ufrj.br.